THE COMING STORM

A Journey into the Conspiracy Machine

GABRIEL GATEHOUSE

BBC Books, an imprint of Ebury Publishing
Penguin Random House UK
One Embassy Gardens, 8 Viaduct Gdns,
Nine Elms, London SW11 7BW

BBC Books is part of the Penguin Random House group of companies whose
addresses can be found at global.penguinrandomhouse.com

Penguin
Random House
UK

First published by BBC Books in 2024

www.penguin.co.uk

A CIP catalogue record for this book is available from the British Library

Hardback ISBN 9781785948152

Trade Paperback ISBN 9781785948169

Printed and bound in Great Britain by Clays Ltd, Elcograf S.p.A.

The authorised representative in the EEA is Penguin Random House Ireland,
Morrison Chambers, 32 Nassau Street, Dublin D02 YH68.

Penguin Random House is committed to a sustainable future
for our business, our readers and our planet. This book is
made from Forest Stewardship Council® certified paper.

For Afsaneh Gray, who shines her light
on the stories I tell, and on my life.

This book evolved out of a radio and podcast series I made for the BBC together with my colleague Lucy Proctor. The journalism we did for that series was a joint endeavour; she was present at many of the weird encounters you will read about, and we spent many fraught hours trying to wrangle the madness into a coherent set of programmes. The volume you are about to read would not exist without her insights, her deep dives into the darker corners of the internet, her camaraderie on the road, her rock-solid editorial nous, and above all her enduring faith in the pot of gold at the end of the rabbit hole.

CONTENTS

PROLOGUE

I pushed through the heavy doors of the campus building and climbed up the stairs. At the top of them was General Michael T. Flynn, a wiry ex-soldier with once-chiselled features and a manic energy. Flynn didn't like me – I knew that much from our last encounter. He thought I was an agent of the Deep State.

The man who had brought me here was Derrick Evans. Evans had the air of a slightly naughty but good-natured puppy dog. He was also a 'Jan-sixer'. He had served his time for that, and was now running for a seat in Congress – the very place he had helped overrun nearly four years previously. 'A storm is coming,' he had written on his Facebook page. A week later, he boarded a bus and travelled to Washington, DC. On 6 January 2021, as the mob scuffled with police outside the Capitol, Evans livestreamed himself shouting, 'The cops are running, the cops are running!' Then, as the doors of the Rotunda were prised open, he made his way inside. 'We're in! Derrick Evans is in the Capitol!' he screamed.

Evans spent less than ten minutes inside the Capitol building. He didn't attack anyone, he didn't smash anything. In fact, on the livestream he can be heard shouting, 'Hey! No destruction of anything. No vandalising property!' But when he got home, he realised he was probably in trouble. For one thing, he was an elected representative himself; he had only recently taken an oath to uphold the Constitution, as he was sworn in as a member of the West Virginia House of Delegates – a small cog in America's vast apparatus of democracy. Now, thanks to his own livestream, he was all over social media, among the crowd of enraged Trump supporters trying to overturn the result of the 2020 presidential election. Also, Derrick had four young kids at home and was facing years behind bars. His wife was pretty furious.

'I take full responsibility for my actions,' Evans wrote when he resigned his seat two days later, 'and deeply regret any hurt, pain or embarrassment I may have caused my family, my friends, constituents and fellow West Virginians.' In court, he pleaded guilty; the judge, impressed by his contrition, gave him a relatively light sentence: three months in prison.

By the time I met him in Charleston, Derrick Evans was telling a very different story – no more Mr Contrite Guy. He and the other Jan-sixers were 'political prisoners', he told me, hostages of the 'Biden regime'. 'We're collateral damage to them,' he said. 'They're using all of us to build a case to ultimately get to President Trump.' Now he was running for US Congress himself. (His opponent in the West Virginia Republican primary had been inside the House on January 6th, among other lawmakers hiding in fear of their lives.)

I asked him what he wanted to do if he got elected. His answer wasn't 'build the wall' or 'tackle the debt', or any of the standard responses trotted out by Republicans. Instead, he pledged to defund the FBI, the CIA and the DOJ (Department of Justice). 'I want to completely abolish these unconstitutional three-letter agencies,' he said. He wanted to get rid of the Federal Reserve and return the dollar to the gold standard. He wanted to put public health officials on trial in military tribunals, a 'Nuremberg 2.0' for people he said were involved in deploying bioweapons that killed millions across the world (he was referring to COVID vaccines). 'We're living under tyranny,' he said, 'way more tyranny today than our Founding Fathers did in 1775.'

Really?

Derrick Evans was not joking. Nor did his ideas seem particularly fringe to me, at least not anymore. By now I'd spent enough time hanging out in the fevered conspiracy swamps of MAGA world to recognise what we were dealing with here. In the 2010s, America had been devastated by an opioid epidemic, as ruthless pharmaceutical companies bent on profit relentlessly pushed fentanyl on communities in pain; now Americans were in the grip of another drug, equally powerful and perhaps harder to kick: the red pill.

It had been a quarter of a century since a Hollywood blockbuster, *The Matrix*, had introduced this drug into the bloodstream. The red pill was a meme, a cultural virus. Once you took it, there was no going back. It was a promise of revelation. It sent you down a series of labyrinthine rabbit holes, at the end of which you would see the world as it really is. Salvation.

In reality, the effect was the opposite. As America hurtled towards the 2024 election, with its very democracy at stake, it was in the grip of an epidemic of confusion, an eclipse of reason. Nearly half the country believed the 2020 election had been stolen in a vast conspiracy for which there was no evidence. And they believed that a convicted felon who openly threatened to dismantle the institutions of democracy was in fact the one to save it. (The producers of *The Matrix* could hardly have predicted how COVID and the internet would combine to unleash an unstoppable firehose of conspiratorial madness. Nevertheless, perhaps in hindsight it would have been better if Neo had taken the blue pill.)

'You start doing some research and you start seeing truth and start seeing facts and you're like: *this is unbelievable*,' Derrick told me. Like millions of others, Evans believed that the instruments of the state – the courts, the judges, law enforcement, the media, most elected officials – were nothing more than a façade. America's vaunted democracy had been hollowed out; in the language of Jean Baudrillard (whose book *Simulacra and Simulation* serves as hiding place for Neo's thumb drive in *The Matrix*) it was a simulacrum, a representation of something that had once existed but was no longer there. Behind the scenes, hiding in the shadows, the Deep State was pulling the strings.

And I was part of the conspiracy.

I followed Evans up the stairs and into a long corridor leading to an auditorium. From behind a door off to the side I could hear snatches of General Flynn's military staccato, lecturing an audience of 'VIP' ticket holders who had paid $200 each for the privilege. Flynn had come to West Virginia to endorse Derrick Evans as a candidate for Congress. Principally though, he was here as part of a nationwide tour to promote a self-produced documentary, modestly entitled *Flynn – Deliver the Truth. Whatever the Cost.*

Michael T. Flynn had had his own run-in with the 'Deep State'. After a successful career as a battlefield commander, he rose to head of the DIA (Defense Intelligence Agency – another three-letter agency) under Barack Obama. But he was ill-suited to the corridors of power. His abrasive style earned him enemies; colleagues spoke of 'Flynn facts', suggesting his grip on reality was not always what you might want in a head of military intelligence.[1] He was ousted from his position in 2014 and fell in with Donald Trump, which is where his real troubles began.

It's easy to forget now, after all that has passed, the crazed intensity of those first few months of the Trump presidency. Ten days before his inauguration, a leaked intelligence dossier was published online that suggested the man who was about to become president of the United States was in fact a Kremlin agent. Mike Flynn lasted just 22 days as Trump's national security advisor before being fired (again) for lying about his contacts with Russian officials. He was the first casualty of the Russia furore.

As a BBC foreign correspondent with a specialisation in Russia, I spent much of the following year trying to uncover evidence that would support this extraordinary story. I pumped my contacts in Moscow; I travelled to former Soviet states to meet politicians and spies and even an eccentric arms dealer. Convincing proof never materialised. Donald Trump and his supporters suspected the whole story was cooked up by the intelligence agencies and the media in a coordinated attempt to delegitimise and possibly oust a duly elected president.

Mike Flynn's experience in the eye of the legal and media firestorm led him down a deep rabbit hole. He got mixed up in QAnon, a crazed movement whose members believed a cabal of satanic paedophiles was secretly running the world. By now he had disavowed Q and was travelling the country on a battle bus emblazoned with his own profile, a retinue of acolytes in tow, preaching his own increasingly elaborate conspiracy theory to anyone who was willing to listen (and pay).

While Flynn held forth behind closed doors, a sidekick by the name of Ivan Raiklin was standing in the corridor in front of a giant board, six feet high and about thirty feet long, covered in names and dates, photographs and newspaper clippings, dotted with pins and crisscrossed by pieces of string. Short and bald with a pugnacious jaw, Raiklin looked like another military man. (I checked his Twitter – the bio said he was a former

Green Beret, a 'Deep State marauder' and the future 'Secretary of Retribution' – whatever that meant.)

Raiklin reeled off names of obscure FBI agents like a chef listing exotic ingredients in his spice cupboard. A small but earnest audience nodded along. It was clearly a well-practised shtick. Raiklin had his own vocabulary: there was the 'FBLie', the 'CLieA' and the 'censorship industrial complex'; Barack Obama was 'Hussein'; and January 6th was the 'fedsurrection', a false-flag operation conceived by Nancy Pelosi and carried out by the FBI to ensure that Trump (and Flynn) never again got near the levers of power. If they did, he said, they would blow the whistle on a mind-bending string of cover-ups involving COVID lockdowns, Hunter Biden's laptop, the Russia dossier and lots more.

If that all seems incoherent or confusing, don't worry. Keep reading and you'll soon get the hang of it. The point was, anyone could become a target of the Deep State, as Derrick Evans told the audience later that evening: 'What they did to General Flynn, he was the first. Then they came after myself and the other January 6th political prisoners. Now they're going after President Trump. And – guess what – tomorrow, if they have their way, they're going to go after every single person in this room.'

Sadly, I didn't get to stay for the screening of Flynn's documentary. After what seemed like hours taking selfies with the VIP ticket holders, the general emerged from the side room.

We crossed paths in the narrow corridor on the way to the auditorium. His eyes narrowed. Perhaps he recognised me from Dallas, where I had met him two years earlier, when he was headlining a QAnon convention. Suddenly, I was being ejected from the hall. Raiklin followed me towards the exit, his minions gleefully filming it all on their mobile phones, delighted at having unmasked an agent of the cabal.

What Flynn didn't know was that, in a strange way, I was coming round to his way of seeing things. Not literally – I didn't believe the election had been stolen or that January 6th was a false-flag operation aimed at keeping Donald Trump out of the White House. That was nonsense. But there were things I'd discovered while researching this story that led me to believe that maybe there *was* a plot against America. It involved not a secret society of satanic paedophiles but a constellation of characters spanning decades. And I was beginning to wonder whether the wild fantasies of Mike Flynn and Derrick Evans, of QAnon and all the rest of it, were in fact a decoy, a conjuror's trick of misdirection, designed to distract people from the real forces at work, forces of disruption powered by new technology, that were the real threat to democracy.

But perhaps I too had swallowed the red pill ...

PART I

FOLLOW THE WHITE RABBIT

CHAPTER 1

THE
ENEMY
WITHIN

It was the night of Halloween, 2020, the height of the pandemic. I was supposed to be flying to the US to cover the 2020 presidential election for BBC News. Donald Trump had been talking up the idea of voter fraud. If he lost, he said, it could only be because of cheating. Asked whether he would commit to a peaceful transfer of power, the president of the United States had answered, 'We're gonna have to see what happens.' Even after four turbulent years, Trump still had an ability to shock, to break with the conventions of American democracy so profoundly that you really began to wonder: what might he do? If he lost, I was convinced there would be trouble. And if there was trouble, I wanted to be there. Instead, I was stuck on the wrong side of the Atlantic with a visa that had expired.

To take my mind off things, I signed up for an online drawing class. The session had a Halloween theme: *Witches: Drawing and Storytelling.* It was one of those spur-of-the-moment things, a random decision. Drawing isn't even a hobby of mine, nor did I have any particular interest in witches. Perhaps it was the word 'storytelling' that lured me to it. Whatever the reason, on the evening of 31 October 2020, I sat down, as per the instructions in the email I'd been sent, with some sheets of blank paper and an assortment of pencils and erasers, and clicked the Zoom link.

The class was run by three women, founders of a feminist collective called the London Drawing Group. Two of them took turns setting us exercises. They got us copying details from various works of art from the height of the European witch-craze of the sixteenth and seventeenth centuries, examining marks and brushstrokes up close, then zooming out to see how the separate elements made up the whole. I got going on a woodcut from 1510 entitled *The Witches* by the German artist Hans Baldung. It was a groundbreaking work for its time, using a pioneering technique that achieved the kind of dramatic chiaroscuro effect usually associated with the great Renaissance painters. There's a lot going on in the picture: out of an intricate mass of whorls and lines the figures of three women emerge, sitting naked in a wood, huddled around some kind of pot or cauldron out of which a powerful concoction is escaping. Above them, a fourth woman flies through the air, riding backwards on a goat, a pitchfork held erect between her legs. The ground is littered with the detritus of unholy ritual: animal bones, a pestle, a cat.

While I was scribbling away, the third member of the collective, Luisa-Maria MacCormack, gave a talk on the theme of witches in European art. Hans Baldung's print depicted preparations for a 'witches' Sabbath' – women gathered in a clearing in the forest, performing their satanic rites: offering up human sacrifices, sometimes the flesh of their own children, before copulating with the Devil in animal form. Baldung was a pioneer not just technically, but conceptually as well. At the time that he made his woodcut, the image of the witch as an old hag who flew about on a broomstick and brewed noxious potions was not yet widespread. At the turn of the sixteenth century, people in Europe believed in magic in a broad and varied sense. They also believed in people who engaged in magic – witches – but these were generally tolerated as part of the tapestry of medieval life. They were seldom prosecuted, and might even be welcomed as purveyors of certain services: layers of charms, lifters of spells. But then, quite suddenly, something changed. The idea of the witch that Hans Baldung depicted, of a sex-obsessed, child-murdering, Devil-worshipping incarnation of evil, an existential threat to all that is good and holy, had come from a book, recently published by an obscure German priest by the name of Heinrich Kramer.

Kramer was born around 1430 in Schlettstadt, now Sélestat in Alsace, on the border between modern France and

Germany, in what was then the Holy Roman Empire. A studious boy, he was admitted into the Dominican order. By his mid-forties, he had been appointed by the Pope as an inquisitor. As such, Kramer was tasked with ensuring the Vatican's ideological control in an age of rising political turbulence. The Reformation was on the horizon, dissenters were chafing at the writ of Rome, and Kramer's job was to root them out. There existed various heretical sects that were fighting back against widespread corruption in the Catholic Church, movements that challenged both the ecclesiastical and secular order of the late feudal period. But Kramer focused his efforts elsewhere, becoming increasingly obsessed with witches. Convinced there had been an outbreak of witchcraft along the Rhine Valley, he mounted a series of zealous prosecutions. The local authorities quickly concluded that Kramer was a crank and asked him to leave.

But Heinrich Kramer was not to be deterred. He obtained a papal bull, a note from the Pope, confirming his authority to pursue witches. He headed to Innsbruck, in present-day Austria, where he hoped to put on a big show trial, a paradigm for other witch trials to come. His attention alighted upon a woman by the name of Helena Scheuberin, the wife of a prosperous local burgher, whom he accused of witchcraft. Why, exactly, he picked on her is a matter of some dispute, but the story goes that Kramer had made advances on her. Scheuberin rebuffed him, cursing and spitting at him in the street, embarrassing him in public. The trial began in 1485. Kramer's methods were brutal: witnesses were threatened, suspects tortured, their testimony twisted to suit his case. But in court, proceedings did not go well. Kramer focused heavily on speculative questions about Scheuberin's sex life. The local bishop disapproved, telling him to stick to the facts. But Kramer ploughed on, interrogating more and more suspects. In 1486, the authorities decided enough was enough. The trial was declared void and Kramer was ordered to leave town.

Professionally defeated and personally rejected, Heinrich Kramer retreated to Cologne. For the next six months, he went dark. Did he rent rooms in the upper floors of a merchant's house overlooking the city's giant cathedral, then still under construction, crawling with craftsmen and surrounded by cranes? Or did he lodge at the university, his old alma mater, where a fellow inquisitor, Jacob Sprenger, was dean of the faculty of theology? We do not know the answers to these questions. We do know that Kramer wrote feverishly over the spring and summer of 1486, working from his notes from the Innsbruck trial and from previous prosecutions. He gathered them together with other inquisitors' accounts as well as folktales he had collected on his travels; he scoured the canonical texts for references that would support his theory – Thomas Aquinas, St Augustine, Aristotle, and of course the Bible itself. Towards the end of the year, he emerged with a manuscript. He titled it *Malleus Maleficarum*, or *Hammer of Witches*.

The *Malleus Maleficarum* tells a frightening story, a dark and twisted fantasy about vast numbers of women, old and young, who have sealed a pact with the Devil. Traversing vast distances on their flying objects, they raise storms and kill livestock, driving horses mad and making cows' udders run dry. They devour babies at their satanic gatherings and offer up toddlers to the Devil in return for sex; they kill infants in the womb and cause impotence in men, keeping nests of penises in trees; they bewitch judges so that they may continue their crimes unmolested. The fact that you may not be able to find evidence linking them to their crimes is but further proof of their diabolical abilities. And the scariest part of it is, they're everywhere. They look just like your neighbour or the milk-maid or your landlord's wife. They are hiding in plain sight, an enemy within, growing like a cancer, engaged in a vast conspiracy directed against all of Christian civilisation and good God-fearing folk like you. Having identified the powers and attributes of the witch, the *Malleus Maleficarum* stipulates how to capture, interrogate and torture her, how to proceed in her prosecution, and how she should be executed.

The clerical establishment, by and large, thought Kramer was mad. And his crazed screed might have vanished as quickly as it was written, were it not for a piece of historical serendipity. Four decades earlier, in the nearby town of Mainz, a goldsmith had come up with an invention that would revolutionise European society: the printing press. Johannes Gutenberg's invention radically changed not only what stories could be told, but who could tell them, and in what quantities those stories could be distributed. In the years since its invention, while Heinrich Kramer was building his career as an inquisitor, 20 million volumes were printed in Europe, most of them in Germany and Italy.[1] Previously, production of the written word, painstakingly copied by hand, had been the preserve of the Church or legal authorities. Suddenly anyone could produce a book, as long as they could write and pay for it to be printed.

Kramer's book landed at a time of upheaval, a perfect storm of technological change and political uncertainty, I heard Luisa saying as I tried to focus on my drawing. The feudal system was breaking down, the old social safety nets were vanishing as common lands were expropriated. These were the beginnings of what we now know as capitalism, the dawn of the modern age. Power was shifting from feudal landlords to urban merchants. Europe was in flux. Towns and cities were flooded with vagrants, peasants who had once been tied to the land were now uprooted and homeless, the harsh but stable certainties of generations vanishing before their eyes. Amid all this turbulence, the *Malleus Maleficarum* travelled from town to town, from printing press to printing press, spreading like a virus along the major arteries of Western Europe. Over the next two centuries, dozens of editions were produced.[2] At some point Jacob Sprenger, Kramer's colleague from the University of Cologne, was added as a co-author. It became one of the most printed books in Europe, by some counts second only to the Bible itself. Of its impact, an English theologian wrote: 'For nearly three centuries [...] the *Malleus* lay on the bench of every judge, on the desk of every magistrate. It was the ultimate, irrefutable, unarguable authority'.[3] Kramer's dark fantasy infected the minds of millions. Over the next two centuries, tens, maybe hundreds of thousands of people – most of them women – were tortured and killed, as witch fever spread from the Old World to the New, borne across the Atlantic aboard colonists' ships. At the dawn of the age of enlightenment, the Western world was in the grip of a diabolical delusion, an eclipse of reason. The opening chapter of the modern age was written in blood.

I looked down at my drawing. It bore little resemblance to the Hans Baldung woodcut I'd been working from. My sheet of paper was covered in dark scrawls and smudges, spirals and angry hatched lines. Distracted by the story of Heinrich Kramer, I'd lost sight of what I was supposed to be doing. Far from honing my skills, my ability to draw seemed to have suffered a catastrophic collapse.

The class ended. I shut my laptop; darkness flooded the room. Sounds of revelry wafted in from outside. Somewhere out there people were celebrating Halloween, the day when we dress up as the things we fear most in order to exorcise their power for the year to come. How many, I wondered, now wearing pointy black hats and carrying broomsticks, knew the sinister origins of their outfits? The *Malleus Maleficarum* had seeped into the culture. Kramer's dark fantasy had morphed into a murderous reality half a millennium ago, just as the old order was crumbling and a new one was taking shape. And it was still with us.

. . .

A week later I was in Arizona, standing outside the Maricopa County vote tabulation centre in Phoenix, staring at a bare-chested man draped in furs, with horns on his head and a spear in his hand, holding a sign that read: Q SENT ME.

It was 7 November 2020. I'd missed the election by a few days, but the fact that I was there at all felt like a small miracle. I'd prevailed upon the BBC's management to put pressure on the US State Department to grant me an interview at the US embassy in London, which was effectively closed due to COVID. I had persuaded them to issue me with a new visa and to waive travel restrictions. It had taken some convincing for my editors to send me out at all. With the voting done, wasn't it just a question of waiting for the results? 'Remember the principle of Chekhov's gun,' I'd said, thinking it sounded clever. *If there's a pistol on stage in Act I, it must go off before the end of the play.* The gun in this case was the spectre of voter fraud, and I was convinced it had been placed there for a reason. In the run-up to polling day Donald Trump had focused on the postal vote, so-called 'mail-in ballots', as the most likely way the Democrats would try to steal the vote. Amid the COVID pandemic, many states had made it easier for people to vote by post. The number of mail-in ballots would be significantly higher than in previous years, and it was likely those ballots would favour the Democratic Party candidate. So, the stage was set. 'If Trump loses,' I told my editor, 'there will be trouble.'

I stood outside the counting centre in Phoenix surrounded by a small group of protestors wearing MAGA caps and chanting slogans: *Stop the Steal!* and *Where's Our Votes?* They were a mixed bunch. Apart from the eye-catching guy in the furs and horns, there were families with kids in tow mixing with men sporting Hawaiian shirts and big guns. A man dressed all in black had climbed up a lamp post and was shouting into a loudhailer. 'They're trying to suppress us. They're trying to break us,' he bellowed. Many waved yellow flags depicting a coiled rattlesnake over the words DON'T TREAD ON ME: the Gadsden flag, flown during the War of Independence against the British and now brandished as a symbol of resistance to their own government.

The votes were still being counted but Fox News had called Arizona for Joe Biden, and Donald Trump's supporters sensed victory slipping away. They felt betrayed by a network they had thought was unshakably loyal to their man. Stories circulated among the crowd as if gospel, passed on by social media, gaining traction with every passing hour: ballots for Trump had been found dumped in the trash in Oklahoma; in Michigan and Wisconsin there had been sudden surges in the Biden vote in the dead of night; electronic vote-counting machines were deleting Trump votes; and in several battleground districts, thousands of people had voted who were in fact dead. In Arizona itself, the biggest story was *Sharpiegate* – a theory that voters had been given a specific brand of black pen to mark their ballots that couldn't be read by the electronic vote-counting machines. None of these tales of electoral black magic were first-hand accounts. They came from Facebook and other platforms and had been picked up and then amplified by high-profile Trump supporters, in some cases by the president himself. Most had been quickly investigated and debunked by reputable news outlets (including my own).

'In one county in Michigan, six thousand votes were changed to Biden that voted for Trump,' one man told me authoritatively, gesticulating with a chunky vape. This story did have some basis in fact: unofficial results in Antrim County, a small Republican-leaning county in northern Michigan, had initially reported a mini-landslide for Joe Biden. Local election officials had spotted the error, I pointed out, and corrected it before the final results were announced. But facts didn't cut much ice with the crowd. 'You're fucking full of shit,' shouted a man who looked like he was auditioning for the part of Hunter S. Thompson in Terry Gilliam's movie *Fear and Loathing in Las Vegas*. 'The queen of England,' he added inexplicably, 'has more dominion over this country right now than Joe Biden.' I looked at the yellow Gadsden flags fluttering in the breeze, confused.

Beyond the specific, refutable allegations of systematic voter fraud, many in the crowd seemed to be experiencing profound cognitive dissonance, a jarring sense of narrative disconnect. 'Somewhere, something's not right,' explained a third man in wraparound shades and a Harley Davidson T-shirt. 'There's no way Trump lost Arizona. Here in Phoenix there was a 200-mile-long Trump train. It was crazy, like thousands and thousands of cars.' For him, the idea that Biden could win here just didn't add up. Trump's supporters were so passionate, so fired up, so engaged; Biden, by contrast, was low-energy: he wasn't even holding rallies, and when he did, they were sparsely attended gatherings where everyone sat subdued in socially distanced rows wearing face masks. How could *that guy* win? Answer: he couldn't, at least not honestly. It was a vast conspiracy by all the people who never liked Trump anyway: the lawyers, the lobbyists, the liberals, the mainstream media, the special-interest groups in the pay of global corporations, big tech, or China. In other words, the Swamp (which Trump had tried and so-far failed to drain). The establishment had been hell-bent on delegitimising his presidency from day one, with the Russiagate conspiracy crap, the phoney Steele dossier with its fantasy video of hookers peeing in a Moscow hotel room, the collusion delusion, the Mueller investigation that came to nothing, the impeachment that went nowhere. Trump himself had called it the 'greatest witch-hunt in American history'. If Donald Trump ended up not being declared president, then it could only be because of fraud. Anyone who couldn't see that was either deluded – or complicit.

I had been reporting from America for many years. It was a paradise for journalists, a land full of great stories and colourful characters who were often only too happy to tell them. But this felt different. I was surrounded by paranoia and suspicion, and it quickly became clear that politely fact checking or rebutting their claims of voter fraud was not only pointless but counter-productive. Indeed, the fact that 'mainstream media' journalists like me and others were so keen to discredit the allegations seemed to them further proof of the Deep State at work.

I wandered over to the man in the horns with the Q sign. He was friendly enough and I thought of calling my cameraman over to film an interview. Television journalism is as much about the visuals as anything else and he *looked* fantastic, his bare chest covered in tattoos, his face painted in the stars and stripes. But then he started talking: *5G vaccines human trafficking new world order look at the connections Hillary Clinton underground bunkers military industrial complex JFK top security clearance sealed indictments central banking system trail of breadcrumbs* ... It was as if he had eaten an encyclopaedia of conspiracy theories for breakfast and was now regurgitating the contents in a random order.

As far as I could make out, the story he was trying to tell was this: Hillary Clinton was, apparently, the central figure in a cabal of Satan-worshipping paedophiles. The cabal consisted of some of the most powerful people in America, with members in politics and the media, business and law enforcement.

Donald Trump, he believed, was fighting a secret campaign to expose them. There was a storm coming. Soon the cabal would be arrested and tried in military tribunals; the worst offenders would be executed. The attempt to steal the election was a desperate rear-guard action by the Deep State to protect the cabal and maintain their grip on power. He flipped his sign around. HOLD THE LINE, PATRIOTS, it read, GOD WINS.

Unlike some of the other people at the protest, he wasn't hostile. He seemed like a good-natured oddball. But his story was just too weird to put in a news report. It made no sense and seemed irrelevant to the matter in hand. Allegations of voter fraud were sweeping the country, and though they appeared spurious they nevertheless had the potential for far-reaching political ramifications. I was vaguely aware of a sprawling conspiracy theory called QAnon that was gaining popularity among some Trump supporters. Sticking an amiable weirdo on camera with a wild tale about a cabal of satanic paedophiles would undermine the seriousness of my reporting. Or so I thought. So I decided not to interview him.

Big mistake.

. . .

During those turbulent weeks following the election in November 2020, Trump and his team of advisors clung desperately to power. As the postal votes flooded in and the president's early lead evaporated, fierce battles were fought behind closed doors, between the pragmatists in the administration who backed the president but drew the line at sacrificing American democracy to a second Trump term, and the nihilists, who were willing to see the White House go up in flames – metaphorically speaking – rather than be evicted from it. The latter group included the disgraced former army general Michael Flynn; the ex-mayor of New York Rudy Giuliani; Sidney Powell, a once respected attorney from Texas who seemed to have fallen down a labyrinthine rabbit hole; and – bizarrely – a multi-millionaire pillow salesman by the name of Mike Lindell. These characters were putting forward increasingly outlandish theories about how the election had been stolen. Things were getting weirder by the day.

Meanwhile, I was travelling across the United States. I had promised my editor trouble and I was trying to figure out when and where Chekhov's gun might go off. Guns were not hard to find: Arizona is an 'open carry' state, which means it's legal to turn up at a protest with an assault rifle strapped to your chest. Outside the voting centre in Phoenix they were almost as numerous as the yellow revolutionary rattlesnake flags. In Georgia, outside the state capitol building in Atlanta, an armoured Humvee painted with the logo of the far-right conspiracy website InfoWars rolled up to join a Stop the Steal caravan. It was headed to Washington for what was billed as a 'Million MAGA March', playing on the 1995 'Million Man March' organised by the Black nationalist Louis Farrakhan. It was a weird reference, given that almost everyone there was white.

'We've been robbed,' said an older lady with a twinkle in her eye who looked like she would have invited me in for tea had there not been a revolution brewing. 'We're coming from the ditches,' she warned, 'we're coming from the woods, we're coming from Alabama!' This felt like groundswell, the beginnings of a powerful movement. And among it all I kept coming across people holding homemade signs emblazoned with the letter Q. 'The plan to save the world,' one young woman told me when I asked her what it meant. 'They're just trying to get Trump out of office because they don't want him exposing what the real endgame of the left wing is, and that's to normalise paedophilia.' She wasn't the kind of person I'd typically expect at a pro-Trump event. She had voted for Obama in 2012 and Hillary Clinton in 2016, but had since become convinced of the existence of a wide-ranging child-trafficking conspiracy at the heart of the American establishment. Another woman held up a placard that read: THEY'RE KEEPING BABIES ALIVE AND STEAL-ING THEIR BODY PARTS! A man stood by the side of the road with a crudely painted sign that said simply: THE STORM IS HERE. #FIGHTBACK.

In Georgia, I'd spoken by phone to members of several militia groups. Some talked about secession or armed resistance. Only one agreed to meet me, a man called Chris Hill, who also went by the *nom de guerre* 'General Bloodagent'. He was the leader of a group called the 'III% Security Force' – so named because of their belief that only three per cent of the North American colonists rose up against the British in the American Revolution. We met in a parking lot on the outskirts of Jonesboro, a small town south of Atlanta. I followed his pickup truck for half an hour as we headed east along the highway at dusk, stopping off briefly to pick up some ribs at a strip mall on the way. We arrived at his home after dark and he showed us into his garage. He'd converted the place into a kind of revolutionary HQ, with flags and banners, two laptops and a comfortable sofa. Before sitting down to talk he offered me, for some reason, a glass of Japanese sake. 'Our country is falling apart,' he told me, as he peered over the top of a pair of reading glasses. 'We no longer have Democrats and Republicans.' Like many others, Chris Hill had lost faith in the whole political system. 'Either President Trump leads us, or We the People will lead ourselves.' He talked about the Constitution. A lot. In fact, almost everyone I would meet over the next few years while reporting this story would turn out to be obsessed with the Constitution of the United States, as if somehow that document anchored them to a past they feared was slipping away.

Perhaps because he had agreed to talk to me on camera, I suspected Chris of being a blowhard, a self-publicist who was more interested in the media attention than anything else. But there was something interesting in the performative way he spoke. When I asked him whether there were any circumstances under which he would accept a Biden victory, he replied: 'Verily I would say to you, I will not fucking accept it'. 'Verily'?

'We the People'? It felt like he was acting out a fantasy, a role-play game in which he was the hero in some kind of steampunk historical epic where eighteenth-century manners and twenty-first-century technology come together to bring about a new American Revolution.

I followed the Stop the Steal caravan to Washington, DC, arriving on 13 November, the day before the 'Million MAGA March' was due to converge on the nation's capital. The result of the election had by now been decided, but Donald Trump was refusing to concede. I checked into a hotel opposite the White House. The lobby bar was full of noisy Trump fans dressed in red, white and blue. They didn't look like the supporters of a defeated president. They were in high spirits, confident that their man would prevail. I went up to my room and switched on the TV. In the hyperbolic, hyper-polarised world of cable news it seemed as if America had made a choice not between two centrist parties in a long-established and stable political system, but between something much more fundamental. Fox News ranted about the Democrats as the party of socialists and rioters; CNN saw in Donald Trump and the Republicans the spectre of the Nazis and an assault on truth itself. These increasingly feverish narratives were driven, I suspected, as much by the need to boost viewing figures as they were by the imperatives of political journalism. The networks were competing for America's attention with social media giants whose whole business model depended on clicks, on feeding the outrage machine. Perhaps, I thought as I flicked through the channels, it was inevitable that a country that had elected a reality TV star as president four years earlier was now being consumed by the inexorable logic of the infotainment industry. Perhaps I too was getting swept up in the hyperbole, because it seemed to me at that moment that the two halves of America, the political binary that for more than two centuries had been the engine of its democracy and its prosperity, had parted ways, no longer sharing a common moral or even factual frame of reference. It felt like end times.

People started gathering early the next morning on Freedom Plaza. Trump had been uncharacteristically subdued the previous few days – plenty of tweeting, but few public appearances. Suddenly the small crowd was abuzz: a motorcade had been spotted heading in their direction. There were shrieks of excitement as the presidential limo did a lap of the square. Inside it, Donald Trump gave the crowd the thumbs up behind the bullet-proof glass, Secret Service agents in COVID masks jogging alongside. 'Oh my God, I'm so happy,' a woman panted, wearing a Trump flag like a superhero cape over her shoulders. 'They're trying to steal it from him. We can't have that. He's our president and our commander in chief. And always will be.' At that point it felt like that could actually be the case, that if a peaceful transition of power was not achieved, the democratically elected 45th president of the American Republic might indeed be its last.

It wasn't a million people, but it was a sizable crowd. Amid the Trump flags and the MAGA hats and the stars and stripes there were banners that read EXPOSE THE TRAITOROUS DEEP STATE COUP – EXPOSE CNN and THE ACTUAL VIRUS IS THE NEW WORLD ORDER + GLOBAL ELITES. DEATH IS THE REMEDY. A line-up of speakers talked about election fraud and creeping socialism. The media were 'enemies of the people'. The speaker of honour was a blonde woman in aviator shades and a bright red coat. She was Marjorie Taylor Greene, a gun-toting businesswoman and mother of three from Georgia who had just been elected to Congress. 'The Democrat Party is no longer an American Party,' she announced, to cheers from the crowd. Donald Trump himself had called her a 'rising Republican star', but her real claim to fame was that she was one of a handful of Congressional candidates to have endorsed the QAnon conspiracy theory, calling the movement 'a once-in-a-lifetime opportunity to take this global cabal of Satan-worshipping paedophiles out'.

Was QAnon *a thing*? Was it becoming a genuine force in American politics? I squeezed my way through the crowd to try to speak to Ms Taylor Greene. Did she *really* believe Donald Trump was fighting a cabal of satanic paedophiles? 'Trump is fighting to save America and stop socialism', she told me. And then she flipped the conspiracy theory accusation back on me: 'Why don't you go and cover Russian collusion conspiracy theory lies? Fake news media!' She turned to the crowd, pointing at me and my cameraman and producer, shouting 'Get them out, kick them out!'

Unnerved, I tried to keep a low profile. After the speeches, the crowd marched towards the Supreme Court. There were scuffles involving members of another militia, the white-supremacist Proud Boys, dressed in black and yellow sweat-shirts emblazoned with the words STAND BACK, STAND BY – a reference to Donald Trump's response during one of the presidential debates when he was asked to condemn far-right groups. They had heard his words as an endorsement. Later that night, fighting broke out between Trump's supporters and left-wing activists: Antifa. I spent a few hours chasing the brawlers round the streets of Washington. It looked dramatic but it was small in scale and soon over.

I'd promised my editors trouble, invoking the spectre of Chekhov's gun. I thought it sounded clever at the time. Now I googled the actual quote. 'One must never place a loaded rifle on the stage if it isn't going to go off,' Anton Chekhov wrote to a fellow Russian playwright in 1889. 'It's wrong to make promises you don't mean to keep.' Well, there were plenty of loaded guns on stage, but so far it didn't look like anyone was actually going to fire them. At least, the consensus in newsrooms on both sides of the Atlantic was that large-scale unrest seemed unlikely. I felt like I was the one who'd made a promise I couldn't keep and, towards the end of November 2020, I flew back home, feeling both a little foolish and a little uneasy.

· · ·

I was back in London on 6 January 2021, when the mob stormed the Capitol. I cursed inwardly as I watched events unfold, stuck on the wrong side of the Atlantic, a distant spectator to an epoch-defining event, consumed by a sense of impotent vindication.

And then I saw him on my TV screen: the same furs, the same horns, the same bare tattooed chest: the man I'd met outside the vote counting centre in Phoenix, Arizona. There he stood, inside the Senate chamber, behind the desk reserved for the vice president of the United States, who moments earlier had fled in fear of his life. The Q Shaman, whom I'd dismissed as too mad to interview, had forced his way into the heart of the citadel of American democracy and, together with hundreds of others, was threatening to bring it down from within. He'd been driven there by a story so preposterous, so implausible, so *insane*, it couldn't possibly be true. Despite the lack of any credible evidence, he and his fellow insurrectionists were convinced the 2020 presidential election had been stolen in a massive and convoluted conspiracy, a plot involving politicians and election workers, journalists and judges, a vast operation in which tens, maybe hundreds of thousands of people would have to be complicit, all in order to protect a secret cabal of Satan-worshipping paedophiles at the heart of the American establishment. And the only person they believed could save them was a fake-tanned real-estate mogul turned reality TV star turned politician by the name of Donald J. Trump.

I had a sudden realisation: all that time I was in America, trying to figure out when and how the trouble might start, I was looking for the wrong thing. I thought I was reporting on a story about election fraud – or rather, a cynical ploy to invent cases of election fraud, a win-at-all-costs battle between Republicans and Democrats, in a political contest that got out of hand. And at one level, that *was* the story. But there was something bigger afoot. That tale the Q Shaman told me, about the Deep State cabal of Satan-worshipping paedophiles, was a significant detail.

QAnon had taken hold of the American psyche not because the *facts* seemed believable but because something about the *story* did. The important questions to ask about the gun on stage were not when exactly it would go off, or even who would get shot. They were about why it was there, what it was supposed to tell us. In any good story, every detail is there for a reason, no matter how small or weird. As I waited for an actual gun to be fired, I'd missed the point: the Q Shaman *was* Chekhov's gun, the minor detail that was there for a reason because it was trying to tell me something important about the bigger story unfolding before my eyes. I had been given a glimpse of the future and had failed to pick up on it. It wasn't until after the gun had gone off that I realised its significance.

What else had I missed? The memory of the drawing class came flooding back to me, the crazy story about the witches and their satanic conspiracy that had landed 500 years ago and had spread like a malignant virus thanks to a new piece of communications technology, just as the old order was dying and a new world was being born. What if the witches in the drawing class were there for a reason too? A serendipitous detail, a sign that the wheels of history were turning again. I had a sudden flash of clarity: January 6th wasn't the main event but a harbinger of something bigger. It was a once-in-half-a-millennium epochal shift, powered by a noxious narrative brew, a bubbling cauldron of conspiracy theories. These half-hidden stories had their origins in the 1990s, when the battle against totalitarianism appeared to have been won and the liberal establishment, drunk on victory, had declared the end of history.

CHAPTER 2

LIGHTING
THE MATCH

It was the summer of 1993. Bill Clinton's presidency was not yet six months old but already the new administration was beset by petty scandal. The political press obsessed over a series of mini-'gates': *Hairgate* (had Clinton closed the runway at Los Angeles International Airport in order to have a haircut aboard *Air Force One*?); *Travelgate* (were the Clintons trying to staff White House departments with their cronies?); *Whitewater* (a convoluted financial scandal more than a decade old that no one really understood). Watergate they were not. But it took the shine off what should have been a honeymoon period, the start of a new era. The Cold War was over. The road ahead appeared full of possibilities.

One man was being given a particularly hard time in the press: Vince Foster – an old friend of Bill and Hillary's from their

Arkansas days, now deputy White House counsel, the second most senior lawyer in the administration.[1] His colleagues had noticed he seemed down. One evening in mid-July, Bill Clinton was having a few of his old Arkansas buddies over to the White House residence to watch a newly released blockbuster, *In the Line of Fire*, a thriller about a rogue ex-CIA agent and a plot to kill the president starring Clint Eastwood and John Malkovich. Bill called Vince and invited him to come along. He thought the film might cheer his old pal up. Gallows humour from a president under fire. But Foster made some excuse. He never came. It was the last time the two of them ever spoke.

Vince Foster arrived at his office in the White House as usual on the morning of 20 July. He ate lunch at his desk and went out at around 1pm. Five hours later, his dead body was found in Fort Marcy Park, just across the Potomac River in Virginia. He had shot himself. He was 48.

The following day, Bill Clinton gathered shocked White House staff. None of them had seen this coming. The reason why Vince Foster had taken his own life, the president said, would likely remain a mystery. But in the right-wing media, on radio talk shows and conservative newsletters, a different narrative took shape. Investigations were looming into the Clintons' financial dealings in Arkansas in the 1970s and '80s. Did Vince Foster, the loyal ally from Arkansas, *know too much*? If his death really was suicide, then why did the facts keep on changing?

Spend enough time on the weirder end of the American political spectrum and soon enough you will come across a conspiracy theory called the 'Clinton Body Count', a trail of dead bodies, supposedly scattered in the wake of Bill and Hillary Clinton's quest for power. Depending on who's counting, the list can stretch to more than 50 names. Vince Foster is not chronologically the first body on the list, but he is perhaps the most important: ground zero for a series of interlinked and increasingly wild stories centred on the Clintons.

●　　●　　●

Vincent Walker Foster Jr and William Jefferson Clinton had known each other since childhood. They were both born in the small town of Hope, Arkansas; they were at kindergarten together, attending Miss Marie Purkins' School for Little Folks. Later, when Foster became a lawyer, he went to work for the Rose Law Firm in Little Rock, where Hillary Clinton was a partner. Vince became, according to various sources, a 'confidant',[2] Hillary's 'close friend', both personally and professionally.[3] Vince married Lisa, they had three children. The Fosters and the Clintons were part of a tight circle at the top of Arkansas society who worked together and socialised together, who trusted each other, whose lives were intertwined like vines in the small world of Little Rock. As Bill Clinton's political star rose (elected attorney general of the state in 1976 and governor in 1978 at the age of only 31) many from that circle rose with him. When Bill became president in 1993, he took some of his most trusted Arkansas buddies with him to Washington, DC, to build his administration. Vince Foster was one of them.

Many in the Washington establishment were suspicious of this new band of Arkies that swept into town. People I spoke to about Arkansas in the 1980s and '90s referred to it as 'terra incognita': a place of corruption and connections, where loyalty was highly valued and a high price was exacted for betrayal. The feeling of suspicion was mutual. In those early days, after 12 years of Republican rule, some in Clinton's circle began to feel the establishment was engaged in a conspiracy against *them*, a plot to keep power in the hands of the Washington political and bureaucrat class, away from the upstart newcomers from the South.

That was the atmosphere into which Vince Foster arrived. He was a mild-mannered man inclined toward privacy, who found himself embroiled in controversy. It started with *Travelgate*, a minor affair involving the White House travel office, the department whose job it was to take care of travel arrangements for the White House press corps whenever the president went on a trip. The travel office consisted of seven dedicated employees, old-timers who had worked for successive presidents. Some had been there since the 1960s. But when the Clintons arrived in Washington, they got wind of financial irregularities. For years the travel office had been handing out lucrative travel contracts to a single firm without competitive tender. Kickbacks were suspected. An audit found an $18,000 hole in the finances. The FBI was called in to investigate. The travel office staff were fired. The White House saw it as house-cleaning. The press saw things differently.

The new woman the Clintonites had brought in to run the travel office turned out to be Bill Clinton's third cousin, who had been in charge of organising travel for the Clinton campaign. Worse, it appeared she had been coordinating with another friend of the Clintons, a Hollywood producer who was also partner in an aviation consulting firm that had been trying to win the White House travel contract. Furthermore, FBI agents later suggested that the White House had pressured them into starting an improper investigation, saying the 'highest levels' were interested. It looked like the Clintons were using the FBI to secure government contracts for their friends. The affair got out of hand. In the frenzied atmosphere surrounding the start of a new presidency, it felt like a firestorm. And Hillary Clinton had lit the match.

From the very beginning of her husband's presidency, Hillary became the focal point of tensions. The most overtly political First Lady since Eleanor Roosevelt, a high-powered lawyer in her own right, she was not content with picking curtains in the presidential residence. Her first act upon arrival in the White House was to establish her own office with its own staff in the West Wing, the political heart of the presidency. No First Lady had ever done such a thing before.

In her memoir, Clinton recounts a story about how naïve she was, in those early days, about her power. She was taking one of her first solo trips as First Lady. A young aide asked her what she would like to drink in her hotel suite. Hillary replied, 'You know, I really feel like a Diet Dr Pepper.'[4] From that day on, she recalled, she couldn't enter a hotel room without finding the fridge filled with the weird-tasting soda. 'I had to recognise,' she wrote, 'how many people wanted to do whatever they could to please me and how seriously they might misinterpret what I wanted.' She felt, she said, like the sorcerer's apprentice in the 1940 Disney cartoon *Fantasia*.

I hadn't seen *Fantasia* since I was a kid, but as far as I remembered, that particular sequence involved ... a broomstick. Focused as I was on the central role of Hillary Clinton as a child-murdering witch in the QAnon story, this seemed like a significant detail. My memory had not deceived me: the Mickey Mouse character puts on the wizard's hat and tries out his magical powers. First, he casts a spell to bring a broomstick to life; then he falls asleep and dreams he is raising storms. When he awakes, he finds he cannot turn off the magic. He hacks the broom to pieces with an axe, only to find the brooms have multiplied and taken over, causing a flood that threatens to engulf him.

What was going on with this Disney metaphor? Was Hillary comparing herself to a witch? One who would struggle to control the forces of magic she unleashed, rampaging broomsticks that would eventually bring her down? I had probably spent too much time pickling in conspiracy theories, finding significance in random details. But Clinton does write that the incident with the Dr Pepper was a warning whose significance she appreciated only later, when she was 'struck by the consequences of an offhand comment' she had made after hearing about concerns of financial mismanagement in the White House travel office.

What appears as an offhand comment in Hillary Clinton's memoir* looked somewhat different to Vince Foster. Clinton had in fact taken a keen interest in the travel office affair; she and Foster had several meetings on the issue, and Foster's notes suggested he felt under pressure to do something about it. When the White House conducted its own inquiry into the *Travelgate* fiasco, it was – according to PBS – 'aimed at pointing the finger some place besides at Hillary'.[5] And so Vince Foster found himself taking some of the blame.

In June 1993, the *Wall Street Journal*, the paper of record for America's financial elite, began preparing a profile of Foster. They contacted the White House for a picture, who declined to provide one. The paper ran an editorial under the headline 'Who Is Vincent Foster?', accompanied by an anonymous outline of a man's head. Foster thus appeared as a shadowy figure, one whose integrity as a lawyer was questionable, the

---

* She recalls telling White House chief of staff Mack McLarty that she hoped he would 'look into it'. (Hillary Clinton, *Living History*).

perfect tool for the new Clinton administration and its cabal of crooked Arkansans.

Foster's reputation meant everything to him. Days before his death, he travelled back home to deliver a commencement address to students at his alma mater, the University of Arkansas Law School. 'I cannot make this point to you too strongly,' he said. 'There is no victory, no advantage, no fee, no favour which is worth even a blemish on your reputation for intellect and integrity.' The grubby world of Washington politics was clearly on his mind.

Colleagues began to notice that Foster was struggling at work. At his wife's urging, he wrote a list of things that were bothering him. The list was later found in his briefcase, torn into little squares. 'The FBI lied ... the press is covering up ... the *WSJ* editors lie without consequence.' Then he wrote, 'I was not meant for the job or the spotlight of public life in Washington. Here ruining people is considered sport.' Days later, he shot himself.

Foster died by his own hand. Five separate official investigations agreed with that conclusion. And yet the conspiracy theories surrounding his death refuse to go away. Donald Trump brought them up in the 2016 campaign. I wanted to know where they were coming from, so I started digging. And the more I dug, the more confused I became. Because, while there is no convincing evidence at all that he died by anything other than suicide, reports into the circumstances surrounding his death are riddled with holes, errors and contradictory testimony – fertile ground for conspiracy theorists.

Take the apparently trivial question of what Foster ate for lunch while sitting at his desk that fateful day in 1993. The *New York Times* reported that an aide brought him a hamburger with onions from the White House canteen, and that Foster removed the onions;[6] the *Washington Post* says it was a cheeseburger and a handful of M&M's.[7] Both quote the same aide, Linda Tripp, a woman who would go on to play a significant role in the Clinton saga. Does it matter what Foster ate for lunch? Not really. But when the details don't add up, people begin asking questions.

Because the body was discovered in a National Park, the initial investigation into Vince Foster's death was carried out by the United States Park Police. More used to dealing with antisocial behaviour in and around the nation's parks and monuments, they appear not to have done a very professional job. Photographs from the scene were underexposed; backup Polaroids were missing; none of the investigators from the scene were at the autopsy; Foster's clothes were dumped in a pile, leaving them exposed to contamination.

In the White House, senior staff blocked investigators from entering Foster's office while they removed piles of documents. The reason, according to Bernie Nussbaum, then White House counsel and Foster's boss, was to protect papers pertaining to the Clintons' *personal* affairs from scrutiny. Exactly what documents they removed was never made clear. Later, when the Whitewater investigation into the Clintons' involvement in a failed real-estate deal gathered pace, people began asking questions. Foster had acted for the Clintons in a personal capacity. Now the line between lawyer-friend and senior government official was becoming blurred.

After the Park Police, the FBI undertook its own investigation into Vince Foster's death, which similarly returned a conclusion of suicide. According to their detailed report,[8] Vince Foster drove up to Fort Marcy Park, placed the muzzle of a .38 revolver in his mouth and pulled the trigger. His body was discovered at around 5.45pm by a man described in the FBI report as a 'CW' or 'confidential witness'. According to the report, this unnamed witness told the FBI he had stopped off in Fort Marcy Park to pee. He walked up a hill towards the old fort and saw what he initially thought was a pile of rubbish. On closer inspection, it turned out to be a body. He alerted the Park Police and drove away, without leaving his details. The report states that the man didn't want his identity revealed. In a footnote, however, the report mentions that the confidential witness 'initially provided this information to G Gordon Liddy, who hosts a radio call in program broadcast from the Washington, DC area'.

Liddy wasn't just any old radio talk-show host. He was an ex-FBI agent turned political operative who headed the bungled burglary of the Democratic Party headquarters in 1972 that eventually led to President Nixon's downfall. He spent four years in jail for his part in the Watergate conspiracy.* In his autobiography, he wrote about his early obsession with Hitler. In jail, he said, he would sing the Nazi 'Horst Wessel' anthem to Black prisoners. By the early 1990s he had reinvented himself as a successful radio talk-show host. He boasted of using effigies of Bill and Hillary Clinton for target practice.

So the first person to apparently see Vince Foster's body was unearthed not by police but by a notorious practitioner of the political dark arts who appeared to have a psychopathic grudge against the Clintons. This seemed to me significant. Especially since, after appearing on Liddy's talk show (in April 1994), and subsequently giving his testimony to the FBI, this confidential witness went on to cast doubt on the whole official narrative surrounding Vince Foster's death. And he did so with the help of an unexpected character, a figure not from the fringes, but from the establishment.

A small band of journalists and citizen investigators coalesced around the Foster case. One was a British reporter by the name of Ambrose Evans-Pritchard. Evans-Pritchard

---

* Liddy had far greater ambitions for Watergate. He initially proposed a wide-ranging, million-dollar sabotage and intelligence-gathering operation aimed against the Democrats. He code-named his scheme 'Gemstone', and his vision included black-bag ops, kidnapping, illegal wiretaps and sting operations involving sex workers. He even volunteered to assassinate an unfriendly newspaper columnist. Richard Nixon himself, with almost comic understatement, called him 'a little nuts'.

was the Washington correspondent for the *Sunday Telegraph*, the venerable mouthpiece of Britain's Tory establishment. Most British journalists followed the lead of the respectable American papers like the *New York Times* and the *Washington Post*. But Evans-Pritchard went his own way. He tracked down G. Gordon Liddy's confidential witness, who told him something potentially explosive: according to the FBI investigation, Foster was found lying on his back with the gun in his hand. But the confidential witness stated that he saw no gun. Something didn't add up. The man told Evans-Pritchard he believed he had 'disturbed the crime scene before it was ready'. 'The whole thing stinks,' he said, 'he clearly didn't shoot himself there. You can't shoot yourself without a gun. The man had no gun. End of story.'⁹

The more Evans-Pritchard pulled at the threads of the Foster story, the more suspicious he became. Apart from the poor record keeping and handling of evidence, there seemed to him to be other holes in the official narrative. Investigators searched the surrounding woods; they were pretty thorough, unearthing old bits of ordnance from the Civil War, but they could not find the bullet that killed Foster. Nor could they explain a blood smear on Foster's right cheek which appeared inconsistent with his injuries and the position of the body. (One likely explanation could be that the inexperienced Park Police had disturbed the body before photographing the scene – but if so, no one admitted to such an elementary error.) The FBI could not locate the man who had initially alerted the police to the body (until he turned up as the confidential witness on a radio talk show), and they ignored or failed to follow up with witnesses who claimed to have seen people in the park behaving suspiciously. Most of these failings could be attributed to the errors of an inexperienced force. But to Ambrose Evans-Pritchard, that was just too convenient. Why didn't the FBI take over the case immediately, he wondered? As it turned out, the day before Foster's death, Bill Clinton had fired the FBI director, William Sessions, over allegations of financial improprieties which came from a report commissioned by Clinton's predecessor, George H.W. Bush. But it was the first time an American president had sacked the head of the FBI. Coincidence? Evans-Pritchard thought not.

He continued digging. He found witnesses who said that the gun appeared at different angles in different crime-scene photos; he reported how Foster's wife initially told investigators she didn't recognise the gun, and later said she did. He tore holes in the 'amateurish' and 'self-evidently mendacious' report by special counsel Robert Fiske, tasked with investigating Foster's death as well as allegations of criminal financial misconduct by the Clintons in Arkansas. He excoriated the Park Police for losing the original photographs of the crime scene. He interviewed a prosecutor who claimed he had found a folder of files that had been deliberately withheld from him by the FBI, which appeared to show a different wound on Vince Foster's neck (according to the official version, he shot himself in the mouth). According to Evans-Pritchard, the prosecutor wanted to open a murder investigation, but 'the FBI cut him off at the knees. They sabotaged the investigation and eventually forced him out of office'.*

Ambrose Evans-Pritchard wasn't making things up.[10] He was diligently uncovering genuine inconsistencies in the various investigations into Vince Foster's death. If I'd found all these holes in the police investigation, I'd have pursued the story too. It seems odd that the likes of the *New York Times* weren't interested. But instead of being congratulated on his scoops in the *Sunday Telegraph*, he was becoming increasingly isolated. His colleagues in the American press had long ago moved on from the Vince Foster story. On the weirder fringes of the right-wing media, wild stories were circulating: *Foster and Hillary had been lovers; Hillary had had him killed in a 'safe house' in Virginia; Foster's body had been transported inside a roll of carpet and dumped in Fort Marcy Park.* In the minds of most establishment journalists, to keep poking away at the minor holes in the Foster case, when the police and everyone else had concluded that he had taken his own life, meant you were associating yourself with conspiracy theorists. People began describing Evans-Pritchard and his friends as 'Foster crazies'.

---

* Author interview with Ambrose Evans-Pritchard. A prosecutor called Miquel Rodriguez resigned from the Starr investigation in 1995, claiming he had been forced out for raising questions about inconsistencies in previous investigations. But in the Office of the Independent Counsel, people were questioning Rodriguez's own professional judgement, suggesting he had fallen for a conspiracy theory.

Evans-Pritchard, for his part, began to suspect a cover-up.

He tracked down a man named Patrick Knowlton. Like the confidential witness, Knowlton had pulled into Fort Marcy Park that summer afternoon in 1993. He too needed a pee. He had spotted Vince Foster's 1989 Honda in the car park, and noticed a suspicious-looking character hanging around. Feeling a little threatened, he quickly found a tree, relieved himself, and left. When he heard about the death of a senior White House aide the following evening, he put two and two together and called the police. Apparently, they weren't interested. Nine months later, the FBI called him and asked him to come in for questioning. He told them about the car. It was brown, he said. The FBI told him he was mistaken – they said the car was blue. None of this made any sense because, according to the registration certificate and all the official accounts, Foster's car was grey.

Evans-Pritchard had some difficulty in locating Patrick Knowlton. Investigators had misspelled his name 'Nolton' in their files. Evans-Pritchard came to believe this was a deliberate ploy. The 'political police' had 'laundered' his name in order to put journalists off the scent, he wrote. When he finally tracked Knowlton down, Evans-Pritchard showed him the FBI transcripts of his interview. He recalled Knowlton's reaction in his book, *The Secret Life of Bill Clinton*: "'a 1988 to 1990 brown or rust brown Honda ..." I never said that, Knowlton muttered.' The FBI transcript went on to suggest that Knowlton said he wouldn't be able to identify the threatening-looking man he'd spotted in the car park. 'That's an outright lie,' he told Evans-Pritchard. 'I told them I could pick him out of a line-up.' Knowlton believed the FBI had deliberately falsified his testimony.

When Knowlton was eventually called in to give evidence to a grand jury, strange things started happening. According to Evans-Pritchard it was Knowlton's girlfriend, Kathryn, who noticed it first.[11] The couple were walking through Dupont Circle, an upscale neighbourhood of Washington, DC, when a middle-aged man in a brown suit stopped and stared at Patrick. Then it happened again. And again. And again. Knowlton telephoned Chris Ruddy, a pugnacious former reporter for the tabloid *New York Post* and fellow 'Foster crazy'. Ruddy joined Knowlton and his girlfriend on their stroll; after half an hour he was apparently so worried by what he saw he called Evans-Pritchard for backup. 'There's a surveillance net of at least thirty people harassing Patrick,' he said. 'I've never seen anything like it in my life.' Later that night, Evans-Pritchard writes, Knowlton called him from his home. He seemed on the verge of a nervous breakdown. Someone, Knowlton said, had got inside his apartment building and was banging on the door. When he answered there was no one there. Outside his window he could see a man in a green trench coat staring up at him. His phone kept ringing. When he picked up, there was no one at the other end. Evans-Pritchard told Patrick to sit tight while he drove over to his apartment. On the way he used his car telephone to 'round up a posse', consisting of himself, an accountant turned amateur detective by the name of Hugh Sprunt who had joined the Foster conspiracy brigade, and – for some reason – a professional clown. Armed with umbrellas, this 'truth militia' mounted a guard outside Knowlton's apartment building, convinced 'the ruling class was going to crush' their friend, a dissident witness in the Foster case.

Evans-Pritchard now believed he, Chris Ruddy and Patrick Knowlton were battling a grand conspiracy. It was scary, but also exciting. In his book, he described a joyful 'sense of camaraderie, when you find yourselves thrown together, fighting on every front at once: against the White House, against the Republicans, against the FBI, against the Justice Department, against the whole power structure of the United States'.[12]

When I spoke to Evans-Pritchard on the phone, he told me this period had been a difficult one for him. He was swimming against the tide, he said, with the White House attacking him and the rest of the press pack ridiculing him. 'The *Washington Post* and the *New York Times*, the "big boys", took the official version. And once those reporters were committed to that position, they didn't want their own work challenged as journalists. They didn't probe anything. And so, among the American people there was a growing suspicion that things weren't being covered. Especially if it didn't go along with their ideological agenda.'

He told me he was reluctant to go back into it all. 'It's a long time ago, I'm a dinosaur now,' he said. But after nearly three decades, his memory was still formidable. He could recall details from FBI transcripts, witness testimonies, crime scene photographs. He said he was still confused by the inconsistencies he and others uncovered. 'I believe the crime scene was falsified for whatever reason.' Some of Starr's investigators believed that too. But wasn't a more likely explanation that inexperienced Park Police officers moved the body when they shouldn't have, and then tried to cover up the mistake? Evans-Pritchard conceded that was possible, perhaps even likely. But I got the sense he didn't really believe it. 'Be careful of Starr,' he warned me. 'He jumped on the Lewinsky stuff because it was fundamentally trivial. Starr wanted to take down Clinton on some sex thing, a surgical strike: keep it limited, don't overcomplicate and don't get into murky waters. The problem is,' he added, 'once you get into this other stuff, you get into Deep State stuff.'

I wanted to hear more from Ambrose Evans-Pritchard. He seemed to me to be an honest broker, a diligent if perhaps impressionable journalist following up leads. But clearly some of his peers thought he was a spreader of disinformation. I suggested we meet face to face. He said he would check his movements and get back to me. It was the last I heard from him.

But one thing he said, just before our telephone call ended, stuck in my mind. 'Arkansas, by the way, is the Sicily of America.

It's completely corrupt. And has been for a very long time. Just bear that in mind.'

The Vince Foster case turned out to be the tip of the conspiratorial iceberg. From the moment Bill Clinton announced his intention to run for the presidency, a cottage industry emerged dedicated to digging up dirt on him and Hillary. Arkansas was the epicentre of those efforts.

* * *

Bill and Hillary Clinton National Airport in Little Rock is a nondescript sort of a place, much like a hundred similar minor airports dotted across America. I walked through the terminal towards the baggage carousel, strolling past a large display extolling the exploits of Arkansas's illustrious former First Couple. The drive downtown takes you down President Clinton Avenue, past the Clinton School of Public Service. The shadow of the Clintons looms large.

I'd come to Arkansas hoping to speak to a lawyer called Cliff Jackson. He lived in Hot Springs, the resort town where Bill Clinton grew up, nestled in the Ouachita Mountains on the shores of Lake Hamilton. Jackson's listing on Google suggested he specialised in personal injury cases, a small-town attorney in an Arkansas backwater. But for a brief period in the 1990s, Jackson had enjoyed a moment of fame, or notoriety, as Bill Clinton's arch enemy: the friend who had stabbed him in the back.

I found Jackson's office by the side of the highway. It was shuttered and looked like it hadn't been used in a while. When I eventually reached him on the phone he was reluctant to talk. I twisted his arm: I'd come all the way from England, I said plaintively, and in the end he agreed to meet me at a rib joint in a strip mall on the outskirts of town.

We queued up at the hatch and ordered a mountain of ribs. I told him I was searching for the origins of a monstrous fantasy about a cabal of satanic paedophiles stealing the 2020 election. I was interested in the boundary between truth and fantasy, I said, and wondered if he could help me locate it. 'I think I bear some responsibility for where we are today,' Cliff said, as a waitress stacked chairs in the half-empty diner. 'But for what I did in the early 1990s, I don't think we would have had Donald Trump.' QAnon, he said, was just a logical extension of the madness he had helped unleash. I was a little startled by his frankness. As he told his story, the ribs sat uneaten on the tabletop, getting cold.

Cliff and Bill met at Oxford in 1968. Bill was a Rhodes scholar, Cliff on a Fulbright: two Arkansas boys in England, thrown together by a shared love of politics and basketball. Bill was a Democrat, Cliff a Republican. But that didn't matter. It was on the court that their rivalry emerged. They played together on the university basketball team. In their spare time they would play endless rounds of HORSE, a one-on-one hoop-shooting contest. Bill did not like to lose, Cliff recalled.

'Bill and I are different,' Cliff reflected, sucking on the end of a congealed pork rib. 'Bill is gregarious and charismatic. I don't consider myself either gregarious or charismatic.' Still, they became friends. The Vietnam war was intensifying. Bill had deferred his military service while at Oxford. In 1969, he was due to return to the United States. In the spring of that year, Bill was sent a draft notice. Like many Americans, Clinton opposed the war. Cliff had a connection in Arkansas who, he thought, might be able to help his friend. So he wrote some letters. Made some calls. And in the end Bill Clinton managed to avoid serving in Vietnam. He played the system, as thousands of others did.

When they returned to America, Cliff Jackson built himself a decent career as a lawyer. But Bill Clinton went into politics and catapulted himself into the stratosphere. Cliff said Bill's success never bothered him. He was happy with his life. But when Bill announced he was running for the presidency, journalists started asking about his Vietnam service. Cliff watched his old friend ducking and diving on TV, dodging the question, suggesting he never received that draft notification that Cliff had helped him avoid. That wasn't how Cliff remembered it. He searched through his old correspondence and found letters from the summer of 1969 detailing his efforts on Clinton's behalf. He had been getting calls from journalists looking for stories about Clinton's past. Now he had a choice to make. 'I'm a person who, once my head hits the pillow, I usually go to sleep,' he told me.

'I sleep the sleep of the innocent – or the sleep of the damned. This night, I couldn't get to sleep. Because I knew that I had a duty to speak up. And yet I knew that if I did, I would be crossing the Rubicon with my friend Bill Clinton.'

Cliff slept on it. The next morning, his mind was made up. He gave his story to the *LA Times*. He went on TV. It was big news for a while, calling into question not just Bill Clinton's patriotism, his fitness to serve as commander in chief, but his relationship with the truth. But Bill weathered the storm and was duly elected as America's 42nd president. Cliff Jackson's act of betrayal had had no effect. Or so it seemed. Sitting in the deserted Arkansas rib joint all those years later, I asked Cliff about his motivation in that moment. Did having this little piece of secret knowledge make him feel powerful? Did it somehow help bridge the enormous gulf of power and success that had developed between him and his erstwhile friend in the two decades since they were shooting hoops together in Oxford? Was he trying to *get even*? Cliff looked at me with his long, thin face. He was silent for a few moments. 'I don't think it makes me feel more powerful,' he said eventually. Then, beneath the dome of his bald head, behind their hooded lids his eyes seem to twinkle, momentarily. 'Now, once the cameras started rolling, did a part of me enjoy it? Yeah, I suppose I did. Yeah ...'

After his moment of TV fame, Cliff became the go-to guy for others with tales to tell about Bill Clinton. A group of Arkansas state troopers came to see him. They had been assigned to

Clinton's security detail as governor. They told how, while on official duty, they would 'procure' women for Bill Clinton: getting phone numbers, arranging motel rooms for sexual trysts, smuggling women into the governor's mansion, and helping Bill keep his liaisons secret from his wife. 'I'm a trial lawyer,' Jackson told me, 'I've been trained to gauge truthfulness and to sense deception. I have learned to trust my intuition. And my gut told me these men were telling God's truth.'

Cliff agreed to represent the troopers and to help get their stories into the media. He wanted the story to appear in one of the establishment papers – better for credibility, he thought, harder for the Clinton machine to spin it as a political hit-job. Cliff introduced the troopers to the *LA Times* reporter he'd spoken to about the draft story. But the *LA Times* editors kept prevaricating, delaying publication. In the meantime, someone else had come to see him: a journalist by the name of David Brock. Brock worked for the *American Spectator*, a conservative magazine that had built up a formidable reputation in the 1970s and '80s featuring writing by the likes of Tom Wolfe and P. J. O'Rourke. By the early 1990s the magazine had become one of the principal exponents of a new and burgeoning genre of journalism: the Clinton hit-piece. In the end, the *LA Times* delayed so long that Brock got his story out first. 'His Cheatin' Heart' was a 12,000-word epic, stuffed with colourful detail depicting Bill Clinton as a serial philanderer. Brock described a man of 'gargantuan appetites and enormous drive', and not just in the bedroom.

One of the troopers told of how, when Clinton ate an apple, he would devour the whole thing, core, stem and seeds. 'He would pick up a baked potato with his hands and eat it in two bites. I've never seen anything like it.' Bill would ingratiate himself with the troopers by engaging in 'locker-room' banter. On one occasion, a trooper recalled Clinton saying one of the women he was sleeping with 'could suck a tennis ball through a garden hose'. Bill and Hillary's relationship, Brock wrote, was more a business partnership than a marriage. He depicted Hillary as foul-mouthed, demanding and ambitious, more invested in her husband's political career than even Bill himself. Hillary tolerated Bill's behaviour 'much as eighteenth century aristocrats maintained marriages of convenience,' Brock wrote, 'to suit the social and material needs of both parties.'

When the *American Spectator* story came out, Cliff said, it was a firestorm, 'a feeding-frenzy, a hurricane, a category-five'. The press descended on Little Rock, Ambrose Evans-Pritchard among them. Everyone wanted to speak to Cliff Jackson and the troopers. And just like Evans-Pritchard, Cliff was feeling jittery. He was fearful of what he called the 'Clinton machine'. At one point he thought he was being followed by a car with Texas plates that traced back to some shadowy government agency. He believed his phone was being bugged. 'I'm not paranoid,' he told me, but 'I guess I was a little scared. I mean, you're dealing with the president of the United States and with people around him who want to cling to power.' Some of those people, he worried, might not 'know their limits'. The troopers told of threatening phone calls from people purporting to represent Clinton. Cliff Jackson thought it as well to put an 'insurance policy' in place. He let it be known that he had much more material, tape recordings, locked in a bank vault in Beverly Hills. Just in case something should happen to him.

When Brock's article came out, Cliff didn't like the tone of it – too much emphasis on sex, he felt, not enough on questions about Clinton's moral fibre. But he couldn't fault Brock on the facts. He had reported the troopers' story accurately enough, he thought. David Brock had made a brief mention of a woman called Paula. One of the troopers said he had propositioned this Paula on Clinton's behalf at a hotel in Little Rock and had subsequently procured a room for Clinton to have sex with her. That woman turned out to be Paula Jones, an Arkansas state employee. After her name appeared in the *American Spectator*, she went public with her story – with the help of Cliff Jackson. She accused Bill Clinton of sexual harassment, of summoning her to his hotel room and exposing himself. Bill Clinton denied the allegations. Over the course of a protracted legal case, Paula Jones's lawyers sought to establish a pattern of behaviour. They asked Clinton whether he had ever had 'sexual relations' with another woman, a White House intern by the name of Monica Lewinsky. Clinton denied it.

Enter Linda Tripp, the one-time White House aide who had brought Vince Foster his last ever lunch of hamburger-

or-cheeseburger. Lewinsky had told her all about her affair with the president, and Tripp had taped the conversations.* Clinton, it appeared, had lied under oath. (In his defence, he claimed he didn't think oral sex constituted 'sexual relations'.) And so Kenneth Starr, the independent counsel who had dug into the Vince Foster story and found nothing untoward, who had spent years investigating Whitewater and had found nothing that would stick to the Clintons, finally had something. Bill Clinton's impeachment was the long tail of Cliff Jackson's decision, all those years earlier, to call his old friend out for being *economical with the truth*. The troopers' story was like a ball of thread that, when pulled at, led – almost – to the unravelling of a presidency, the undoing of a president.

But when the troopers' story came out, something strange happened to the narrative: it split in two. Down one road lay Paula Jones, Monica Lewinsky and impeachment. This was the narrative about the Clintons that came to dominate liberal mainstream America: Bill as the supremely talented but flawed politician whose political enemies had tried everything they could to bring him down (and whose efforts had almost succeeded thanks to

---

* Tripp, whose desk in the White House was positioned just outside Vince Foster's office, was also suspicious about his death. According to an FBI report, it struck her as odd that Foster should remove the onions from his burger: 'She couldn't understand why he would do that if he was planning to commit suicide. It did not make sense to her that he might be worried about his breath if that were the case.' The report added that Tripp did not know whether Foster actually liked onions.

Bill's inability to keep it in his pants). Hillary, meanwhile, having stood by her husband as governor and president, was blazing a trail for women and, by the start of the 2000s, embarking on a promising political career of her own.

Down another road lay an altogether darker tale: a narrative cooked up using many of the same ingredients but with added spice, creating a toxic broth that bubbled away beneath the surface of mainstream America.

CHAPTER 3

THE
SCANDAL
FACTORY

At some point during the category-five hurricane feeding frenzy following the release of David Brock's story, Cliff Jackson had a visit from a film producer. Patrick Matrisciana was 'tall, tanned and smooth, California-looking', Jackson remembered. He was a former boxer who had converted to evangelical Christianity during the 1960s, when the anti-war, left-wing counterculture was sweeping college campuses. Matrisciana would show up at student gatherings and wrangle the loudhailer off whoever was speaking to spread his message of God-fearing conservatism. In the 1980s, with the advent of the VHS video tape, Matrisciana decided he could reach more people through their television screens. He set up a company, Jeremiah Films, and started making a series called *Pagan Invasions*, films with dramatic soundtracks and portentous narration on subjects like the occult. He boasted of infiltrating witch covens.

Matrisciana told Cliff Jackson he was making a documentary about the Clintons, and that he wanted to interview the troopers. Cliff, whose intuition had never failed him, didn't trust him and advised his clients to steer clear. But the troopers didn't listen. Matrisciana flew them out to his ranch – 240 remote acres in southern California, where they and others told their stories on camera. The result was *The Clinton Chronicles*: not so much a documentary as a carnival of conspiracy theory.

The film opens in much the same vein as the *Pagan Invasion* films: brooding synth and strings to a 1980s rock drumbeat. The narrator begins: 'On January 20th, 1993, William Jefferson Clinton became the 42nd president of the United States.' There's a shot of Bill, smiling, walking towards his inauguration ceremony in slow-motion, Hillary visible over his left shoulder. The narrator continues: 'At the time, most Americans were not aware of the extent of the Clintons' criminal background. Nor were they aware of the media blackout, which kept this information from the public.' From there, *The Clinton Chronicles* unfolds like a horror movie. It tells the tale of two young boys whose bodies were found dead on the railway tracks outside a small airfield in Arkansas: murdered because they stumbled upon a multi-million-dollar drug-smuggling operation. 'The fact is, we know who killed these kids,' a former Arkansas police officer tells the camera. '[We] can't do anything with it as long as Clinton's in office. Because it tracks right back to Bill Clinton being involved in the cover-up.' People who tried to alert the police were themselves murdered, the narrator adds. 'Witnesses' come forward, people somehow connected to the Clintons in Arkansas. They talk about how Clinton controlled the legal system, judges, lawyers, the banks; they tell of being intimidated, violently assaulted and left for dead, or their relatives murdered. Somewhere in the midst of all of this, the troopers tell their stories. They are the same stories they told to David Brock, give or take a few minor details; the stories Cliff Jackson's intuition told him were 'God's truth'. But now, they seem less like the peccadillos of a serial philanderer. They appear more sinister, part of a pattern of behaviour from a man drunk on sex and power. The troopers appear as ballast, lending weight to the wild, murderous fantasies about the Clintons as a demonic couple of unchristian appetites at the head of a corrupt cabal. *The Clinton Chronicles* shines a different light on that apple anecdote from the *American Spectator*: Bill in the Garden of Eden, taking the forbidden fruit proffered by Hillary, the apple of American innocence, and devouring it whole.

The film ends with a stark message, white letters against a black screen: 'Since August 1991, an alarming number of Clinton associates have died of unnatural causes. The following is a partial list …' It's the original Clinton Body Count. Vince Foster is there, along with the boys on the train tracks and two dozen others, including one man who supposedly died in a plane crash 'while enroute to interview for this film'. On the internet,

30 years later, people are still maintaining that list. They talk of people connected to the Clintons 'being suicided' – people like Jeffrey Epstein, the financier and paedophile who trafficked young women to satisfy his own desires (and possibly those of his rich and famous friends), and who killed himself in his jail cell in 2019. The list keeps on growing.

Patrick Matrisciana sent VHS copies of *The Clinton Chronicles* to every member of Congress. But his film barely made an impression on mainstream America. Even for a Washington press corps hungry for scandal stories involving the Clintons, the whole thing was so outrageous, so obviously bogus as to be unworthy of the attention of serious journalists.

Matrisciana's film was a flop in Washington, but found its audience elsewhere: in the Church. Jerry Falwell, the influential evangelical preacher and pioneer televangelist, began promoting *The Clinton Chronicles* on his show. Falwell's *Old Time Gospel Hour* was shown on hundreds of TV networks around the country to audiences of up to 10 million viewers. He sold tapes by mail order. He boasted about sending out hundreds of thousands of copies, saying other people had copied them so that the number in circulation eventually numbered in the millions. Falwell not only helped promote the film, he had helped finance it. Between 1994 and 1996 he contributed $200,000 to Matrisciana's anti-Clinton documentaries. The money came via an organisation called 'Citizens for Honest Government'. Along with Matrisciana, another signatory on the account was Chris Ruddy, the tabloid reporter who had joined forces with Ambrose Evans-Pritchard on the Vince Foster conspiracy theory. Ruddy was working for Richard Mellon Scaife, heir to an old banking fortune who owned the *Pittsburgh Tribune-Review*, which published his Foster investigations. And Mellon Scaife was funding David Brock of the *American Spectator.*

Cliff Jackson had been the midwife to a diabolical fantasy. What he didn't know at the time – or at least he told me he didn't know – was that amid all the deranged conspiracy theories, there was an actual conspiracy at work. Not directed *by* the Clintons, but *against* them. And at the centre of the conspiracy was David Brock.

• • •

According to Brock, the Arkansas Project was hatched around the same time that Foster killed himself in a park in Virginia, mid-1993, on a boat trip around Chesapeake Bay off the coast of Maryland. On the boat were Bob Tyrrell, Brock's boss at the *American Spectator*, and three other men, political enemies of the Clintons. The initial impetus for the project was to provide covert support for a disgraced Arkansas judge, David Hale, who was promising to implicate Bill Clinton in the Whitewater financial scandal. Over a number of years it would grow into a much wider cloak and dagger operation, involving informants, safe houses and secret payments.

The Arkansas Project was largely run through the *American Spectator*, even though its existence remained a secret from most of the magazine's staff. Brock claimed he wasn't informed about the details, but pieced together the outlines of the scheme through documents he found lying around on a photocopier at the magazine's office. Richard Mellon Scaife was funnelling cheques of up to $50,000 through the magazine disguised as 'legal fees'. That money made its way to an assortment of dubious characters in Arkansas. They included Rex Armistead, a former Mississippi Highway Patrol officer turned private detective who had caught the Vince Foster bug off Chris Ruddy, and a man named Parker Dozhier, who ran a shop selling bait and fishing tackle on the shores of Lake Catherine in Hot Springs. These people had little in common other than a visceral hatred of the Clintons. Dozier was the project's 'eyes and ears' on the ground in Arkansas. A trapper and furrier by trade, he was a semi-professional spinner of tales with an active imagination who wrote a novel entitled *Pelts: Murder and Mayhem in the Fur Trade*. Dozhier would send tips to the *American Spectator*'s office in Washington, information he had gleaned from local court proceedings or conversations with other 'informants' in Arkansas (including Cliff Jackson.) Dozhier also played host – and paid thousands of dollars – to David Hale, who had become a key witness in Ken Starr's Whitewater inquiry, leaking titbits of information to journalists via classified ads in local newspapers. Brock's job was to travel to Arkansas to 'investigate' these stories – wild rumours about corruption, sex, violence and murder – and turn them into colourful copy for the magazine. He and other members of the conspiracy would stay at a 'safe house', a ramshackle ranch on the outskirts of Little Rock. They would gather at Dozhier's bait shop in Hot Springs, which Brock remembered was littered with copies of *Soldier of Fortune* magazine and other right-wing militia paraphernalia. David Brock knew that much of the 'information' being pumped out by the Arkansas Project was bogus. But there was good money in it.

Brock said he and others at the *American Spectator* were sceptical of the Vince Foster story. But Richard Mellon Scaife was obsessed with it. He called it the 'Rosetta Stone of the Clinton administration': the key to deciphering a secret code.[1] 'Once you solve that one mystery, you'll know everything that's going on or went on,' he said. 'I think there's been a massive coverup about what Bill Clinton's administration has been doing, and what he was doing when he was governor of Arkansas.' Scaife claimed Clinton could 'order people done away with at his will. He's got the entire federal government behind him. [...] God, there must be 60 people [associated with Bill Clinton] who have died mysteriously.'*

---

* Scaife interview with John F. Kennedy Jr, quoted in 'Scaife: Funding Father of the Right' by Robert G. Kaiser and Ira Chinoy, *Washington Post*, 2 May 1999. In a strange twist of fate, JFK Jr, the son of President Kennedy, died in a plane crash in 1999, a year after that interview with Scaife. Conspiracy theorists added his name to the Clinton Body Count. And when QAnon emerged, some of the movement's adherents would claim that JFK Jr had faked his own death. They believed JFK Jr was, in fact, the mysterious person known as 'Q', the secretive figure on a crusade against the Deep State, leaving cryptic clues on the internet about a cabal of satanic paedophiles and a coming storm that would sweep them from power.

Richard Mellon Scaife spent between 1.7^2 and $2.5 million on the Arkansas Project.[3] The aim, David Brock told me, was to create 'a kind of scandal factory', to dig up stories from the Clintons' past – true or false – and 'inject them into the bloodstream of the main media'. Brock eventually turned on his right-wing paymasters and became an acolyte of the Clintons. Reflecting on his efforts a quarter of a century later, he told me you could divide the Arkansas Project's conspirators into two categories: the cynics and the Clinton crazies. Ambrose Evans-Pritchard, he claimed, fell into the latter category: people who genuinely believed the wild conspiracy theories they promoted. In his book *Blinded by the Right*, a mea culpa memoir published in 2002, he described Evans-Pritchard as 'the least cynical of the bunch'. But he thought Ambrose was completely bamboozled by the wild tales he heard from an assortment of Arkansas con men. He had 'no capacity to judge the credibility of sources', Brock wrote. 'To him, the word of a drug-addled ex-con was as good as anybody else's, or perhaps better. I began to think that Ambrose had spent too much time in Nicaragua, a Third World dictatorship where truth was more easily gleaned from the streets than from the government or its agents. He distrusted anyone – right, left, it didn't matter – who was tied into the American political system, which he viewed as thoroughly corrupt. Ambrose's work would condition the movement to believe that Arkansas was a mirror image of Sandinista Nicaragua, a corrupt, backward, one-party state.'

David Brock's scathing assessment of Evans-Pritchard reflects some of the hyperpolarisation that was already creeping into American journalism at the time: two groups of people, each sincere in their view that the other was deluded.

By his own admission, Brock was more cynical. 'I definitely belonged to the group that was in it to do political damage to the Clintons,' Brock told me. 'There was a coordinated operation that was well-funded, that was relentless, that would say and do anything to try to defeat them.' Part of Bill Clinton's success, he said, was 'triangulation' – the effort to distil the essence of both the left and right into a single political force. Triangulation left the Republicans with little to campaign on apart from scandal. The cynics were essentially using the crazies as a means to an end. In the process, Brock said, the politics of the right had become 'unmoored from any concern about reason or fact'.

· · ·

As fast as the Clintons' enemies could make up stories, there were legions of people, 'friends of Bill', who were on hand to rebut them. One of the most enthusiastic rebutters was Gene Lyons, columnist and literary essayist, an establishment figure in Little Rock.

I found Lyons at his home on a quiet tree-lined street: a few steps up to a raised porch leading to a modest front door. I rang the bell, and Lyons shuffled up to greet me wearing a stained T-shirt and a couple of days' worth of stubble. I went inside and said hello to his wife, Diane, whose eyesight was failing, and two tubby Labradors, who ate out of a pair of old frying pans on the kitchen floor. Gene made coffee and we sat on the porch to talk about old times.

Lyons had written a review of Ambrose Evans-Pritchard's book about the Clinton years. He called it 'a militiaman's wet dream [...] the moral equivalent of leaving a loaded pistol in a psychiatric ward'. Like David Brock, he was willing to give Evans-Pritchard the benefit of the doubt: perhaps he was just an impressionable journalist who flew down to Arkansas and found it teeming with stories, a gullible foreigner who took 'every bar-room fabulist and boat-dock novelist' at face value, he said.

I asked Lyons about the general air of corruption that always seemed to surround the Clintons in Arkansas. Forget about the murders, the baseless conspiracy theories, I said. What about the time, for example, just after Bill was elected governor in 1978, that Hillary Clinton made a $1,000 investment in cattle futures, an investment that miraculously netted her $100,000 a few months later? It turned out she had made the investment through an advisor linked to a large Arkansas food producer. The company stood to gain from legislation her husband might enact as governor. Some suspected the lucky windfall had less to do with savvy investing and more to do with political favours. It certainly looked fishy. But the beneficial legislation never materialised, the company's owner ended up backing one of Clinton's rivals, and the minor scandal fizzled out. What about

Whitewater, the complex scandal about a disastrous real-estate venture that got caught up in the collapse of a savings and loan company? The Clintons' business partners in that venture, Jim and Susan McDougal, were convicted and sent to jail (Susan for refusing to answer questions about the veracity of Bill Clinton's testimony under oath). But nothing ever seemed to stick to the Clintons themselves. What about the fact that Hillary – the wife of the governor – was also a partner in one of the state's biggest legal companies, the Rose Law Firm? They represented some of Arkansas's most powerful businesses, some of which also funded her husband's political campaigns; the same firm also did legal work relating to the Clintons' personal business dealings, blurring the line between politics and family interests.

'Realistically, looking back, she probably should have resigned when he became governor,' Gene allowed. 'That would have prevented a lot of trouble.' But Lyons said the salary of the Arkansas governor in the 1980s was small. 'If they were going to have any life after politics, not understanding where it would all end up, Hillary needed to make money.' Bill liked to talk about how he was born to a single mother in a little town called Hope, and grew up in his grandparents' home with little money. But Hillary came from a middle-class family in a prosperous Chicago suburb. 'She was seen as having sacrificed a great deal by burying her light in darkest Arkansas,' said Lyons, whose wife had been on friendly terms with Hillary back in the day. As far as he was concerned, even Bill's sexual 'adventures', were the product of malicious rumour and insinuation. 'One doesn't know exactly who Clinton canoodled with and who he didn't, but you can't believe every single thing you hear.'

. . .

Despite the best efforts of the Clinton crazies, none of the allegations of criminal behaviour ever stuck. The drug running, the murders – it was all fantasy. The best Bill Clinton's political enemies could do was to say that he had lied under oath about his affair with Monica Lewinsky. There were other women, like Paula Jones, who said he had sexually harassed them.* But for many of Clinton's supporters these stories became subsumed into the wider cesspit of nonsense peddled by his enemies.

There was one story, however, that I could not ignore: Juanita Broaddrick.

It was a fine spring day when I set off in my hire car, heading west out of Little Rock towards the state border with Oklahoma. Around an hour into the journey, somewhere south of the Ozarks, there was an abrupt change in the weather. It rained so hard I could barely see the cars in front of me. I slowed down almost to walking speed. The wipers juddered impotently across the windscreen. Giant trucks, huge silver beasts festooned with exhaust tubes and lights, thundered past. I felt isolated and vulnerable in my little tin can on wheels.

---

* Clinton settled the Paula Jones claim – a civil suit – out of court, paying Jones $850,000 while his lawyer maintained her claim was baseless.

By the time I arrived, the rain had vanished again, as abruptly as it had appeared.

Juanita Broaddrick was nearly 80 years old when we met. She welcomed me into her home, a nice house in a small gated community just a few miles from where she grew up. 'Are you rushed for time,' she said, giggling as she poured me a glass of water. 'Because I'll absolutely talk your ear off.'

In 1978, Juanita owned and ran a nursing home; she was an energetic businesswoman in an unhappy marriage. She and her husband were beginning the process of getting divorced, living separate lives under the same roof. She was having an affair, with a man called David Broaddrick, whom she would later marry. It was a busy time for Juanita. As well as raising a son and running her own business, she was active in the local community. Bill Clinton, then attorney general of Arkansas, was running for governor, and Juanita was volunteering for the campaign.

One day she got a phone call from campaign HQ: Clinton was going to be making a stop in the area, could they come to her nursing home and meet some of the staff and residents? Juanita and her colleagues were delighted. They were excited to meet this promising young man who might become governor of their state. When the big day came, they put a large campaign sign out in front of the nursing home, put on their CLINTON FOR GOVERNOR badges, and gathered in the main hall to greet him. Bill Clinton did not disappoint. He was charismatic and charming. He and Juanita shook hands for the press photographers.

Afterwards, Clinton came over to chat. 'I just remember that whole time he talked to me, he never lost eye contact,' she said, more than four decades later. 'It was like what you were saying was the most important thing in the world.'

Juanita does not remember the exact words of that first conversation, but she says she told Clinton in broad terms about the challenges facing the nursing home sector in Arkansas. 'He sort of stops me mid-sentence and says, "Are you ever in Little Rock?" And I said, "Yes, my nurse and I will be there in about three weeks." And he said, "Call my office and let's get together and talk about this. I'm very interested in this."'

Juanita was due to attend a seminar on nursing in the state capital, together with a colleague, Norma Rogers. On 24 April 1978, they set off after work and drove to Little Rock. They checked into the Camelot Hotel. Juanita had put together a presentation to show to Clinton, and the following morning, she phoned his office. Bill wasn't in. But the woman who answered the phone said she had been told to expect a call from Juanita, and to pass on a number for Mr Clinton's apartment. Juanita was a little surprised. She called the number and Bill picked up almost immediately. Juanita explained about the presentation and suggested she stop by his office to talk him through it. As Juanita remembers it, there was a silence at the other end of the line, and then Bill Clinton said: 'You know, I'm not going to be there today.' Juanita was disappointed. Then Clinton said: 'Why don't I come to your hotel right now?' Bill said he would call from the lobby when he got there and suggested they meet in the coffee shop.

Juanita told her colleague Norma to go along to the conference, sign both of them in, and she would join her as soon as she had finished in the coffee shop. A little while later, the phone rang in her room. It was Clinton. He said the lobby was crowded, there were reporters down there, would it be OK to get coffee in her room and discuss it there? 'And I can remember is as though it was yesterday, because I was not a real extroverted person, I'd never been alone in a hotel room with a man I didn't know. And that feeling just sort of goes through you: *Oh … this is my hotel room.*' But Juanita pushed her misgivings aside.

'I was just as nervous as could be,' she remembered. Clinton was standing by the window and Juanita was pouring the coffee, when he said, 'Come here a minute, I want to show you something down here.' Clinton pointed to a building across the street. He said it was an old nineteenth-century jailhouse, which he intended to restore if he got elected. Then he put his arm around her shoulders. Juanita wanted to get away from his embrace. She started to make her way back to the table and the coffee cups. 'And that's when he grabs me and starts to pull me into him.'

She pushed Bill Clinton off her, she remembered. But Clinton pulled her back and started trying to kiss her. 'And that's when I told him, I screamed, "No!"' Every time she screamed, she said, Clinton would bite on her lip. 'I thought, *My God, he's going to bite my lip off.*'

Juanita Broaddrick said Clinton shoved her onto the bed, ripping away at her clothes. 'I am screaming bloody murder. I don't know to this day why someone didn't hear me. I'm struggling and I remember that I could hardly breathe. Because he was so heavy. And that he kept pushing down with one hand on my shoulder and ripping my clothes with the other.'

Then, she said, he raped her.

'When the rape was over, my mouth was bleeding, I could tell it was swollen and painful and I just hurt all over. I was gutturally crying.' Clinton got up to leave. At the door he turned around, motioned towards her swollen lip, and said, 'You'd better put some ice on that.' Then he left.

As soon as she heard the door close, she got up and locked it. Then she lay back down on the bed and tried to comprehend what had happened to her. 'I felt like ... I didn't even hardly exist anymore. That I was just this this lump of flesh laying there on the bed.' Part of her blamed herself. She shouldn't have allowed him to come up to her room, she thought. But alongside the hurt and pain and self-doubt sat another feeling: fear. 'I just kept thinking, when I locked the door: *Somebody is going to come in and get rid of the body. Because this is the attorney general, this man is running for governor. This is serious.* I was so afraid that, if anybody knew about this, is there somebody with him that's going to come in and do something to me so I won't tell?'

Eventually, her colleague Norma Rogers returned. Norma went to fetch ice to put on her mouth and Juanita told her what had happened. They sat at the foot of the bed, she remembered, and Norma said, 'What do you want to do?' Juanita said: 'I just want to go home.'

In the days that followed, Juanita told four more people about the rape, all close friends. She did not tell her husband, and she did not go to the police. 'How could I go to the police?' she said. 'He *was* the police. He was the attorney general of my state. And he regulated nursing homes as attorney general. You know, he could have shut me down at a moment's notice for any reason whatsoever.' Besides that, she had another fear: 'Who in the hell is going to believe me? Who's going to believe that this fine young man, who's running for governor as attorney general, did this to me? I just wanted to go on with my life and accept the mistake I made letting that man come to my room.'

Juanita wanted to move on. But that was not to be. Rumours began to circulate in Arkansas.

In 1992, during Clinton's presidential campaign, Juanita was approached by two men who wanted her to tell her story. She refused. Throughout the 1990s, the story would surface from time to time. Sometimes journalists would call. Juanita ignored them, or if challenged outright, denied it had happened. She had seen what happened to other women who spoke out – they would be attacked in the media, their reputations trashed. She wanted no part of it.

When Paula Jones filed her case, her lawyers sought to establish a pattern of sexually predatory behaviour by Clinton.

They issued a subpoena, and in January 1998, Juanita filed an affidavit, as 'Jane Doe #5', in which she denied any 'unwelcome sexual advances' by Bill Clinton. But in April that year, Kenneth Starr's Office of the Independent Counsel also subpoenaed Broaddrick. Her son, Kevin, intervened. Juanita had told him about the rape when he was 19 years old. Now 28 and a qualified lawyer, Kevin told her: 'Mom, Paula Jones was a civil suit. This is federal. This is serious. You've got to tell the truth.'

But now Juanita Broaddrick had a problem. Just three months earlier she had told Paula Jones's lawyers, under oath, that nothing had happened. If she changed her story, she would be vulnerable to charges of perjury. The FBI officers sent by Starr gave her assurances they would protect her from prosecution in return for the truth. And so she told them. The truth, she said, was that Bill Clinton had raped her. For 20 years she had kept her secret. For nearly a decade, she had been under mounting pressure to tell her story – from Clinton's political enemies, from journalists, from lawyers. She had resisted them all. It was only the sheer blunt force of the Starr inquiry, which thundered like a juggernaut through the politics of the 1990s, that forced the story out of her. 'There I was,' she remembered years later, as we sat in her living room in Arkansas, 'crying in a deposition with people that I didn't know. It was awful.'

Kenneth Starr submitted his report to Congress on 9 September 1998. Over 222 pages he laid out the grounds for impeachment. There was no mention of Juanita Broaddrick.

The report came with seven appendices: a further 3,183 pages of notes, emails, faxes, evidence logs and interview transcripts that are now part of the public record. Buried in page 74 of the second appendix is single clue: 'Jane Doe #5 signed an affidavit in which she denied that the president made "unwelcome sexual advances toward me in the late seventies." (On April 8, 1998, however, Jane Doe #5 stated to OIC investigators that this affidavit was false.)' And then a footnote, which pointed the attentive reader to the full transcript of Juanita Broaddrick's interview with the FBI, in which she told of being raped by Bill Clinton.

Why had Starr not made more of her explosive allegation? 'The main thing that Ken Starr's people wanted to know was if there was any obstruction of justice,' Juanita told me. '*Has anyone ever threatened you? Have you received anything monetarily from the Clinton campaign? Has anyone offered anything to you to not say anything?*' After four years, during which the Office of the Independent Counsel had investigated corruption in the Whitewater affair, the death of Vince Foster and numerous other allegations of abuse of power, it had all boiled down to two questions: had Bill Clinton lied under oath about his affair with a White House intern, and had he obstructed justice by urging others to lie on his behalf?

If Juanita had invented her story in order to damage Bill Clinton, now was her chance. But she didn't take it. No one had threatened her, she said, no one had offered her anything. 'I had nothing for Ken Starr.'

As impeachment approached, Juanita Broaddrick's name was again circulating among journalists. She continued to rebuff their requests. But one reporter would not take no for an answer. Lisa Myers, a well-respected reporter for NBC News, wrote her a long letter. One way or another, Myers argued, her story was going to come out. She urged Juanita to take control. 'The worst thing that can happen is if the story starts to come out in pieces, or inaccurately,' she wrote. 'Your name and allegations will be known to the world ... but in a form that the White House has time to pick apart.' Lisa Myers said she had been through a similar though – as she put it – less traumatic experience. She *believed* her.

On 20 January 1999, Myers, accompanied by producers and a camera crew, arrived at Juanita Broaddrick's home and started setting up for an interview in her living room. Juanita was in the bathroom, getting ready. Suddenly, it seemed too daunting, too traumatic. She broke down in tears. *I've got to go out there and tell Lisa to pack up and go home*, she thought. It was her husband, David Broaddrick, who persuaded her to go through with it. So, she re-did her make-up, sat down in front of the cameras, and let it all out.

NBC knew they were sitting on a bombshell. If it aired before the Senate vote, Juanita Broaddrick's story could, conceivably, bring down the president. Lisa Myers and her team had work to do. Apart from Broaddrick herself, there were no direct witnesses. They contacted the women Juanita said she had told about the rape at the time. Four of the five backed up her story. The NBC team went through the records and found there was indeed a nursing seminar at the Camelot Hotel in Little Rock in the spring of 1978. They found Juanita's name on the list of attendees. Other details checked out too: the building Juanita said Clinton had pointed to from the window of her hotel room just before he assaulted her had since been demolished, but in 1978 the old county jailhouse had been visible from the hotel.

Juanita was given to understand the interview would be aired on *Dateline* nine days later, on 29 January 1999. The Senate was due to vote in mid-February. As they waited, she and her husband went skiing in Colorado with their kids. She got a phone call. It was Lisa Myers. 'I have good news and bad news,' Myers told her. Juanita's heart sank. 'The good news is, you're credible. The bad news is, you're very credible.'

NBC News executives were wrestling with the question of what to do with the interview. Myers was convinced Broaddrick was telling the truth. She tested her story every way she could think of. Nothing had emerged to cast doubt upon its veracity, and Juanita's telling of it had never wavered. 'It never got better. It never got worse. It was always the same.'[4] It was the exact same story she told me more than 20 years later. Myers had her supporters at the network. But others at NBC headquarters in New York wanted to kill the story without even seeing the interview.[5] Executives were concerned: how could they prove a rape allegation that was 20 years old, let alone one against a sitting president facing trial in the Senate? As executives watched and re-watched the tape, as they went back over all the evidence Myers had gathered, they kept asking for more.

As January turned to February and the day of the Senate vote approached, news of the Broaddrick interview started to leak. Matt Drudge, who had broken the Monica Lewinsky story, reported that NBC had come under pressure from the White House not to air the story. The White House refused to comment. NBC denied it emphatically. The delay, they said, was purely the product of journalistic rigour and due diligence. A campaign sprang up. On Fox News, then still a fledgling insurgent TV network, anchors wore 'Free Lisa Myers' badges. Now some familiar characters started crawling out of the woodwork. Rush Limbaugh was talking about Lisa Myers on his radio show – the same Limbaugh who in 1993 had told his listeners that Vince Foster had been murdered in an apartment belonging to Hillary Clinton, and that his body had been rolled up in a carpet and subsequently dumped in a park; Jerry Falwell, who had financed and distributed *The Clinton Chronicles*, told the millions of viewers of his *Old Time Gospel Hour* to flood the NBC switchboard with calls. If these efforts were aimed at prodding NBC into airing the story before the Senate vote, they were likely counterproductive.

Juanita's story was becoming bound up not only with the highly politicised drama of the Starr report, but also with the characters on the fringes, the oddballs and fantasists, the hucksters and shadowy operatives whose stories had come crawling out of the Arkansas swamps and infected the high-minded world of Washington politics. As one journalist wrote in a contemporary account, Juanita Broaddrick's story was now 'fruit from a poisoned tree'.[6]

And so, NBC sat on it. On 12 February 1999, as expected, the Senate voted to acquit Bill Clinton. A week later, the *Wall Street Journal* scooped NBC and published Juanita Broaddrick's story. Bill Clinton's lawyer, David Kendall, responded: 'Any allegation that the president assaulted Ms. Broaddrick more than 20 years ago is absolutely false.' When Clinton himself was asked about it at a press conference, he said he had nothing to add. Lisa Myers's report finally aired a few days after that. It ran opposite the Grammy Awards, which was dubbed the 'Grammy Year of Women' because every artist nominated for Album of the Year was female. Madonna opened the show with a performance of 'Nothing Really Matters'. A week later, Monica Lewinsky's first TV interview pushed Juanita Broaddrick off the front pages and out of the public consciousness. And so the story faded away. For the Washington establishment, the politicians, the media, it wasn't the right ending to the impeachment story. And with impeachment out of the way, even Clinton's enemies seemed to have no more use for it. Juanita Broaddrick watched the *Dateline* interview at home with her family when it aired. At the point when she broke down in tears in front of the cameras, she said, she had to leave the room. The whole saga put a strain on her marriage. She and David Broaddrick separated in 2002. Juanita Broaddrick says she didn't watch the end of the *Dateline* report until many years later.

But then, someone did find a use for her story. And they would wield it as a weapon, not against Bill but against Hillary.

CHAPTER 4

PERSISTENT
MAKE-BELIEVE

The more I looked at it, the more it seemed like the 1990s existed on two separate planes of reality. I was 12 when the Berlin Wall came down, 16 when Bill Clinton first took office, 21 when he emerged from the other side of the Monica Lewinsky scandal and impeachment. The 1990s was the decade when I came of age. From my vantage point, the collapse of Communism in the East had been the harbinger of a total victory for liberalism in the West: not just economic but social and political as well. The world was run by liberals, from the people in the banks on Wall Street to the people who made the films in Hollywood. And the Clintons were their avatars: smart, urbane, progressive, successful, even a little bit cool. They seemed to have won the arguments. All of them. And as the millennium approached and one Clinton prepared to leave the stage, another was waiting in the wings. Could she go all the way? Perhaps. If you lived along America's coastlines, east or west, and you got the *New York Times* delivered to your door every morning, you might have been forgiven for thinking that the churn of history had indeed come to a halt. The dramatic tension between left and right that had powered the story of the post-war years, the grit in the global oyster, had produced a shimmering pearl: global, free-market capitalism with a social democratic face. The business of democracy, at home and abroad, was now merely a question of management. The fundamental question of what *system* worked had been settled. And so, China joined the WTO, Russia began its (ill-fated) experiment with extreme capitalism, while America led the world as the sole global superpower. The tide was inexorably rising.

But between the Atlantic and Pacific Oceans there was another universe entirely. Bill Clinton's fabled strategy of triangulation, of adopting some of his opponents' policies while pursuing enough of the causes dear to his base not to alienate them, made him an unbeatable political force. He weakened the Democrats' traditional support for labour unions, while promoting progressive social policies that kept minority and working-class Americans within the Democrat fold. Clinton alighted on this election-winning strategy in the 1970s and 1980s. As governor of Arkansas he had supported union-busting legislation favoured by the state's big businesses in the hope of dissuading them from supporting his opponents. Arkansas may have been a political backwater, but it was home to two of America's biggest companies: Walmart and Tyson Foods. As Clinton's political fortunes prospered, these companies grew into giant global corporations.*

While in the rust belt jobs were exported to China and other parts of the booming global market, the weakened US labour movement was shedding membership. Whole swathes of America were being left behind. Over the same period, from the 1970s onwards, the country's plethora of small, local, family-owned newspapers, which had nurtured an engaged democratic populace, were rapidly being consolidated into corporate behemoths. By 1990, 14 companies controlled half of America's 1,600 daily newspapers.[1] Over the following three decades, the rise of the internet would further hollow out the remaining purveyors of serious local journalism. The mechanism whereby citizens were informed about the decisions made on their behalf was becoming increasingly centralised.

Boats that do not rise on the tide sink beneath the surface. Many of the stories that made up the rich and varied tapestry of American life existed out of sight of the people who decided what passed for news, either because they didn't know about

---

* Hillary Clinton was appointed to the board of Walmart in 1986 and remained there until she took up residence in the White House six years later. The Clintons' relationship with Tyson Foods was bumpier. But the minor scandal about cattle futures – in which Hillary's $1,000 bet on the cattle market miraculously netted her a $100,000 profit – would likely never have become a scandal in the first place had the trade not been organised by an investment advisor who also worked as a lawyer for Tyson Foods, at a time when the company stood to gain from policies Bill Clinton might enact as governor.

them, or because they didn't fit the bigger national narrative. These stories told of an America slowly sinking in terminal decline. Many who lived that reality were experiencing a jarring sense of cognitive dissonance. On their TV screens they heard experts telling an optimistic story of America's undisputed leadership in the world fuelling a new age of prosperity as globalisation took hold. The reality of their daily lives was different: disappearing jobs and wage stagnation, as the middle classes fled to the suburbs and the once-prosperous downtowns of Middle America emptied out.

From the dawn of civilisation, from the *Ramayana* to the *Odyssey*, from the Nordic sagas to the tales of the Old Testament, people have turned to stories. The tellers of these tales weren't there just to while away the long winter nights. They had a crucial function in human society: they helped their communities to understand their environment, to navigate an often-hostile world. When Homo americanus looked into the mirror the 1990s corporate media held up to their lives, many saw something that was barely recognisable: a grotesque, distorted image. How could these stories help them understand their condition? How could they trust what these people were telling them? They began to look elsewhere.

. . .

One hot Saturday afternoon in the summer of 1995, Chris Lehane climbed up to the fourth floor of the Old Executive

Office Building in Washington, DC. A late nineteenth-century edifice in the ornate French Second Empire style, the building stands out among the neo-classical power architecture that dominates this part of DC. It looks more like a grand European hotel or railway terminus than what it really is: the overspill office for the executive branch of the United States government, where most of the White House staff actually work.

Lehane was special assistant to President Clinton. That was his official job title. In reality, he was an attack dog. His role, he told me when I spoke to him a quarter of a century later, was managing the White House's response to what he called 'the various Republican-generated controversies of the era'. This was 'pre-Monica', he added: Monica Lewinsky was 19 years old, still in college, her ill-fated White House internship two years off.

Lehane's time was mostly consumed by Whitewater. His office was located in room 488 – a spinners' HQ piled high with Whitewater cartoons and documents, pie charts detailing the amount of money Congress had spent on what the Clinton administration was keen to portray as a politically motivated non-story. He was part of a two-man unit variously known as the 'garbage men' or 'masters of disaster'. Many years later he co-wrote a film based on his time at the White House. '[T]he film shows that to win in politics you sometimes have to use the hardest blows to get people in office who will achieve the highest ends,' he wrote. 'This is politics not how you wish it were played, but how it really is played – a knife fight in a telephone booth.'[2]

This particular Saturday morning, Chris Lehane wasn't heading to his office. He was heading to a small room with no windows, a closet really. Inside there were a dozen or so computers – among only a handful in the whole White House complex that were hooked up to what was then called the 'World Wide Web'. Lehane's mission that day had – at first sight – nothing to do with Whitewater. Two years after his death, the White House was still getting calls about Vince Foster. These questions, Lehane said, were 'off the wall'. He wanted to know where they were coming from. And he suspected he knew where to find the answer: this new technology known as 'the internet'.

Lehane sat down behind one of the computer terminals and went online. He found himself in a series of chat rooms, the ancestors of today's social media platforms. People swapped theories about how and why Vince Foster had been killed, the sex scandals, the corruption allegations of Whitewater, the smuggling of guns and drugs through Mena Airport, the dead boys on the railway tracks; in this world these stories were all connected. It was a parallel reality, a self-sustaining information ecosystem that existed entirely outside of the world of establishment journalism that occupied most of Chris Lehane's time.

When he emerged into the hot and humid air of the DC summer afternoon, he stood outside the Old Executive Office Building, blinking, feeling like he had just glimpsed the future.

The top-down model of communication, in which officials could control the message through the medium of radio, television and the political press corps, was coming to an end. In that moment, Lehane realised that under the surface of Washington politics, buried beneath the phone boxes in which political operatives and their proxies in the old media were busy slashing each other in a semi-choreographed blood-spattered tango, a whole other world was taking shape, a primordial digital soup where stories germinated and multiplied like bacteria in a Petri dish.

The Arkansas Project was still a closely guarded secret. But Lehane had figured out the contours of it. And he had seen how the internet had the potential to spread these stories beyond the wildest dreams of David Brock and his colleagues. Working through the night, he compiled a dossier. It was 331 pages long. He titled it 'The Communication Stream of Conspiracy Commerce'.

Lehane outlined what he called the 'blow-back strategy': political mischief-makers would feed stories to the British press. (The *Sunday Telegraph* is extensively featured. To Ambrose Evans-Pritchard's fury, Lehane refers to this venerable old broadsheet as a 'British tabloid'.) Once the story was printed on the other side of the Atlantic, Lehane wrote, it was picked up on the internet and then reprinted by right-wing papers in the US. From there the story bounced to the Republican-controlled Congress, where a committee would be set up to investigate. And once that happened, the mainstream press – the *New York Times* and the *Washington Post* – would have no option but to report on it.

Lehane called it 'conspiracy laundering'. Many of the central characters in Lehane's conspiracy were by now familiar to me. Lehane identified Richard Mellon Scaife as the ringleader. The dossier describes him as a little-known recluse, a 'Wizard of Oz' figure, orchestrating the machinations of the conspiracy industry. Ambrose Evans-Pritchard also features prominently. So does Chris Ruddy. Newt Gingrich – the Republican speaker of the house and thorn in the side of Bill Clinton – looms large. Cliff Jackson is there, as are some of his state troopers, and of course an assortment of women who had accused Bill Clinton of sexual impropriety of one kind or another.

Lehane's dossier circulated through the White House; it would be shown to other journalists as a warning against falling into the conspiracy-theory trap. Some would use it as the basis for stories about the Clinton crazies. Evans-Pritchard started getting calls from other reporters asking him whether he had ever accepted money from Scaife. He suspected the White House of orchestrating hit pieces against him and Ruddy. When Evans-Pritchard learned the contents of the dossier, he wrote, he found it revealing. 'What came through strongest was the growing alarm that the investigative journalism on Foster's death was striking close to home. Clearly someone was awake at night in the White House fretting.'[3] As for the American media, he came to believe it behaved 'as an adjunct of the governing elite'. It was 'incurious, slothful, consensual, pedestrian, biased without acknowledgment, fearful of challenging power, and not particularly honest.'⁴ Eventually the dossier landed on the First Lady's desk. Hillary Clinton's famous remark – in a 1998 TV interview after the Lewinsky story broke – about a 'vast right-wing conspiracy' had its origin in Chris Lehane's dossier.

Was it really a conspiracy though, I wondered as I leafed through the dossier? Certainly, people were coordinating with each other to spread negative stories about the Clintons. And certainly, some of those stories were bogus. But some weren't. The White House treated conspiracy theories about Vince Foster's death and stories about Bill Clinton's sexual transgressions with exactly the same disdain. As far as the White House was concerned, all these stories – beginning with the wild fantasies about murder and drug-running emanating from the swamps of Arkansas and ending with Ken Starr's legal enquiries about perjury and obstruction of justice – were indeed part of the same conspiracy. They involved some of the same protagonists and they had the same aim: to bring down the Clintons. But in my mind there was a crucial difference: while Vince Foster had *not* been murdered, Bill Clinton *had* had sex with Monica Lewinsky. And then there was Juanita Broaddrick's story.

In other words – it wasn't just the co-conspirators of the Arkansas Project who deliberately mixed truth with lies, reality with fantasy. The Clintons were at it too, and they had a whole political and media machine behind them. In my mind, a proper conspiracy had to have some hidden purpose at first sight unconnected to events playing themselves out on the surface, some nefarious cause prosecuted by unseen hands. This did not seem to qualify. This looked like the rough and tumble of politics. A knife fight in a telephone booth.

But there were two names that kept appearing in Chris Lehane's dossier that seemed out of place in this company of over-credulous reporters and partisan political actors: James Dale Davidson and William Rees-Mogg.

Rees-Mogg was the former editor of *The Times* of London, another figure of the British establishment (and father of Jacob Rees-Mogg, MP). I was less familiar with Davidson, though I had come across his name in Evans-Pritchard's book. He described Davidson as a 'tall, slender, elegant man of dry humour and considerable wealth'. It seemed the two were friends. Davidson would 'wine and dine' Evans-Pritchard at the best restaurants in DC.

Davidson and Rees-Mogg published a newsletter called *Strategic Investment*. There were hundreds of similar publications circulating in the 1990s, subscription services for investors that sent out monthly tips on stocks and shares, as well as analysis of the political and economic environment. But the reason this particular newsletter had come to Chris Lehane's attention was that it was also peddling the Vince Foster conspiracy theory.

This seemed like strange fare for an investment newsletter. But Davidson had caught the Vince Foster bug. He used his money, among other things, to pay for independent experts to examine the handwriting in the torn-up 'suicide note' found in Foster's briefcase.* Evans-Pritchard described *Strategic Investment* as part of a new American samizdat media, an information ecosystem driven by the internet resembling the faxes and xeroxed literature that circulated in the dying years of the Soviet Union. 'What was bothering the White House most about the internet was the enormous amplification it gives to newsletters like *Strategic Investment*,' Evans-Pritchard wrote. 'The effect was highly subversive and the White House was having great trouble jamming the broadcast mechanism.'[5]

What were an investor and a British Tory grandee doing swimming in these conspiratorial waters? Why were they perpetuating this bogus theory, that Vince Foster had been murdered at the behest of the Clintons, when multiple investigations had concluded there was no foul play? Alongside their newsletter, Davidson and Rees-Mogg wrote a book called *The Sovereign Individual*. In the years since it was first published in 1997, this book has become something of a cult classic, a guidebook to the future, among a powerful group of people: the crypto bros and tech accelerationists of Silicon Valley.

In the very first chapter, the book appears to predict a coming storm. The opening pages seem suffused with millennial angst: 'Just as an invisible, physical change of ions in the

---

* Evans-Pritchard and the 'Foster crazies' were suspicious of the note. It came to light only several days after Foster's death, despite the extensive search of his office, and when it did, White House staff were evasive about it. The experts James Dale Davidson employed claimed the note was a forgery.

atmosphere signals that a thunderstorm is imminent even before the clouds darken and lightning strikes, so now in the twilight of the millennium, premonitions of change are in the air. One person after another, each in his own way, senses that time is running out on a dying way of life.' And then Davidson and Rees-Mogg deliver a history lesson, focusing on the end of the fifteenth century. (*Witches and the printing press*, I thought, *the start of my own journey.*)

In the late medieval period, Davidson and Rees-Mogg write, the Catholic Church was haemorrhaging credibility. The paramount institution of the age, it was riddled with corruption and moral decay, from the lower ranks of the clergy right to the very top, selling indulgences and fathering children out of wedlock. History, they predict, is about to take another turn. For yesterday's priests and bishops, read today's bureaucrats and politicians. Enter the Clintons.

The book talks of Bill's 'fatherless childhood in Hot Springs, Arkansas, a centre of gambling, prostitution, and organised crime to which most of his family had some connection.'[6] Some of the details read like the script of *The Clinton Chronicles* – such as the smuggling of drugs and guns through Mena Airport in Arkansas. Citing Bob Tyrrell, whose magazine the *American Spectator* played host to the Arkansas Project, they claim one of Bill Clinton's former bodyguards alleged he was 'complicit in death-squad activity', to prevent anyone from talking. And then there is Vince Foster. Referencing Ambrose Evans-Pritchard's work in the *Sunday Telegraph*, they say Foster – at the behest of Hillary Clinton – hired a former security guard to spy on Bill Clinton. That security guard, a man by the name of Jerry Parks, was later found dead in his car, shot in a 'gangland-style assassination.'[7] US politics, they write, was entirely penetrated by drug money. Bill Clinton was the leader of a system that was riddled with corruption, irredeemably hollowed out, its inevitable demise only a matter of time.

The fact that these 'crimes' were not more widely known, the authors claimed, was another feature of a system on the verge of implosion: persistent make-believe. After the fall of Rome, Rees-Mogg and Davidson write, the emperors in the West had been deposed by German kings. But the new rulers pretended nothing had changed: the old imperial insignia was still displayed on public occasions; the Senate continued to meet. It was the 'preservation of the façade of the old system.'[8] In the twentieth century, they write, the corporate media was engaged in a similar deception, depicting a country at the peak of its power, a democracy working as it should, ignoring any stories that might undermine the system.

The most important engine of change was technology, they write. That applied as much at the end of the fifteenth century – the printing press, the gunpowder revolution – as it did at the end of the twentieth. Now, the agent of change was the internet. And here is where the book becomes a little more ominous. Because unlike the far-fetched conspiracy theories about Vince Foster,

Davidson and Rees-Mogg's predictions about the imminent future – published in 1997 – look pretty accurate 25 years later.

They predict the internet will abolish the job-for-life to be replaced by a gig economy; they foresee the expansion in off-shoring, with the super-wealthy moving their assets around from jurisdiction to jurisdiction at the click of a button. This in turn will hurt governments' abilities to collect taxes, shrinking the state. They predict digital currencies will lead to a privatisation of money, reducing the ability of governments and nation-states to solve their crises by printing cash. They predict that artificial reality and computer game technology will 'liberate information from the bounds of reality'. In the future, they write, you will be able to watch 'any story you wish, true or false, unfold on your television/computer with greater verisimilitude than anything that NBC or the BBC can now muster'.[9]

All of these changes, they write, will lead to an 'epidemic of disorientation'. They predict a wave of resentment from those they describe as being of middle talent in industrialised countries where the 'national economy brought high income to unskilled work in the twentieth century'.[10] They predict 'an intense and even violent nationalist reaction [...] suspicion of and opposition to globalization, free trade [...] hostility to immigration [...] popular hatred of the information elite, rich people, the well-educated, and complaints about capital flight and disappearing jobs'. The list goes on. I wondered how many of the people who voted for Donald

Trump would recognise themselves in that description? How many who stormed the Capitol on 6 January 2021? Had Davidson and Rees-Mogg identified the Trump wave 20 years before it became a reality? And if so, how many of their other predictions were also about to be realised? Because *The Sovereign Individual*'s main message is this: the nation-state is collapsing; democracy is dead. And if you don't want to get screwed, you'd better get ready.

The Sovereign Individual is as much a prophecy as a handbook. Davidson and Rees-Mogg believe that if you can glimpse the future, you can prepare for it, to weather the coming storm. A select few will be able to profit in almost unimaginable ways: 'The most obvious benefits will flow to the "cognitive elite", who will increasingly operate outside political boundaries'.[11] Once they have let slip the 'shackles of politics', once they are liberated from the bounds of reality, these individuals will help radically shrink the power of the state and increase private control over resources. In place of the collective power of the nation state, a new power will rise: the sovereign individual. 'What mythology described as the province of the gods will become a viable option for the individual,'[12] they write. These sovereign individuals will, they say, 'compete and interact on terms that echo the relations among the gods in Greek myth. The elusive Mount Olympus of the next millennium will be in cyberspace.'[13]

The book ends with a prediction:

The shift from an Industrial to an Information society is bound to be breathtaking. The transition from one stage of economic life to another has always involved revolution. We think that the Information Revolution is likely to be the most far-reaching of all. It will reorganise life more thoroughly than either the Agricultural Revolution or the Industrial Revolution. And its impact will be felt in a fraction of the time. Fasten your seat belts.[14]

After reading *The Sovereign Individual*, I felt the same way I did at the end of the drawing class months earlier – like I had just glimpsed the contours of something significant. What if, I wondered, James Dale Davidson and William Rees-Mogg were anxious about missing out? What if history turned too slowly for them to profit from it? Were they trying to accelerate the future, to bring about the very revolution they foretold?

Looking back over old copies of their *Strategic Investment* newsletter, its pages are filled with anti-democratic sentiment. In the November 1999 issue, Davidson writes from New Zealand, where he says he was witnessing 'the damage that an anachronistic electoral process imposes on countries that otherwise have a good head start in preparing for the competitive conditions of the Information Age'. He was referring to that country's general election, in which the free-market-oriented National Party was defeated at the polls by the Labour Party. Democracy, he is telling his readers, is bad for business. To say this, he adds with a knowing wink, is heresy: 'A perfunctory cheer for Democracy is "the public cant" of the modern nation-state system.'

'The future is disorder,' they quote Tom Stoppard at the beginning of their book. 'A door like this has cracked open five or six times since we got up on our hind legs. It is the best possible time to be alive ...'

William Rees-Mogg died in 2012. He missed the turmoil of Trump, the shock of January 6th. I contacted his son. Jacob was polite but busy with a new job at the time (minister for Brexit opportunities) and regretted he didn't have time to talk about his father's old writings. The book is in fact dedicated to Jacob's younger sister, Annunziata Rees-Mogg. I drove out to see her at her medieval home in Lincolnshire. She could shed little light on her father's intentions. She hadn't read the book, she told me. In 1994, when she was 15 years old, her father had given her a copy of *Brave New World* for Christmas, signifying – she thought – his interest in texts that see into the future. He himself was a Luddite, she remembered: he never learned to type; when his family finally persuaded him to get a mobile phone, he wanted the oldest model he could get. As for making profits out of chaos, he was 'jolly bad at it', Annunziata said, far too interested in ideas to make much money from disaster. In Annunziata's telling, William Rees-Mogg – or Baron Rees-Mogg of Hinton Blewitt in the County of Avon, to give him his proper title – was a Tory of the old school, a Somerset man through and through, a conservative whose love of family and place, whose reverence for history, did not accord to my idea of a burn-it-all-down accelerationist. 'I think, overall, the book is more sensationalist than was my father's nature,' she concluded. She implied, I think, that any revolutionary zeal had come from his co-author.

James Dale Davidson was still alive, still editing his *Strategic Investment* newsletter. The great prognosticator claimed he called Donald Trump a day *before* the 2016 election to congratulate him on his victory. 'I think he sussed out the fact that the whole business model of Western civilisation is kaput,' he said.[15] Brexit and the election of Donald Trump was evidence that the central prophecy of *The Sovereign Individual* was correct. What did he make of January 6th? What did he think when he saw all those old conspiracy theories about the murderous Clintons, wild tales he had helped to spread, erupting again all over the Capitol in Washington, DC? Did he rejoice?

Davidson did not want to speak to me. In an email, he said he wasn't spinning any conspiracy; he was simply trying to get to the bottom of a mystery that was close to the president and First Lady of the day. Then he flipped my question back onto me. 'Blaming me, my newsletter or *The Sovereign Individual* for conspiracy theories including QAnon is ridiculous,' he wrote. 'Insinuating that I could be part of a plan to deliberately seed chaos in order to profit from it later is the ravings of a tin foil hatted lunatic. Any sane person knows QAnon is malarkey.'

Perhaps he was right. Perhaps I had spent too much time wading through the murky swamps of Arkansas conspiracy theories. But I couldn't quite shake the nagging suspicion that Davidson and Rees-Mogg's dream, of a world unshackled from democracy, had come perilously close to realisation when the mob stormed the Capitol in Washington, DC, on January 6th. And it did seem to me that some of the key protagonists in this drama were avoiding me: James Dale Davidson, Ambrose Evans-Pritchard, and now another – Chris Ruddy.

•   •   •

Ruddy, even more than Evans-Pritchard, was the driving force behind the Vince Foster conspiracy theory. I had emailed him right at the start of my investigation, asking if he would speak to me. He politely declined. So I started digging.

Having exhausted the Vince Foster story, Ruddy decided on a change of direction. It was 1998. Matt Drudge had just broken the Monica Lewinsky story, and Ruddy had seen how the Drudge Report had transformed itself from an insurgent online operation into a massive force. If Drudge could do this as a one-man band, Ruddy thought, what might *he* do with a better-resourced operation? He wanted to set up a website: Newsmax. It would be a kind of hybrid – an 'alternative' news website that also sold newsletters, hard copies of which would be mailed out to subscribers, covering subjects as far-reaching as politics, economics and health. Ruddy pitched his idea to two familiar figures: Richard Mellon Scaife and James Dale Davidson. The former would put up some money; the latter contributed his soothsayer's vision of the growing power of the internet, and agreed to join the board. He was later joined by William Rees-Mogg, who became chairman.

Newsmax thrived. Ruddy was a phenomenal networker with a huge email distribution list. In the first decade of the new century, he had had something of a rapprochement with the Clintons. He travelled with Bill Clinton to Africa as part of the Clinton Foundation; he favoured Hillary for the Democratic nomination against Obama in 2008 and even considered supporting her for president in 2016 before switching to Trump. But if you could ever properly have called Ruddy a 'newsman', he no longer was. Newsmax was a business, and the business model was to sell stuff to a boomer audience hungry for the kind of content they weren't getting from the establishment media. By 2013 the company had revenue of $104 million, generated by a monthly magazine with a circulation of 200,000, 17 separate subscription newsletters and $6 million worth of vitamin supplements sales. In 2016, Bloomberg described Newsmax as less of a news business and more of a strange hybrid of the conservative think tank the Heritage Foundation and Amway, the giant multi-level marketing company selling health, beauty and home-care products. Now Ruddy was expanding into the 24-hour cable news business, telling interviewers he wanted create a kinder, gentler version of Fox News. 'Our goal is to be a little more boomer-oriented, more information-based rather than being vituperative and polarizing,' he said.[16] He added that his aim was not to beat his giant Murdoch rival, just to shave off some of their audience, particularly among conservatives who felt that Fox had drifted too far to the right.

But somewhere during the course of the Trump presidency, that changed. By the 2020 presidential election, Newsmax had become a major player, poaching hosts – and viewers – from its rival. And when Fox News called Arizona for Joe Biden, on 7 November 2020, Newsmax went in for the kill. They pushed Donald Trump's stolen-election narrative, pulling in millions of enraged Fox viewers who thought their once-favoured channel had betrayed their hero. (I remember the moment well, standing outside the counting house in Phoenix, as the chants switched from *CNN Sucks!* to *Fox News Sucks!*) Inside the Fox News headquarters, the effect was electrifying. Anchors like Tucker Carlson, megastars in the conservative, 'alternative' media ecosystem at the time, panicked. They worried they were losing their audience to Newsmax, and doubled down on the theory themselves, even though, privately, they thought it was bogus. Newsmax, the company founded by a bunch of Clinton conspiracy theorists at the tail end of the 1990s, was now the outrider, the tail that wagged the dog.

PART II

THE OPERATION

CHAPTER 5

REHEARSAL

On 31 December 1999, people watched nervously as the seconds ticked towards midnight. Experts had predicted that when the numbers on the global network of computers flipped from 99 to 00, there would be a nervous breakdown in cyberspace. A *millennium bug* was going to wipe the slate clean: a great reset, causing chaos on the financial markets and planes to drop out of the sky. They were wrong. In Hong Kong some police breathalysers failed; in New York, a video rental store sent out a fine of $91,250 for a VHS tape because the computer system thought it was 100 years overdue; and in Berlin, the computers at the *Deutsche Oper* decided they had returned to the year 1900. But instead of commissioning a new work from some long-dead composer, all that happened was that some employees didn't receive the correct pay that month. The mistake was swiftly rectified. And that was more or less it. The new millennium seemed to get off to a smooth start. It wasn't until later that year, in November 2000, that a computer glitch of a much more basic kind started causing some real political turbulence that would put America's faith in its own democracy under strain.

Bill Clinton was stepping down after two successful terms in office. The presidential election on 7 November pitted Al Gore for the Democrats against his Republican challenger, George W. Bush. Both were, in a way, continuity candidates: Gore was Clinton's vice president, while Bush promised to pick up where his father – H.W. – had left off when he was so rudely interrupted by the Clinton juggernaut. But election night was a mess. In Florida, ten minutes before the end of voting, all the major news networks called the state for Gore. They had based their calculation on exit polls. Two hours later they retracted their prediction as Bush's tally began to grow. In the middle of the night, at around half past two, the networks declared that in fact Bush had won Florida, and therefore the presidency. Gore phoned Bush to concede. He then retracted his concession as his own vote tally began to creep up in heavily Democratic counties like Palm Beach and Miami-Dade. By the following morning, the race was officially too close to call. There would be a recount.

The stakes were impossibly high. A few hundred votes either way could decide the next president of the United States. The media descended on Miami, at the heart of one of the most contested counties. Among the journalists was a young reporter by the name of Nicholas Kulish. I knew Nick from my days as a foreign correspondent in East Africa – we'd reported on a mutiny in the Democratic Republic of Congo. In November 2000, Nick was a young reporter at the *Wall Street Journal*, sent to cover the Florida recount. He would end up playing a tiny role in the whole fraught business. And he would witness something that seemed quite minor at the time, no more than a scuffle, but which, in hindsight, acquired greater significance.

For a long time afterwards, Nick carried around with him in his wallet a little rectangle of paper, a memento from his first big story. Florida was experimenting with some new ballot designs. Instead of using a pen to mark a cross in a box next to your preferred candidate, voters were instructed to punch through a little perforated section on the ballot paper. The ballots could then be read by computers that would tally the vote. But the perforated sections didn't always entirely separate from the rest of the ballot card, leaving little pieces of paper still attached. These little rectangles were known as 'chads', and they became a media obsession. There were hanging chads (still attached by one corner) and swinging chads (attached on one whole side), dimpled chads and pregnant chads (still entirely attached to the ballot paper but bearing the imprint of having been poked at by some pointed implement). Like ancient soothsayers or tea-leaf readers, electoral officials had to try to interpret the meaning of these slivers of paper. On these chads hinged the outcome of the 2000 presidential election.

Nick stationed himself at the Stephen P. Clark Government Center, a drab concrete monolith in downtown Miami where the recount was being held. At first things appeared to be going smoothly. The recount was being done in a large hall with room for observers from the media and both parties. Occasionally someone would challenge a decision, which would then be adjudicated to everyone's satisfaction. But the election workers were up against a deadline. It was Wednesday, 22 November. The recount had to be done by the Sunday evening. They had hundreds of thousands of ballots to get through. They simply weren't going to make it. So election officials decided that, instead of re-counting every single vote, they would only go back over the really controversial ones, the ones the computers found hard to read. And they would move proceedings to a smaller room elsewhere in the building. The media would have to wait outside.

This was far from ideal. The journalists called it the aquarium because it felt like they were staring into a fish-tank: Nick and his colleagues could see through the thick glass windows, people gesticulating, remonstrating, getting angry, but they couldn't hear anything. It was hard to figure out what was going on. Every once in a while, one of the Republican observers would emerge accusing their Democrat counterparts of foul play: stealing ballots or, on one occasion Nick remembered, eating chads. How exactly the Democrats hoped to secure electoral advantage by gobbling up little rectangles of paper, no one could figure out. Things were getting tetchy. The Republicans wanted to stop the recount. Bush was ahead anyway; any recount could only hurt their chances. The Democrats on the other hand needed the recount to continue if they were to have any hope of winning.

Nick and a group of other journalists decided they needed access to the room where the recount was happening. Together they drafted a petition to the electoral authorities reminding them that, according to Florida law, the recount had to happen in public, and warning them that the present arrangement was undermining confidence in the electoral process. They scribbled their petition on a page from a notebook and Nick, as one of the more junior reporters, was dispatched to present the petition.

For several days, protestors had gathered in front of the building where the recount was being held. They held up plac-ards mocked up to look like Gore–Lieberman signs that read: SORE–LOSERMAN. Also out front was a large camper-van, a mobile home that was the Republicans' field HQ. From time to time a representative would emerge to give a quote to the press. It struck Nick at the time that the Democrats were fighting this battle solely on the legal front. The Republicans were doing that too – they had sent down a team of lawyers who were arguing their case in the courts and representing their interests at the recount. But they were also fighting on another front: they were fighting for the *story*, the narrative that they had already won the election and any other outcome would repre-sent a perversion of the course of democracy, an overthrow of the will of the people.

Not long after Nick handed in his petition, the protests took an uglier turn. He was outside the fish tank, watching what was going on inside, when he heard a commotion in the corridor. He went over to see what was going on. Some of the protestors had got inside the building and were chanting slogans in front of the election commission main offices. He recognised a few of them, people he'd chatted to over the course of long hours and days waiting for something to happen. What with the Winnebago parked out the front stuffed with Republican operatives, he was already beginning to suspect that there was something distinctly inorganic about the protest. 'You'd ask where a person was from,' he remembered, 'and they'd be like: *I'm just a concerned voter.* And I'd be like: *You're a very familiar-looking concerned voter. Do you live in Washington, DC?* And there was a little bit of a wink and a nod. You kind of picked up along the way that these were not local people from Miami rising up for the legitimacy of their vote count.' They didn't look like typical protestors either, dressed in smart slacks and Oxford shirts.

Now these 'concerned voters' were inside the building. At first, Nick said, the atmosphere was jovial, it all seemed like a bit of a joke, as if they were play-acting at being angry protestors. But then the mood soured. A local Democrat emerged from the fish tank with a sample ballot. The crowd turned on him, chasing him down the corridor, accusing him of tampering with the count. A Democrat spokesman was bundled to the ground while making a statement to the press and set upon by the mob. The crowd was screaming *Stop the Count! Voter Fraud! Let Us In!* By now, Nick had got inside the aquarium. He could see a group of red-faced men pulling at the door trying to yank it open, pounding on the glass. 'I remember so vividly looking over at one of the police officers. He put his hand on his service pistol.' The officer was scared, and so were the election workers.

The Republican operatives in the camper-van outside eventually called for calm. The mini-riot died down as quickly as it had erupted. But not long afterwards, the Miami-Dade election board announced they were abandoning the recount. 'We simply can't get it done,' the local elections supervisor said, looking drawn and exhausted.[1] The implication was that the board could not satisfy the competing demands of the press and Republican operatives for access to the counting process and the deadline imposed by the court. But Nick was in no doubt – they had been spooked by the violence and the protestors. 'When it was claimed that it was all kind of a big joke: *Ha, ha, ha! Who's afraid of men in khakis and pink button-down shirts?* I would always remember that moment. Because why would a trained police officer put his hand on his gun?'

The decision to stop the count was met with jubilation by Republicans in Washington, as pictures of the protest were beamed around the nation. Also watching in the *Wall Street Journal*'s offices in DC was Nick's colleague, Jim VandeHei, an experienced Capitol Hill reporter. He too thought he recognised some of the protestors. At least two of them were staffers in the office of Tom DeLay, the house majority whip in the Republican-controlled Congress. VandeHei flew out to Miami and together he and Nick began digging. It turned out the staffers from the whip's office were just the tip of the iceberg. In the days leading up to the riot, DeLay's office had passed on a tempting offer to Republican staffers in the chill of a Washington November: a trip to Florida, airfare, accommodation and food in the sunshine state all paid for by the Bush campaign. They arrived not in Cuban shirts but dressed for the business of Washington, DC: sports jackets, suit coats, slacks and button-down shirts. The kind of apparel you might purchase at Brooks Brothers, the reasonably priced purveyor of office-wear. The incident became known as the 'Brooks Brothers riot'. 'Once word leaked out, everybody wanted in,' one operative involved told Kulish and VandeHei.[2] They estimated more than 200 staffers signed on, housed in hotels by the beach and getting a per diem of $30 for food. Late at night, instructions would appear on printed sheets of paper, slid under their hotel room doors. One participant said that, upon arrival in Miami, he was told by a Republican official that he and several other volunteers were to become protestors. 'We've never done this before,' he recalled the official saying. 'Anyone know how to put together a protest?'

As it happened, Al Gore's presidential ambitions ended not in the counting rooms of Florida but the Supreme Court of the United States. The Brooks Brothers riot became a footnote in history. But over the years, Nick Kulish said, the story of how a bunch of DC operatives in chinos shut down the Florida recount morphed from an embarrassing incident into something people liked to brag about. Years later, the infamous Republican operative and 'dirty trickster' Roger Stone would claim it was he who had directed the protestors from the Winnebago parked outside. 'I set up my command centre there,' he told the *New Yorker*. 'I had walkie-talkies and cell phones, and I was in touch with our people in the building. Our whole idea was to shut the recount down.'[3] It was he, Stone said, who radioed his 'pimply-faced contacts' inside the building to pursue the Democrat with the sample ballot. Others said that was nonsense. Brad Blakeman, another Republican operative, later claimed *he* was coordinating efforts from the camper-van: 'Roger did not have a role that I know of [...] I never saw or heard from him.'

Roger Stone is a myth-maker. His reliability as a witness is contested in almost everything he says. He was already tight with Donald Trump at the time of the Florida recount. 'Roger is a stone-cold loser,' Trump told the *New Yorker* in 2008. 'He always tries taking credit for things he never did.' But in 2016 and 2020 he nevertheless played key roles in Trump's election campaigns. A few days before the 2020 election, Stone was captured on camera by a Danish documentary crew, saying: 'Fuck the voting, get right to the violence.' The remark appears to be in jest. But two months later, on January 6th, he was to be found walking around Washington, DC, with the Proud

Boys militia, whose members would take part in the storming of the Capitol.

I sat drinking coffee with Nick Kulish at his home in Brooklyn, reflecting on how things had turned out. The Brooks Brothers riot, that forgotten footnote in history, served as a sort of template for a new way of conducting politics: 'Almost like an amusing prelude,' Nick said, 'first as comedy, then as tragedy.'

At the time, the Brooks Brothers riot and the Florida recount felt like the biggest story of Nick's journalistic career. Not for long. Less than a year later, he found himself standing outside the smoking embers of the Pentagon; bits of fuselage littered the ground. Then, 18 months after that, he was on his way to Iraq as American forces unleashed shock and awe. Around that time, a Silicon Valley venture capitalist by the name of Peter Thiel invested half a million dollars in a new website set up by a Harvard student called Mark Zuckerberg. Facebook would harness the power of the internet chat rooms that Chris Lehane had seen in the 1990s and grow into a tech behemoth that would soon begin to wreak its own shock and awe on the very fabric of society. Into this fledgling world of online social networks stepped a young boy with a severe disability. His name was Fred Brennan.

CHAPTER 6

ANYONE
CAN BE
ANYTHING

Fred was the first person I talked to when I began my investigation, pulling at the long roots of January 6th. It was two weeks after the storming of the Capitol. I was in Washington for the inauguration of Joe Biden. DC looked like it was on a war footing: Capitol Hill was crawling with soldiers erecting razor wire and barricades. Hours earlier, Donald Trump had left Washington for the last time as president. He'd made a short address at Andrews Air Force Base. It was a lacklustre speech. Trump rambled seemingly impromptu about his great record in government – the economy was a 'rocket ship', the vaccine 'a miracle', and the number of votes he'd won in the election (which he'd just lost) was 'an all-time record by a lot'. He wished everyone a 'good life' and promised: 'We will be back, in some form.' And with that, Donald Trump turned and headed towards Air Force One. The presidential aeroplane gleamed in the late-morning sunlight. Lined up between him and the plane were a dozen or so flags, stars and stripes, fringed with gold tassels and fluttering in the wind. Actually, the precise number of flags is important. There were 17 of them. In the fevered echo chambers of the internet, that number was laden with significance: Q – the seventeenth letter of the alphabet.

'Someone must have done that on purpose,' Fred told me. He believed the 17 flags were a signal to the QAnon crowd. He said that if Trump wasn't fully conscious of what he was doing, then people around him were. And I believed him. Because without Fred, QAnon might never have happened.

Fred Brennan grew up poor in rural upstate New York. He was born with a rare genetic condition – osteogenesis imperfecta, more commonly known as brittle bone disease. From an early age Fred had all the classic symptoms: stunted growth, loose joints and bones that break at the slightest knock. His parents separated when he was five years old. In the ensuing custody battle, Fred was sent to live with his father in a small village. Life was not fun. He did not get to ride horses or milk cows. He rarely got to go outside at all. His father, who had a succession of different girlfriends, was out at work most days. Most of the time, Fred was left indoors to his own devices. He had no friends, no one to play with: a severely disabled kid, locked inside his own body.

I drove out to see Brennan at his home in New Jersey. I turned off the highway, past a drive-thru McDonalds, into a low-rise housing project on the outskirts of Atlantic City. Late spring was turning to summer. Seagulls squawked overhead. A wheelchair ramp led up to a porch overlooking a scrubby baseball pitch. Beyond that, somewhere, lay the ocean. In the distance loomed the skyscrapers and casinos. It felt like an in-between place: neither seaside nor city. The door was on the latch. I pushed it open and went on in. It was dark inside, the curtains drawn. In the kitchen, take-away containers covered the worktop and several days' worth of dirty dishes sat piled up in the sink. Fred lived here with his mother and younger brother, both of whom suffer from the same condition. It didn't look like they got much help.

Fred got into computers through gaming. As a kid, his favourite game was *Sonic*, in which a blue hedgehog superhero battles Doctor Eggman, an evil Humpty Dumpty-like character bent on world domination. It was the early 2000s, the era of faltering dial-up connections. His father would often kick him off the internet to use the phone line. Fred would tinker with the machine, fascinated by how it worked. Later his aunt gave him an old laptop that kept breaking. Fred learned how to fix it. Whenever he could get online, he would spend time on a message board where children swapped tips on how to complete the various levels of *Sonic*. The forum was more than a just place for hedgehog superfans. It became a support network for other lonely, isolated kids. They would share stories about how their parents were fighting or drinking, or how they were being taken into care. It was a lifeline and a place of anonymity, a place where Fred – despite his disability – could be just like other kids. The internet became the home he wished he had, the family he desperately wanted.

Then, one day, when Fred was about nine years old, something unexpected happened in this virtual safe haven: the *Sonic* message board was flooded with porn. The attacks kept on happening, and after a while Fred figured out who was behind it. They came from 4chan, a niche website few people knew about at the time.

. . .

4chan was the creation of another kid called Christopher Poole, who grew up not far from Fred, in New York City. Poole was into anime – Japanese animation – and would spend hours on a Japanese message board called 2channel, and spin-off site called 2chan. One of the things he loved about these internet spaces was the anonymity: under the online handle 'moot', he could be whoever he wanted to be, say whatever he wanted to say, and discuss whatever weird topics he wanted to discuss. His other main hangout was a website called Something Awful, another early internet forum, where he frequented a niche subforum entitled Anime Death Tentacle Rape Whorehouse, or ADTRW for short. (Pay attention to those five words –

they are like strands of DNA within which is encoded what is to come.) In 2003, when moot was 15 years old, he decided to create his own website that would merge the strange anime-obsessed communities he'd befriended on Something Awful with the manga aesthetics of 2chan. He copied the open-source code from the Japanese website, translated the text using Babel Fish, and called it 4chan.[1]

At first the website had just one section (or 'board', in the vernacular): /b/ (Anime/Random). As the name suggested, it was a place to discuss anime and other random topics. By the end of the year, moot had added several more, also dedicated to various aspects of anime culture. 4chan was much like the plethora of other internet forums that sprang up around the same time, except for one crucial thing: users didn't have to register – even under a pseudonymous handle like moot. 4chan was completely anonymous. By default, posts appeared as *Anonymous*; posters were known as *Anons*.

The 4chan ethos was one of Darwinian ruthlessness: popular posts survived, floating to the top of the feed, while those that didn't find favour sank into the oblivion of the primordial digital soup. The aesthetic was user-*un*friendly, stripped down and basic like a website from the 1990s, and made deliberately hard to navigate so that newcomers – or 'newfags' as they were known – could be easily identified and hounded off the site. It was a place of quick, cruel wit that crackled with a fiery energy that was simultaneously creative and performatively offensive, a

Petri dish in which a new online culture was evolving, one that was both hyper-individualistic and at the same time forging a collective identity.

Because of the principle of anonymity, it's hard to say exactly who the early users of 4chan were. But it seems they were mostly young, mostly male, and quite quickly no longer just interested in Japanese cartoons. They spent their days dredging the internet for the detritus of America's corporate entertainment industry – snippets of old movies, video game characters, long-forgotten advertising slogans – mashing them up into new units of pop-culture: memes.

One of the favourite pastimes on early 4chan was *rick-rolling*: a trick in which users sent out a link to some topic of interest but when you clicked on it, it redirected to a YouTube link to Rick Astley's 1987 hit 'Never Gonna Give You Up'. But it wasn't all harmless. 4chan users took a sadistic pleasure in trolling, bombarding each other with insults and grotesque porn, pictures of self-harm, images of child abuse. The denizens of 4chan saw themselves as the outlaws of the internet. As such, they took their anonymity seriously. Like members of Fight Club, they had a dictum: the first rule of 4chan was you didn't talk about 4chan. When they got bored of trolling each other, they would band together in groups to take part in 'raids': coordinated attacks on other websites, flooding more innocent parts of the internet with their insults, their in-jokes and obscene imagery.

It was a 4chan raid that shattered Fred Brennan's childish haven on the *Sonic* forum. At first, Fred and the other kids had no idea who the raiders were or what was going on. They just wanted to be left in peace. But when the raids kept on happening, some of them let it slip they were from 4chan. And Fred figured, if he couldn't beat them, he would join them. So he left behind the childish world of animated hedgehog superheroes, and joined the world of 4chan. He was 12 years old.

4chan was populated by slightly older versions of Fred: kids stuck at home in their parents' basements with nothing but an internet connection for company. Because everyone was anonymous, anyone could be anything: an attractive prospect for a severely disabled boy who didn't get out much and had no friends. A lot of the kids on 4chan had grown up with role-play games like *Dungeons & Dragons*. *D&D* was a pre-internet phenomenon, an imaginary game played mostly indoors. But sometimes *D&D* devotees would don wizard outfits and foam swords and meet up to stage mock battles in the woods. That was known as live action role play – or LARP. On 4chan, LARPing had migrated online. People posted as characters in their favourite video games; when they raided other websites, they appeared as those avatars.

With few rules, 4chan was a frontier town with only one sheriff: moot. Moot decided what topics could be discussed on what boards, what could be said and what couldn't. Inside the world of 4chan, moot was God. Fred threw himself into this new world. He learned its language (*normies*: people who don't get it, don't understand the new online culture; *for the lulz* – to do something mean/destructive, just for laughs, because you can); he adopted its aesthetic (the endlessly shifting memes, simple line drawings of a sad man representing all the myriad facets of millennial despair); he internalised its mores (*fuck the establishment and its politically correct bullshit! Internet freedom! Free speech!*).

Out in the 'real' world, other stuff was happening. There was a subprime mortgage crisis, a banking crisis. While giant corporations were being bailed out with trillions of dollars, people were losing their jobs, their homes. Meanwhile, the kids hanging out on 4chan were growing up. They sat behind their computer screens watching their life-chances vanish before their eyes. Some began to organise, to get together and plot their fightback against the enemy: corporate America. They began with an unlikely target.

In January 2008 – before the financial crisis had erupted in full force – the gossip website Gawker had published a video from the secretive Church of Scientology. The video featured the church's most famous adherent, the Hollywood star Tom Cruise. The church threatened Gawker with legal action unless they took the video down, claiming it was private property. The anonymous free speech absolutists on 4chan were incensed. Within days, a menacing video appeared online. Over pictures of gathering storm clouds, a computerised voice declares:

'Hello, leaders of Scientology. We are Anonymous. Over the years, we have been watching you, your campaigns of misinformation, your suppression of dissent, your litigious nature [...] Anonymous has therefore decided that your organisation should be destroyed.' At first Anonymous confined their activities to cyberspace. They staged coordinated attacks to overload Scientology's servers.

Fred Brennan remembered taking part in these early Anonymous raids as a young teenager, a 4chan newfag. 'This was the first modern trolling, I guess you could say.' At the time, it seemed to Fred that he and the other kids on 4chan had come up with the idea themselves, spontaneously. In hindsight, he said, it seemed there was a small group of anonymous accounts – 'hardcore organisers' – who were pulling the strings behind the scenes, pointing the swarms of 4chan users towards the tools they would need to carry out their raids. The tech-savvy no-hopers suddenly saw how they could marshal their collective superpower to great effect. Then they moved offline, into the real world.

•   •   •

It was a cold February day in New York City. Dale Beran was a young aspiring journalist who had got wind of a story. 4chan had been on his radar for a few years by now. He was intrigued by how people on the site shrouded themselves in secrecy. He wanted to write something about this internet phenomenon, but he couldn't get anyone to talk to him, let alone meet him in real life. Then he saw a call-out on 4chan for people to gather in coordinated protests outside Scientology buildings around the world.

Dale didn't really know how to go about becoming a journalist. He did have a notebook, a long yellow thing, given to him by a friend who was a real reporter, that said 'reporter's notebook' on it. It felt like a prop, good enough to get started. So on the appointed day, at the appointed hour, Dale Beran boarded a subway train heading for 42nd Street hoping to meet some real-life 4chan people.

He persuaded his roommate to come along. They exited the subway. The Scientology HQ building was a few blocks up. As they walked through the freezing streets of midtown Manhattan, pulling their hats down over their heads, they began to have their doubts. Perhaps this was another 4chan prank. 'We're going to get there,' his roommate said, 'and there's going to be one guy standing there mocking us.' But then they rounded a corner and saw a crowd: hundreds of 4chan users, shouting slogans in front of the Scientology building. Many were wearing Guy Fawkes masks, inspired by the film *V for Vendetta*. Others came in suits and Afro wigs, a reference to a character from an online video game 4chan users liked to raid. Dale looked down at his long yellow notebook. He too had come in character. 'I was sort of pretending to be a reporter,' Dale told me. 'Everyone else was pretending to be a hacker or a protestor and would not admit they were from 4chan.' The LARP had leaped off the internet and into real life. 'Everyone was a little surprised and delighted, I think, that it was working.' The protest ended abruptly when a man dressed as the hacker Neo from *The Matrix*, wearing wrap-around sunglasses and a long leather trench coat shouted: 'Now back to our moms' basements!' The mysterious denizens of 4chan melted away into the New York subway.

Was it all a game, a joke? Perhaps. But some of the LARPers from 4chan would go on to become real hackers. These young tech-savvy geeks dressed as superheroes from movies and video games would use their powers – their knowledge of computers, of coding, of the internet – to target big financial institutions: PayPal, Mastercard, the World Bank. They were no match for the power of big finance. The FBI soon put a stop to Anonymous and their campaign against global capitalism, arresting its leaders. But role play had become reality – and Dale Beran would go on to become a real reporter, one who, with Fred Brennan, would help uncover the identity of the people behind QAnon.

. . .

Fred Brennan was 13 at the time of the Scientology protests. Being severely disabled, he watched them unfold from behind his computer screen. Not long after, his father confiscated his computer. Already depressed, Fred's mental condition worsened. 'I was hospitalised for cutting myself and saying I was going to kill myself,' he told me. He spent a month in hospital, and the next two years in foster care, during which time he had less access to the internet. When he came out of the care system, aged 16, he moved back in with his mother at her home outside Atlantic City. When he came back to 4chan, things had changed. 'All the old memes were out. I had to kind of relearn the culture.'

Fred described it as one of the most depressing places on the internet: people talking about how miserable their lives were, posting pictures of themselves surrounded by piles of rubbish and old fast-food containers, others competing to comment on how disgusting they looked. 'It's all these men in their twenties that are maybe overweight and have a huge beard and seem like they haven't gone outside in ten years.'

This was where Fred felt at home. Gone were the lefty, anti-capitalist idealists of Anonymous. The anons who remained were drifting in a nihilistic direction. 4chan became a place populated by kids-who-weren't-kids-any-more, but still stuck in their parents' basements. In their virtual, online worlds they could be superheroes or supervillains. But in the real world, post-financial-crisis, they were nothing, powerless. It was a largely male space, awash with the smashed-up detritus of popular culture glued together with far-right imagery, violence and porn. The culture of performative offensiveness had descended into wanton cruelty (4chan users once hacked the website of the Epilepsy Foundation, flooding the site with flashing animations designed to trigger seizures). It was a place of conspiracy theories and nihilistic trolling. Their targets were feminists and liberals, people the denizens of 4chan thought were in league with big business to keep them at the bottom of the pile.

Fred started hanging out on a board called /pol/. This was the section of 4chan dedicated to discussing politics. 'Pol' stood for 'politically incorrect'. 'A lot of people just assumed this was the racist board, the Nazi board,' Fred said. Somebody gave the board an emblem: a swastika. But they weren't the old-fashioned type of neo-Nazi, tattooed skinheads. /Pol/ was populated by new breed of right wingers who were articulate and tech-savvy and whose fascist-adjacent worldview was broadcast loud and clear to those insiders who knew their memes and codewords, but could only be discerned by the uninitiated as if through a dense fog. They became known as the 'alt-right' and they adopted a cartoon frog called Pepe as their mascot.

Fred told me he was never a neo-Nazi. But the neo-Nazis liked what he was posting. He started getting into eugenics. In Israel, some disabled people were suing medical authorities for failing to detect abnormalities in the womb and allowing them to be born. It became known as 'wrongful birth'. Fred was fascinated. 'I was very into that, like we should start doing this in America. I was keeping track very closely of these Israeli cases.' He would scan the Israeli press and whenever there was something new to report, he would write about it on /pol/.

The neo-Nazis cheered him on. Eventually, his posts caught the attention of a more old-fashioned publication. The Daily Stormer, a neo-Nazi website, approached him to write an article. Fred obliged. In the article, he argued people like his mother, who had a genetic condition that could be passed on to her offspring, should be paid not to have children. It appeared under the headline 'Why I Support Eugenics'. 'It was really dumb,' Fred told me, with the benefit of hindsight. 'But, you know, I just liked that I was being listened to.'

When Fred Brennan said eugenics should get rid of disabled children like himself, was he really just looking for attention? When other 4chan users posted about a cabal of Jews running the world, did they really believe that or were they just trying to trigger the 'libs'? When they hosted forums dedicated to child pornography, were they really paedophiles or just play-acting for shock value? Perhaps the answer was both. In the twilight zone between fantasy and reality, the difference was sometimes hard to tell.

Christopher 'moot' Poole – lord of 4chan – was walking a tightrope: taking down posts that even he thought crossed the boundaries of acceptable free speech or were outright illegal (images of child sex abuse). At the same time he was trying not to alienate his users and lose them to the plethora of copycat chans that had sprung up: 7chan, 420chan, 4chon. Some of the most offensive stuff tended to appear on boards that Fred Brennan frequented the most. Eventually, instead of deleting individual posts or banning particular users, moot just decided to delete those boards.

For Fred, it was as if his favourite local bar, the place he came for company and conversation, had been closed down at a stroke. He took it personally. He became increasingly angry with Poole, whose actions he saw as arbitrary and against the free-spirited ethos of 4chan. He started hanging out on the other chans, looking into the technical side of things, figuring out how imageboards worked. He taught himself to code. For a while he ran a site called Wizardchan, a 4chan offshoot dedicated to 'incels'. Wizardchan was so named because of a Japanese internet meme that said that any man who reached the age of 30 and was still a virgin would become a wizard. Fred took over the website after the guy who created it disappeared – Fred assumed he had committed suicide. Because of his disability, Fred said, he was seen as somebody who was 'so pathetic they would never have sex. So it was guaranteed I could hold the Wizardchan deed, the domain and the server in perpetuity.'

But that was not to be. Somehow, the chief wizard worked some magic: Fred Brennan found a girlfriend. The world of Wizardchan might have been bitter and twisted, but it was not without its ethics. 'There was a code of honour that Wizardchan's admin cannot be a so-called normie. It would be very dishonest.' Fred lost his virginity. He also resigned his position. Now he was looking for a new project. One day, he and his new girlfriend took some hallucinogenics and, high on a cocktail of sex and magic mushrooms, he found it: 8chan.

Fred created 8chan in October 2013, fuelled by his animosity towards Christopher Poole. As Fred saw it, moot's increasingly authoritarian behaviour was a betrayal of everything he valued about the internet: freedom. 8chan would be just like 4chan, but with even fewer rules. At first, no one paid attention. For months, Fred's new website was getting 50 to 100 posts on good days. Sometimes there were as few as 10. The outlaws were still drinking at *Moot's Saloon* while over at *Fred's Bar* all was quiet. But then came Gamergate.

• • •

It started with a new and somewhat unusual videogame. *Depression Quest* was more like *Dungeons & Dragons* than a traditional videogame: players assume the character of a person suffering from depression. They come up against various real-life scenarios, and their responses influence the course of the game. The game was also unusual in that it was created by a woman, Zoë Quinn.

Quinn, who suffered from depression, hoped the game would raise awareness. *Depression Quest* was not exactly what the male-dominated shoot-it-all-up gaming crowd were looking for, but it received positive reviews in the industry press. But when an ex-boyfriend wrote a blog post claiming that the game had only got good reviews because Quinn was sleeping with an influential gaming critic, he sparked a firestorm. The over-grown kids on 4chan (who may or may not have been suffering from depression themselves) seized this claim and spun it into a conspiracy theory. This sex-for-influence scandal exemplified everything that was wrong with the gaming industry, they said. It was rotten to the core, controlled by a corrupt cabal of elite social justice warriors who were ruining their games with their feminism and so-called progressive values.

The users of 4chan did what they knew how to do best: they organised a trolling campaign. First, they created a hashtag: #Gamergate. Then, using anonymous accounts on Twitter, they pushed it out onto the mainstream internet, where it gained traction. Over the summer of 2014, the rape- and death-threats against Quinn (and any other woman who supported them) turned from a steady flow into a flood. When Quinn was 'doxxed' (their personal details such as address and tele-phone number published online), the harassment started to look dangerous. 'Next time she shows up at a conference,' one poster on 4chan wrote, 'we give her a crippling injury that's never going to fully heal.'[2] The threats were so numerous and so specific Quinn called the FBI and went into hiding.

Christopher Poole watched as 4chan, the website he had built as a place for devotees of Japanese animation, became the engine room of a giant, co-ordinated campaign of misog-ynistic rage and violence. The DNA encoded in those five words that had inspired his creation – *Anime Death Tentacle*

Rape Whorehouse – had sired its inevitable offspring. 4chan had arrived as a force in the mainstream consciousness. It had poked a tentacle above the surface. Suddenly they were writing about 4chan in the *Washington Post* and the *New York Times*. And not in a good way. By now, Poole's ambitions went beyond his early experiment on the frontiers of internet freedom. He wanted to make money. That meant advertising. Few companies wanted to promote their products next to an avalanche of violent threats and toxic bile. So, in September, moot banned all discussion of Gamergate on his website.

Amid howls of outrage and betrayal, thousands of 4chan users deserted the site and began looking for somewhere else to carry on their trolling operation. Christopher Poole's loss was Fred Brennan's gain. 8chan's only real rule was you could not post stuff that was illegal in the United States. That meant copyright infringements were out. So were actual images of child sex abuse. Almost everything else was allowed, including manga-style illustrated images of child porn, doxing and harassment. Almost overnight, Fred said, he was getting 7,000 posts per hour. The company that hosted 8chan kept contacting Fred and demanding he take down the most offensive material. He refused. When they booted 8chan off their platform, he moved it over to another server, only for the same thing to happen again. 'I just took the whole free-speech attitude,' Fred told me. Having set himself up as a haven of freedom after the 4chan 'sell-out', he wasn't about to start censoring his own users. Buoyed by an influx of misogynistic incel refugees from 4chan, Fred Brennan's dream of taking down the tyrant moot and creating the biggest troll-site on the internet seemed within reach.

Looking back, Fred said, he saw Gamergate as 'an operation'. Similar to the Anonymous campaigns, it had the veneer of an anarchic, organic trolling campaign. But behind the curtain, a hard-core of organisers was directing the action, nudging the frenetic swarms on 4chan and 8chan in this direction or that. But Gamergate – like the Brooks Brothers riot – was still just a rehearsal, a testing ground for a much bigger operation to come.

CHAPTER 7

CONFLICT IS ATTENTION, ATTENTION IS INFLUENCE

The riptides of 4chan, the trolling, the feuds, the memes that budded and withered and bloomed again like a time-lapse of the seasons, happened mostly out of sight of mainstream America. Like the wild conspiracy theories of the Arkansas Project years earlier, establishment journalists, the people who saw themselves as the chroniclers of the national narrative, took notice only rarely – and briefly – when a tentacle reached out and poked them in the eye. Vince Foster, Gamergate, these stories would have their moment in the national media and then disappear again when the press moved on to more serious matters. Matters they felt they had a handle on – campaigns, elections, party politics – the plethora of 'pseudo-events'[1] that make up most of what passes for news.

When the Republican Party chose Donald Trump as its candidate in the 2016 presidential election, I joined the majority of my colleagues in the political and media class in assuming the result was inevitable. Of course, we never said so out loud – not even to each other – not in so many words. The show must go on. A democratic election must by definition entail a contest in which the outcome is not predetermined.

Donald Trump looked like a gift to Hillary Clinton. She was a canny operator who had been at the sharp end of politics for 40 years, first as her husband's loyal consigliere, and – for the last 15 – in her own right, as senator for New York and then secretary of state. Hillary was a veteran with a vast political machine behind her. She was running against a novice, a brash ingenu from the world of real estate and reality TV, who appeared to have no grasp of how Washington worked. In my world, a consensus emerged: after Obama, the first Black president, the next chapter in the great story of America was already writing itself. The United States would put a woman in the White House. It was progress, the arc of history.

From the very beginning, Donald Trump's campaign looked like a train wreck. He kicked things off by descending from an escalator in his gilded palace in Manhattan to announce: 'The American Dream is dead.' (*OK*, we thought as we ticked off the traditional voting blocs in our minds, *forget the aspirational middle class.*) He went on: tariffs were good, globalisation was bad (*bye, bye neo-liberals and 'moderate' Republicans*); Mexicans were rapists (*adios, Latino vote*); as for women ... Later on, as the campaign neared its apex, we would find out exactly what he thought of women.

The Republican establishment was deeply ambivalent about Trump. Many of the top operatives thought he was going to lose and didn't want to sully their CVs by working for him. His campaign was staffed by an assortment of oddballs and misfits. At some point, while trying to glean some information about Donald Trump's old business ties to Russia, I ended up speaking to a campaign operative who lived on a boat in Florida with a talkative pet parrot. It was all part of the fun of 2016, which – thanks to Trump – was shaping up to be a much more lively and entertaining contest.

One of the more high-profile and unorthodox members of the Trump campaign was Michael T. Flynn. While running the Defense Intelligence Agency under Barack Obama, he had championed new technologies for intelligence gathering and analysis, promoting an AI surveillance company called Palantir – named after the seeing stone of Sauron in *The Lord of the Rings*. Palantir was careful not to deny the suggestion (strictly off the record of course, for reasons of national security) that its technologies had been crucial to the operation to find and kill Osama Bin Laden – a suggestion that may or may not have had any basis in fact. Nevertheless, the fact that the company was associated with the operation was proving lucrative for Palantir and for its founder, Peter Thiel. After being edged out of the Pentagon, he worked for a stint as a private lobbyist for the Turkish government; he appeared at a high-profile dinner in Moscow, seated next to Vladimir Putin (and got paid $45,000 for the privilege). In 2016 he became the Trump campaign's national security advisor.

Flynn first hit my consciousness at the Republican National Convention, where Trump was to be officially anointed as the Republican Party's candidate in the presidential election. Even though Trump was already the presumptive nominee, having bested his rivals in the primaries, there were suspicions in his camp that the Republican establishment would try to screw him at the last minute, to stitch up the delegates so that someone else might get the nomination. (Roger Stone, the man who claimed to have directed the Brooks Brothers riot, coined the phrase 'Stop the Steal' during the 2016 primaries. The slogan would be repurposed in the aftermath of the 2020 election.)

The event was being held in Cleveland, Ohio. Trump was due to accept the nomination on Thursday, 21 July. Flynn appeared on the Monday, part of a four-day warm-up act that included more than a hundred other speakers. It was nearing the end of day one. Melania Trump had just left the stage. As Flynn came on, he looked a little nervous, out of his element. 'I don't know how you follow an act like Melania Trump ...' he began. The speech started conventionally enough – Flynn the former solider enumerating the failures of Obama's and Clinton's foreign and military policies. But it wasn't firing up the crowd. In the video of the event you can see the hall, no longer full, getting emptier. Flynn tries rallying the remaining faithful with chants of *U-S-A!* Then, from somewhere in the hall, someone shouts something. At first it looks as if he can't quite make it out. His eyes flit across the room. Then people start chanting. A half-smile passes across Flynn's chiselled face. *Lock her up! Lock her up!* He nods his head in time to the chant. 'Lock her up, that's right,' he agrees, and then repeats it with more force, warming to the idea. The delegates are on their feet. The chant spreads. Looking at Flynn's face in that moment you can almost see a realisation dawning on his military commander's brain: foreign policy is not the best line of attack. The weaker flank is elsewhere.

In the Clinton campaign they weren't too worried about Flynn's *Lock her up* chant. Philippe Reines, one of Hillary's most trusted aides, remembered thinking it was 'a bit jarring' at the time. 'It's a little different from *Beat. Her. At. The. Polls,*' he said.

All his political life, Philippe had worked for Hillary: first when she was elected senator in 2000, then when she ran for the Democratic presidential nomination in 2008. He went with her to the State Department when she became secretary of state. In 2016 he was one of the most senior officials on the Clinton campaign. At the time, like me, he knew nothing about 4chan.

He didn't realise the cultural landscape was shifting beneath his feet. He assumed the old rules still applied; that there was an upper limit to how much traction the crazy stuff could ever get. Besides, there were plenty of other things to worry about that seemed more pressing than the ramblings of a retired general. The day after Flynn's speech, WikiLeaks published a batch of emails from inside the Democratic Party. It was just days from the Democrats' own convention. Hillary Clinton had beaten her rival, Bernie Sanders, to the nomination. But the leaked emails revealed the Democratic Party machine had favoured Clinton over Sanders, leading Bernie supporters to accuse the party of a stitch-up.

Philippe and his colleagues thought they knew the origin of the leak: a hack by Russia's military intelligence service, the GRU. That was the conclusion of private investigators and of US intelligence; that was the story told in the newspapers and on establishment news channels. But on the internet, a different story emerged. Seth Rich, a 27-year-old staffer at the Democratic National Committee (DNC) in Washington, had been shot dead in the entrance to his apartment block after a night out in a bar. It was the early hours of the morning of 10 July, less than two weeks before WikiLeaks published the leaked emails. The police concluded it was a botched robbery, but they never found the culprits. On the conspiratorial discussion boards of 4chan and 8chan, Seth Rich was obviously the leaker, and his killing was revenge.

This story spread from 4chan to Facebook and Twitter. A month later, Roger Stone tweeted a picture of Seth Rich next to three other faces and the text: 'Four more dead bodies in the Clinton's [sic] wake. Coincidence? I think not.' Stone by then had been fired by the Trump campaign (he said he had quit) and was operating as a free agent – his preferred modus operandi. But he was still close to Trump and was still trying to find damaging material on Hillary Clinton.* That same day, Julian Assange, the founder of WikiLeaks, suggested in a TV interview that the source of the leak was indeed Seth Rich. WikiLeaks announced it was offering a reward of $20,000 for anyone who could help solve his murder. So now, in the parallel universe that had been germinating beneath the surface, Seth Rich joined Vince Foster on the ever-growing Clinton Body Count.

The DNC leak was an embarrassing episode for the Democrats. They were trying to come together to fight the election behind candidate Hillary. Instead, at their national convention, there was discord within the party. But it was hardly life-threatening for the campaign. After all, the emails simply showed what most people already knew: that the Democratic Party establishment favoured the candidate who had spent her

---

* This had been something of an obsession for Stone for nearly a decade. In 2008 he had set up an anti-Hillary fundraising organisation entitled Citizens United Not Timid. The name was chosen for its richly obscene acronym. He told an interviewer: 'The truth is, we sat around for hours trying to come up with words for BITCH and just couldn't do it.'

entire career at the heart of the Democratic Party establishment over the candidate who had spent his entire career railing against the establishment. What else was new? The damage seemed contained.

• • •

The 2016 campaign was a whirlwind in which the normal rules appeared to have been suspended. As a journalist, events came at you so thick and fast you barely had time to recover from whatever bomb had just dropped, when another would land that seemed to obliterate the first. The 7th of October was such a day. I had spent a week in Youngstown, Ohio, speaking to Trump supporters, trying to get out of my metropolitan bubble and under the skin of the people who saw salvation in a man who seemed to me a chancer and a buffoon, and an offensive one at that.

I'd met a woman called Carrie Pasquale. When she lost her job as a technician in a medical centre, she and her husband Anthony set up a real-estate business. Then came the crash of 2008. They went bankrupt. Now they were struggling with multiple jobs on low wages, trying to raise their children – two daughters and a son. I had asked Carrie about Trump's long history of offensive remarks about women. 'Look at that face,' he'd said about a Republican rival in the primaries. 'Would anyone vote for that?' Of Megyn Kelly, a Fox News anchor, he had said: 'There was blood coming out of her eyes, blood coming out of her wherever,' in an apparent reference to her menstrual cycle. In a normal campaign, these remarks would have been enough to disqualify any candidate. But it didn't bother Carrie. The very fact that Trump was an iconoclast, that he was shaking things up, was what attracted her to him. If he shook things up to such an extent that the whole system started to fall apart, then so be it. 'I don't think things can get any worse than they already are,' she said.

It was just after four o'clock in the afternoon. I was sitting in the BBC's Washington office, editing these clips into a report, when the news broke. An old video tape had emerged in which Donald Trump was caught on microphone while filming an episode of *Access Hollywood*, bragging about sexually assaulting women. 'When you're a star,' he said, 'they let you do it. You can do anything … Grab 'em by the pussy.'

Within minutes, the whole of the American media was talking about nothing else. Speculation swirled. The Republican establishment was urgently considering ditching Trump. Could they find a replacement at such short notice? Would Trump even make it to the second presidential debate, scheduled to take place in two days' time? I turned to my colleague, Warwick Harrington, a veteran of many presidential campaigns. We were both thinking the same thing: *Surely he can't come back from this?* It was a Friday, the feature we were editing was due to air the following Monday. It seemed pointless. By then, we thought, there might no longer be a candidate Trump. We left the office and went to a bar.

We were barely a few sips into our beer when the second story dropped. The Russians had done it again: this time they had hacked directly into Hillary Clinton's campaign. An hour after the *Access Hollywood* tape emerged, WikiLeaks published more than two thousand emails from the account of the campaign chairman, John Podesta. They let it be known they had thousands more. Between now and the election we could expect a daily dribble of sordid and embarrassing revelations from the heart of the Clinton campaign. It was a double October surprise. I phoned Carrie Pasquale, my barometer in Youngstown. Did Trump's talk of pussy-grabbing change her calculus? How would she explain such comments to her daughters? Her answer: that was just locker-room talk, the kind that boys will engage in. The sooner they learned that, the better. Carrie was holding strong. Trump was still in the race. We went back to our edit.

Now Philippe Reines was worried. John Podesta was another Clinton veteran, having shepherded Bill Clinton's administration through the Lewinsky scandal as White House chief of staff. He and Philippe had known each other for years. Philippe knew the kinds of things that were in Podesta's email inbox. There was plenty of petty sniping within the campaign – frank assessments of colleagues and Clinton associates that are one thing to air in private but look embarrassing in public. Worse, the hack would expose the inner workings of the campaign: debates over what donations to accept from what corporate lobbyists; best lines to take to defend Clinton against accusations of being in the pockets of Wall Street and big business. There were emails that seemed to show the Clinton campaign co-ordinating with friendly super PACs, against campaign finance rules. Then there was the issue of the Clinton Foundation, the Clintons' charity that does aid work around the world. Critics had accused the Clintons of using the foundation to exploit their political influence for personal financial gain. The Clintons had always maintained there was no proof of any such thing. But in John Podesta's inbox there were documents that suggested otherwise. A former fundraiser at the Clinton Foundation wrote to Podesta detailing how the former president was personally making millions of dollars from donors, and 'gets many expensive gifts'. An audit by a respected New York law firm that found that the foundation's board had failed to properly oversee potential conflicts of interest and that some donors expected 'quid pro quo benefits'. There was nothing illegal. But it stank. It looked like a repeat of the Arkansas playbook from decades ago, but now on a global scale: while ostensibly engaged in public service, the Clintons somehow kept making lots of money. And no matter how much there appeared to be conflicts of interest, nothing ever seemed to stick to them.

The thing Philippe was most worried about was the 'self-oppo document': a list he and others on the campaign had drawn up detailing all the things the Trump campaign might attack Hillary on. They had gone through her old speeches, many of them attracting hefty fees, looking for off-key remarks.

Like the time she told a joke to a room full of bankers from Goldman Sachs. If the CEO, Lloyd Blankfein, wanted to run for office, she quipped, he should leave the bank 'and start running a soup kitchen somewhere'. Or the time she talked about how 'onerous and unnecessary' it was for businesspeople running for public office to have to divest themselves of their assets, stocks and powerful positions on company boards. The people best equipped to regulate the banking industry, she said in 2013 – five years after the crisis of 2008 – were the bankers themselves. Polling had identified Hillary Clinton's biggest weakness: while millions of Americans struggled to pay their mortgages, taking on second and third jobs to make ends meet, she was perceived to be too cosy with Wall Street. Philippe knew this. He and his colleagues had collated all these damaging snippets in case they somehow came out. Then they would be ready to defend her from that accusation. Now the Russians had handed all this ammunition to the Trump campaign on a plate. And the second presidential debate was just two days away.

Philippe Reines had spent months preparing Hillary for the debates. They dusted off an old mock-up set the Obama campaign had built in 2012. Over the course of about a dozen 'debate-prep' meetings, his job had been to play the role of Donald Trump. It was a daunting task. He had no doubt he would be able to channel Trump's energy on stage. But he and Hillary were friends. They had spent the past 15 years in each other's pockets. It had to feel realistic. 'I went to my tailor and

I said: "I need to look like Donald Trump. And I don't mean in a Halloween kind of way."' So the tailor made him a slightly baggy blue suit. Philippe bought a long red tie. He bought lifts, to make himself appear taller, and leg restrainers to stop himself from swaying about while speaking. He experimented with fake tans, but decided it looked ridiculous. 'I didn't do the hair, because that's a little too comical.' Most importantly, he said, he never broke character. 'I was Donald Trump and I wanted her to see it. I wanted her to dread it.'

That Friday evening, the day of the *Access Hollywood* tape and the second WikiLeaks dump, they had another session. The debate was to take place on Sunday, in St Louis, Missouri. But now people were wondering whether the event would even go ahead. 'Most of the people thought, he's not going to show up. Or if he does show up, he's going to throw himself at the mercy of the audience.' But Philippe thought he knew better. He was convinced Trump would come out swinging, would take aim at Bill Clinton, and his reputation with women.

As part of his preparation for playing the role, he had watched all of Donald Trump's debates in the Republican primaries. Sometimes he would switch off the sound and just focus on body language. The debate was going to be held in a town-hall format, which meant the candidates were free to walk around the stage. From many years' experience, Philippe knew that Hillary was distracted by things in her peripheral vision. He also thought Trump would try to unnerve her. So during prep that night he decided to crowd her, getting up close, distracting her when she was giving her answers. Philippe was confident he had given Hillary all the experience, the ammunition she needed, to go into the debate. 'You can prepare for almost anything, as long as your imagination is broad enough,' he said. But Philippe still thought he was fighting a conventional campaign. Donald Trump had other plans.

On 8 October, the day after the *Access Hollywood* tape appeared, Juanita Broaddrick got a phone call from the office of Steve Bannon. They wanted to invite her to the debate. Juanita was doubtful. As head of Breitbart News, Bannon had proclaimed the site a 'platform for the alt-right'. Now he was in charge of the Trump campaign. Was she getting in over her head? She needed to talk things over with someone she trusted. She called her son, Kevin. It was he who had counselled her to tell the truth to Ken Starr nearly 20 years before. He would know what to do. Kevin told her not to do it. 'Bannon is just using you,' he said. It wasn't the answer Juanita wanted to hear. After all these years of hurt, after decades of being ignored, now was her chance to highlight her story in the most public forum. She wanted to be there. She ignored her son's advice and got on a flight to St Louis.

The operation was kept a secret even from officials in the Trump campaign. Paula Jones was going to be there, as was Kathleen Willey, another woman who had accused Bill Clinton of sexual assault in the 1990s. Bannon wanted to catch the Clinton campaign off their guard. It had to be a surprise. Juanita was told to wear a hat and dark glasses so no one would recognise her at the airport. With less than two hours to go before the debate, Junita and the other women were driven to Donald Trump's hotel. 'It was like *Mission: Impossible*,' Juanita remembered.

Juanita and the others joined the Trump motorcade and headed towards the campus of Washington University, where the debate was to be held. Philippe Reines heard about the stunt about 45 minutes before the debate began, as Hillary was driving towards the venue in her own motorcade. 'You can rehearse or play act as much as you want,' he told me. 'The actual nastiness of it, the hardness of it, isn't evident until you are there.' In the hall, the Trump campaign tried to seat Juanita and the other women next to Bill and Chelsea Clinton. The organisers vetoed it, and Juanita ended up sitting a little further apart, but still within view of both Bill in the audience, and Hillary on stage. 'Trump wanted them to be in physical proximity to Bill Clinton. He wanted them to confront him. And he wanted Hillary to face them the whole time.'

The debate began. Donald Trump did exactly what Philippe had predicted: he came out swinging. He stalked Hillary around the stage. He threatened to put her in jail. When it was over, team Hillary breathed a sigh of relief. But not Philippe. 'It wasn't so much about her performance. It was just so icky. The whole weekend was icky. The pre-debate press event with the women was icky. Trying to get the women in front to accost Bill Clinton was icky. And certainly everything that happened on stage was icky. Everyone felt good. And I just said, "I don't feel good."'

● ● ●

A month later, it was all over. Instead of preparing for a senior job in a new administration, Philippe Reines was left with the bitter taste of defeat. 'I had resolved after the campaign that – win or lose – I was going to clear my head.' He spent 12 days travelling on trains, taking all of Amtrack's long-distance journeys, criss-crossing the country, staring out of the window of his carriage. He called it his 'Redeeming-my-Faith-in-America tour'.

One evening, as the train wended its way through the North Dakota countryside, Philippe got talking to a guy in the restau-rant car. The conversation turned to politics. Philippe chatted away for a while before admitting that he was somewhat close to the subject matter. When the man found out he had worked on the Clinton campaign, he asked if he knew John Podesta. Philippe replied that he had known Podesta for a long time. Then the man said: 'And what's all this about him being a child trafficker and a paedophile?' Philippe had no idea what he was talking about.

The man pulled out his phone and showed him. It was all over the internet: a story about how John Podesta, Hillary Clinton's campaign manager, was running a sadistic ring of child-abusers for a group of elite paedophiles out of the basement of a pizzeria in Washington, DC. Philippe was not expecting this. When the emails were hacked, he had been on the lookout for political bombshells. His boss's inbox was a vault full of political secrets stretching back a decade and more. But pizza?

Podesta was a gourmand. In fact, the whole family was heavily into cooking. His brother, Tony, a bigshot DC Democratic lobbyist who also had an extensive modern art collection, and his mother, who had been a chef, liked to throw dinner parties. They would exchange recipes and menu suggestions over email. At some point there was talk of pizza. Philippe looked at the stories on the man's phone and thought back to the campaign. Had he *missed* something? 'You have the totality of the emails as a problem,' he remembered, still looking bemused. 'I don't remember anyone saying, *Oh God, this pizza thing is getting away from us*. Because you're rational people.' But behind the fog of the campaign, something else had been brewing.

It had begun on 4chan, back in the summer, just before the Republican National Convention at which Gen Mike Flynn led chants of *Lock her up*. Someone appeared on the /pol/ (politically incorrect) board, claiming to be a 'high-level analyst' at the FBI with 'intimate knowledge of the inner workings of the Clinton case'. They called themselves 'FBIAnon'.

The 'case' in question was an FBI investigation into the Clinton Foundation, which had in fact begun in 2015 but had been put on hold during the election.[2] The poster offered to answer 'as many questions as I can without giving too much away'. The first question was classic 4chan snark: 'Will Hillary get pregnant again?' ('Hopefully not,' was the reply.) The second question – quite reasonably – was: 'Why are you on 4chan on a Friday night?' (The poster claimed they had been 'sent home' awaiting word about a 'shitstorm' caused by the attorney general.) The third question was more on-topic for what FBIAnon wanted to talk about: 'Will she be indicted?' Response: the FBI was under intense pressure not to do so. FBIAnon claimed: 'There is enough for her and the entire government to be brought down. People do not realise how enormous this whole situation actually is.'

Some 4chan users saw straight through FBIAnon's faux Deep-Throat shtick: 'Stop LARP-ing and give us something to work with; some good concrete examples,' one replied. Others seemed to be engaging in good faith. Between July and October 2016, FBIAnon hosted at least seven Q&A sessions on 4chan. The posts were all in the same cloak and dagger vein, and suffused with white-supremacist ideology (talk of 'white genocide' and 'deporting all blacks') and antisemitism ('the Holocaust is a lie', '9/11 was Mossad'). There are plenty of references to the Clintons having people murdered. ('People with dirt on the Clintons have a shocking tendency to jump off tall buildings and board faulty aircraft,' one user says. 'We are all worried about that,' answers FBIAnon.) They talk about Hillary Clinton's 'intimidation and silencing of the women Bill has raped/assaulted'. They also talk about child trafficking: 'Pedophiles and sex traffickers everywhere,' they write.

'Many politicians trade girls like cattle.' Another Anon asks: 'Did Hillary have sex with kidnapped girls?' FBIAnon answers, simply: 'Yes.'

When WikiLeaks dropped the Podesta emails in October, FBIAnon wrote: 'When you are reading Podesta's e-mails, remember that the Clintons deal in weapons, drugs and people. Some terminology in use is far more nefarious than many of you suspect.' On the porn-saturated boards of 4chan they went to work, combing through the Podesta files looking for clues. They found one: an invitation from the performance artist, Marina Abramović. In 2015 she had sent John Podesta's brother, Tony, an invitation to attend a 'Spirit Cooking dinner'. 'Do you think you'll be able to let me know if your brother is joining?' she asked, before signing off, 'All my love, Marina.' John Podesta did not attend the dinner, but on 4chan the internet detectives dug out old videos of Abramović's art. An installation from 1996 entitled 'Spirit Cooking' showed text painted in blood red on a white wall: 'With a sharp knife cut deeply into the middle finger of your left hand. Eat the pain,' it read. And: 'Mix fresh breast milk with fresh sperm milk. Drink on earthquake nights.'

This nugget was picked up on a website called dangerand-play.com, which ran an article entitled 'Podesta Spirit Cooking Emails Reveal Clinton's Inner Circle as Sex Cult with Connections to Human Trafficking'. Dangerandplay.com was run by a semi-professional internet troll called Mike Cernovich. In his day job, Cernovich was a lawyer who also published self-help books for men. His maxims included: 'Conflict is attention; attention is influence.' He told the *New Yorker* that he used trolling to 'build his brand'.[3] In 2014 he had been heavily involved with Gamergate. It had helped build his profile. Now he was at it again. From Cernovich's website, the story spread to the Drudge Report. The establishment press knew better than to ignore Matt Drudge (they remembered Monica). On 4 November 2016, days before the election, a column appeared in the *Washington Post* debunking the idea that Podesta was drinking bodily fluids.

While the establishment media was reeling from Hillary's shock defeat, trying to adjust to a new political reality, on the chans they were still digging. 'CP' had long been chan slang for 'child pornography'. For years 4chan users had created nudge-wink memes to refer to pornographic images of children using anything with the initials 'C. P.' Captain Picard from *Star Trek* was one. Cheese pizza was another. Now in Podesta's emails, they found references to pizza. They also found references to a particular pizza restaurant whose initials also consisted of the letters C and P: Comet Ping Pong in Washington, DC. Comet Ping Pong was owned by James Alefantis, who was the ex-boyfriend of David Brock, the former Arkansas Project co-conspirator turned Clinton-defender. Even the initials of the central protagonists suddenly fitted the bill: Clinton, Podesta: CP.

Comet Ping Pong is a family place: a pizzeria in the front, with ping pong tables at the back of the restaurant where kids and their parents can bat balls about while they wait for their food. On 16 November, two men walked into the restaurant. One, wearing a stubbly beard and a preppy pink button-down pink shirt, was filming on his phone. His name was Jack Posobiec, a well-known figure on the alt-right social media scene. On the video you can see him and his friend giggling, as they say they're going to 'infiltrate' the restaurant. They joke about what might happen to them. Might they get killed? They're not kids, they say, so maybe they'll survive. Posobiec is livestreaming all this to his followers online. They look around. There's a secret back door, they say. The staff are on to them. They know about this ridiculous story. They've been getting death threats. It's no joke to them. The restaurant staff call the police and ask them to leave. Outside, Posobiec continues his broadcast. 'There were kids there, little kids going in and out of this back room,' he says. (No kids were visible in the video.) 'So they have a big secret they're trying to hide. It could potentially blow the lid on Hillary Clinton and John Podesta ...' By now, 10,000 people were watching. 'Can you even think of a hashtag to do with all this?' He asks his friend. '#Pizza ... #pizzagate ...?'

Two weeks later, a man by the name of Edgar Maddison Welch, a 28-year-old father of two from North Carolina, packed an assault rifle and a handgun and got in his car. As he drove towards Washington, DC, he recorded a message: 'To my girls,' he said. 'I love you more than anything in the world.' He arrived at the restaurant, got out of his car with his guns and walked straight through to the back. He was looking for the secret room. He wanted to save the children in the basement. He shot open a locked door in the kitchen. It was a store cupboard. There were no captive children. There was no basement.

Welch was arrested. No one was hurt. It was a minor incident. Mainstream America moved on. But the roller-coaster ride of the Trump presidency was just beginning. Posobiec claimed the whole thing was a joke, a 4chan-style prank. But some of the obscure characters behind the Pizzagate hoax weren't just random trolls and LARPers. They were political operatives, and they had bigger plans.

CHAPTER 8

MIMETIC
WARFARE

The night before Donald Trump's inauguration, a group of his supporters gathered for a gala in Washington, DC. The venue was at the National Press Club, an august institution more used to hosting the great and the good of the Washington establishment. This was different. The organisers called it the 'DeploraBall', riffing on an ill-judged comment by Hillary Clinton during the campaign.* Donald Trump's meme-army had adopted the term as a badge of honour. Now the deplorables were in town to celebrate their improbable victory.

Outside, police clashed with protestors who were holding signs that read STOP TRUMP/PENCE FASCIST REGIME BEFORE

---

* 'You could put half of Trump's supporters into what I call the basket of deplorables,' she had said at a fundraiser in New York a month before polling day. 'They're racist, sexist, homophobic, xenophobic, Islamophobic, you name it.'

IT STARTS. Inside, the atmosphere was electric. Dinner jackets and cocktail dresses mixed with kilts and chinos and cheap-looking plastic baseball caps emblazoned with the Trump MAGA slogan. Among the men, there were plenty of 'fashy' haircuts – long on top, very short sides. 'We did it!' one man exclaimed, still in a state of shock and wonder at the political earthquake they had been part of. 'We memed him into the presidency. We memed him into power. We shitposted our way into the future.'[1] Trump had won in a way that was supposed to be impossible according to the rules of conventional politics. The Podesta emails had shown how much time and effort the Clinton campaign had spent trying to figure out what would 'play well', honing and crafting their message to please the largest number of people. Donald Trump had done the opposite. His whole campaign, every utterance, from the scripted speeches to the supposedly embarrassing leaks of 'locker-room talk' had seemed calculated to divide and offend. It was the 4chan playbook. And it had worked.

The evening's host took to the stage. He seemed pumped. 'Are you Twitter trolls?' he asked the crowd, shifting his weight back and forth between his feet like a boxer in the ring before a fight. 'Yes!' shouted half the room. 'No!' thundered the other half. Then they laughed. 'Either answer is correct,' the host responded. 'We're taking over!' Many knew each other, but only from Twitter. Like the Anonymous protest outside the Scientology HQ many years earlier, they were meeting for the first time 'irl' – in real life. The host himself was a minor celebrity on this niche, highly online right-wing scene. He had cut his teeth on the misogynistic battlefields of Gamergate, honed his craft in the meme-swamps of the chans, and helped weaponise the Clinton emails into the surreal LARP/conspiracy theory that was Pizzagate. It was Mike Cernovich.

Cernovich took aim at his enemies: Hillary, the Democrats, and the 'fake news media', of course. But the Republican Party, too. The whole American establishment was in their sights. Little David had wounded Goliath. The giant was down, but not out. The deplorables still had work to do.

Another familiar figure appeared. Dressed in a bright white tuxedo, he bounded onto the stage wearing aviator sunglasses. Gone was the stubbly beard and the preppy pink shirt. But it was unmistakeably the same man from the pizza restaurant video, Jack Posobiec.

'MAGA Three Ex!' he exclaimed. MAGA3X was the organisation that had put on the DeploraBall. It described itself as a 'citizen grassroots movement that helped elect Trump'. It had been set up in October by Cernovich, Posobiec and two other men. The first was Anthime Gionet, aka Tim Treadstone, aka Baked Alaska. Gionet had once worked for BuzzFeed, but he had found the millennial news site's progressive values not to his liking and abandoned them in favour of the far right and open antisemitism. Not in the LARPing, winking, deniable way of the savvier 4chan trolls, but bluntly and directly. So much so that Cernovich had disinvited him to the DeploraBall, sparking a major rift in the alt-right movement.

The other MAGA3X founder didn't seem to fit with the crowd. Jeff Giesea had no big social media presence. When he took to the microphone, he struggled to hold the attention of the assembled trolls. Dressed in a slim-fitting dark suit and tie, he looked more like a corporate exec than a 4chan clown. Which is exactly what he was. At Stanford University he had edited the right-libertarian student paper, the *Stanford Review.* After college he worked for an investment fund before founding several of his own businesses. In 2015, he had written an article for a NATO-affiliated publication under the headline 'It's Time to Embrace Mimetic Warfare'.[2]

Mimetic warfare, Giesea wrote, was about 'taking control of the dialogue, narrative and psychological space. It's about denigrating, disrupting, and subverting the enemy's effort to do the same.' Giesea suggested NATO could play on the prejudices, fears and hypocrisies of the Islamic State terror group by, for example, 'enlisting gay activists worldwide to start and spread an "#ISISisgay" hashtag' to 'denigrate and ridicule' the group and 'weaken its appeal to recruits'. Giesea, who is himself gay, acknowledged such a tactic might be ethically unpalatable to some, and might have unintended consequences. 'But,' he argued, 'as with a company facing a disruptive technology (think of Kodak with the rise of digital photography) member nations must adapt and innovate or get left behind.' Trolling, he said, was cheap and effective. It was already being used to great effect by nations less powerful than those of the collective NATO alliance (Russia, for example), and non-state actors such as ISIS. 'Trolling, it might be said, is the social media equivalent of guerrilla warfare, and memes are its currency of propaganda.'

Giesea and Cernovich had met a few months previously, at a 'Gays for Trump' party during the Republican National Convention in July 2016. By the time Giesea penned his NATO article, Cernovich had been engaged in mimetic warfare for years, even if he hadn't formalised the idea in those terms. Now he, Giesea and a select group of other alt-right figures were going to turn their meme-guns inward, aiming them not at ISIS in Iraq and Syria, but at the American public.

Jack Posobiec embraced the idea. He joined a group called Citizens for Trump. They produced charts and graphs showing how they'd got the #Pizzagate story to trend, bragging about a steep rise in Google searches for the phrase 'Hillary is a witch'. 'Instead of a competition between rival campaigns,' Posobiec wrote, the 2016 election 'became a contest between rival realities.'[3] It was, he said, as if the electorate were watching two different movies, both with the same characters, but completely different plot lines. 'In one movie, Donald Trump was the monstrous villain, and in the other movie, Hillary was the evil gorgon-queen.'[4] The winner of the contest, he posited, got to decide which of those two stories was true. The victor – in effect – got to determine reality.

With the DeploraBall in full swing, Posobiec gushed into the camera. 'After tonight we're talking about getting bigger and better plans. If you think this is big, we're just getting started.' The trolls were emboldened. They weren't just kids sitting behind their computer screens any more. They were kingmakers who had helped install the biggest troll of all in the White House. Aside from the president elect, they had another very powerful ally, a man who was also in the room that night, keeping a low profile.

Peter Thiel was perhaps the most unlikely figure at the DeploraBall. He didn't talk to any of the journalists who attended the event, and he left before the speeches. But his presence hinted at something beyond the image of the plucky meme-insurgents the organisers wanted to portray. One of the most powerful investors in Silicon Valley, Thiel was a contrarian who had built up a fortune by making risky bets.[5] In 2016, he made one of his riskiest: he announced his support for Donald Trump. In October that year, a week after the *Access Hollywood* tape showed Donald Trump bragging about grabbing women by the pussy, Thiel doubled down, giving $1.25 million to the Trump campaign.

Less well known at the time were Thiel's connections to the alt-right. Giesea had been his protégé since his days editing the *Stanford Review*, which Thiel himself had founded back in 1987. After Stanford, Thiel gave Giesea a job at his hedge fund, Thiel Capital Management, and then provided the seed money for Giesea's first venture. Giesea, in turn, helped introduce Thiel to a world that appealed to his self-image as an icono-clastic outsider, a visionary who could sniff change on the wind long before anyone else noticed.

One of the most influential figures on the alt-right scene was Curtis Yarvin. He wrote a blog under the pseudonym Mencius Moldbug, in which he expounded on how the American Republic was a sclerotic shell of its former glory. His posts, which ran into the tens of thousands of words, mashed up obscure nineteenth- and twentieth-century thinkers with references to *Star Wars* and *The Lord of the Rings*. What America needed, he said, was a monarch, a dictator: a Caesar to cross the Rubicon and seize the reins of power. Yarvin said he watched the 2016 election at Peter Thiel's house. 'I think my hangover lasted into Tuesday,' he wrote to another alt-right provocateur. 'He's fully enlightened,' he added, 'just plays it very carefully.'[6]

Like most people, at the time of the DeploraBall, I knew little about Peter Thiel's connections to the alt-right. But now I wondered, was that the plan to Make America Great Again, not under a buffoonish real-estate mogul with weird hair and a fake tan, but under someone much more powerful – a Silicon Valley CEO-king with dreams of becoming a 'sovereign individual'?

There were too many names. Too many connections. I was turning into one of those people whose walls are covered in Post-it notes and string. From my excavations into the murky world of the 1990s, I'd already drawn a spider diagram, a sprawling node that centred around the Arkansas Project and the conspiracy theories about the death of Vince Foster: Ambrose Evans-Pritchard, Chris Ruddy, James Dale Davidson, William Rees-Mogg, with Richard Mellon Scaife, the money man in the middle. I now drew another, centred around Pizzagate: Posobiec, Cernovich, Giesea, Yarvin and – at the centre – Peter Thiel. Both looked like operations aimed at destabilising or 'disrupting' the establishment. Both seemed to bring us one step closer to the prophecy of *The Sovereign Individual*: of an 'epidemic of disorientation' leading to a collapse in our faith in democracy.

I could feel the seductive pull of finding connections. But at the same time I mistrusted that instinct. Wasn't that the conspiracy theorist's game? Was I falling down my own rabbit hole?

· · ·

From a friend, I'd heard about a professor at the University of California, Berkeley, by the name of Tim Tangherlini. A folklorist by training, Tangherlini is an expert in the beguiling power of stories. Lately he had turned his attention toward conspiracy theories. He teamed up with Vwani Roychowdhury, a computer scientist, and together they created a programme that uses artificial intelligence and machine learning to examine the narrative structure of conspiracy theories. This – they claim – can help tell the difference between a conspiracy *theory* and an actual conspiracy.

To create their programme they got a computer to analyse thousands of online posts about Pizzagate. The computer produced a visualisation of the people, places and actions involved in this totally bogus conspiracy theory. It was, essentially, a more scientific iteration of my Post-it-note-and-string method. Then, for comparison, they did the same for news stories about a real conspiracy.

Bridgegate began with a traffic jam. One Monday morning in 2013, without warning, officials in New Jersey closed several lanes leading onto the George Washington Bridge. The crossing is the busiest motor-vehicle bridge in the world, connecting New Jersey to Manhattan. The result was an enormous tailback that lasted until the end of the week. It blocked access to ambulances and emergency services and infuriated commuters. The officials claimed they were conducting a traffic-flow study. This, they said, was the reason they didn't tell anyone about their plans beforehand. But it turned out there was no traffic study. The traffic jam was in fact the whole point of the exercise. The lanes had been closed as a petty act of political revenge. The plot was concocted by allies of Chris Christie, the governor of New Jersey, against a political rival. The story took months to emerge. It was less eye-catching than paedophilia and satanic ritual abuse in a DC pizza parlour, but it was actually true. It was a real conspiracy that was pieced together by dogged local reporters, and it helped put an end to Governor Christie's presidential hopes.

The difference between the conspiracy theory and the actual conspiracy, Professor Tangherlini and his colleagues found, was a question of robustness. For example, the Pizzagate story asked people to believe that a cabal of high-ranking Democrats and other elites were operating a sadistic paedophile ring out of the basement of a pizza restaurant. The key clues, according to adherents, were to be found in coded language in the Podesta emails. The plausibility of the plot rested entirely on the belief that when John Podesta wrote about ordering a cheese pizza, he was in fact talking about child porn. If you removed that element, the story fell down. There was no other 'evidence' for the conspiracy. In the case of Bridgegate, by contrast, journalists had sources who were telling them about the plot to harm the mayor of Fort Lee by causing an epic traffic jam. Those sources, on their own, were insufficient. The journalists dug up documents that corroborated their sources. And later, some of the co-conspirators confessed their involvement. So you could remove one or more elements from the Bridgegate story without the whole narrative collapsing. It was more robust.

I wrote down my emerging thesis, with its actors, plots and subplots, and sent it to Tangherlini. He fed the elements into his computer and came back with a graph: one that looked not unlike my own spider diagram. His verdict: I wasn't a very good conspiracy theorist. The conspiracy theorist, for example, would have jumped straight from William

Rees-Mogg to his son, Jacob, connected the whole plot to Brexit, and thence to the Rothschild family (a favourite of conspiracy theorists) by pointing to Rees-Mogg Jr's work for J. Rothschild Capital Management. My spider diagram by contrast was pretty robust. It didn't rely on hidden knowledge or a secret code, Tangherlini told me, but on leads that were externally verifiable. 'The way it looks is you've got these people who are hiding in plain sight. This small group of wealthy elites want to hasten the end of what they described in *The Sovereign Individual*, so that they could use their strategic investment positions to basically short the Western democratic world.'

I was simultaneously relieved and alarmed. I had secretly hoped that Tangherlini would pour cold water on my theory and pull me out of the rabbit hole. Instead, he seemed to be saying, *keep on digging*.

• • •

In the aftermath of the 2016 election, Facebook came under scrutiny for the avalanche of fake news that plagued the campaign. I wrote to Peter Thiel, the man who saw the site's potential and bought a ten per cent stake when it was still a start-up, to see if he would discuss it. He didn't respond. I wrote to Facebook asking to speak to Mark Zuckerberg. Not a chance. But they did invite me to come and film at their HQ in Palo Alto, California.

From the outside, the Facebook 'campus' at Menlo Park is unobtrusive and low-key. Designed by Frank Gehry, the main building is a long, single-storey box raised on concrete stilts. Upon arrival I was greeted by a fresh-faced young employee who was to be my chaperone. He laid out the ground rules: I could film views of the campus, but I was not allowed to talk to anyone. I wondered why they had invited me.

I wandered along the sun-dappled walkways, past the free restaurants and ping pong tables, through the cavernous open-plan offices and up onto the roof garden planted with wildflowers and oak trees. The place was dotted with notices and slogans that conveyed the company ethos – *Be Bold* and *Move Fast*. (The original Facebook mantra – *Move Fast and Break Things* – had been quietly dropped when it began to look like they were actually breaking things. Like democracy.) These slogans, I was told, were usually based on 'something Mark said'. On campus, Zuckerberg was always just 'Mark'. There seemed to be an unspoken rule that the surname of the company's founder should never be uttered.

I tried to engage my guide on the subject of the election. Facebook's mission, he told me, was to 'make the world more open and connected'. How did he feel that mission was going right now? He couldn't say. I gently probed the subject of the 'filter bubble', the algorithm that ensured Facebook users saw content that tended to confirm their own worldview and filtered out alternative voices. Facebook's mission, he repeated, was to make the world more open and connected. I tried several other avenues of enquiry. I always got the same response. I wanted to record my impressions on camera. My minder stopped me. When I ventured to do so later, on the public highway outside Facebook HQ, a security guard came and tried to chase me off.

My experience on the Facebook campus left me with the impression that there was something else going on behind the mantra of 'open and connected'. What I didn't realise at the time was the extent to which the 2016 election had plunged Facebook into an existential crisis, pitting the values and ideals of its staff against the company's business model. Years later, when I started to pull at the threads of January 6th, I met a woman who had been right at the centre of this battle for the narrative.

Her name was Katie Harbath. In 2021, she had just turned 40 and had spent the past decade working at Facebook, where she was in charge of global election strategy. After the storming of the Capitol, she had one of those *what-am-I-doing-with-my-life* moments and quit. I met her not long after that, at her apartment in a leafy part of Washington, DC.

'Facebook moves at a speed that I've never seen any other company move,' she said, reflecting on the 'move-fast-and-break-things' ethos. She was still adjusting to life on the outside. She showed me into her small study on the upper floor of the flat. On a whiteboard she had drawn a timeline of the interaction between big tech and democracy. The story, in Harbath's telling, began in 1996, when the Clinton campaign first started using a technique known as 'microtargeting': matching up commercial data with election statistics. If you know from market research, for example, that voters of a certain age who lean Republican like to drink beer and buy guns, you can tailor your political advertising to suit that audience. It might, for example, be cheaper and more effective to buy advertising on a small TV channel devoted to hunting, rather than the expensive slots on, say, NBC's nightly news. In the 1990s, microtargeting still largely inhabited the offline world. It was with the advent of Google that microtargeting really took off. By the 2004 election, Harbath was working for the Republican Party. Part of her job was to target bloggers – the new ecosystem of politically engaged 'citizen journalists' whose home-spun efforts were reaching growing audiences. From there, politics began to rip through the online world like a wildfire, fanned by an avalanche of new technology: Facebook in 2004, YouTube in 2005, Twitter in 2006, the iPhone in 2007. It was Barack Obama's savvy use of these new platforms that catapulted him from underdog into the White House in 2008. On Katie Harbath's timeline, 2008 marks the start of what she calls the 'optimism era' of the internet. 'Everyone was like: "Wow, this is amazing. How great is it that you can be building a community online? This can bring down walls."' In a political world dominated by big money and powerful players, the internet was giving a voice back to the people. And it didn't stop there: WhatsApp launched in 2009, Instagram in 2010, Snapchat in

2011. Then came the Arab Spring. In Silicon Valley, the geeky coders, the introverted hackers, the awkward disruptors saw their inventions bringing democracy, hope and change, not just to Americans but to everyone. They were changing the world and making billions of dollars in the process. It was peak optimism. But it was not to last.

There is a little notch on Katie Harbath's timeline. It is marked 'May 9th, 2016'. Harbath was in the Philippines. It was election day. At a TV news station in Manila, she was about to go on air. 'I was going to talk about how much conversation we were seeing on Facebook about the election,' she told me. Facebook was investing heavily in the Philippines – the company had spent millions bringing free network coverage to the country. For many Filipinos, Facebook *was* the internet.

Elections were a big part of the Facebook business model. Katie Harbath's team worked with the advertising team, whose job it was to monetise viral political content. In the run-up to the election, Harbath had sent three members of her team out to the Philippines to train the various presidential campaigns how to use Facebook to greatest effect. They would show campaign officials how to set up an official page on the site, and in how to create content that would be most likely to get clicks. Facebook did not favour any particular candidate – Harbath's team provided their services to any campaign that wanted it. (Indeed, they did the same in the United States that year: the Trump campaign accepted their help; Clinton declined.[7])

But in the Philippines, one campaign in particular turned out to be much better at using Facebook than all the others. Rodrigo Duterte was the former mayor of Davao, a medium-sized city with an outsized drug problem. Duterte's solution was a brutal crackdown on anyone suspected of being involved in the drugs trade – dealers and users alike. He was variously nicknamed 'the Punisher' or the 'death-squad mayor' and was estimated to have presided over more than 1,000 extra-judicial killings in the city. He bragged about killing three people himself. During the campaign, he promised to expand his lethal strategy to the whole country. He built an army of social media foot soldiers who called themselves DDS, which stood for 'Duterte Die-Hard Supporters' but also echoed another acronym: Davao Death Squad. They deluged the campaign with a flood of incendiary and fake posts: from a photo purporting to show the body of a young Filipina woman who had been raped and murdered (the picture had actually been taken in Brazil) to a post claiming the Pope had endorsed Duterte (he hadn't, any more than he would endorse Donald Trump). Facebook loved the engagement. The fake posts were sensational, they were getting attention and clicks – the currency of social media. In April, a month before the vote, a Facebook memo described Duterte as 'the undisputed king of Facebook conversations'.[8] On 9 May, the day Katie Harbath was in Manila to talk about Facebook's role in supercharging democratic engagement, Rodrigo Duterte's supporters, whipped into a frenzy of viral anger and fear, elected him to the presidency.

After the polls had closed, Katie's phone started pinging. People were messaging with a link to an article in the tech website Gizmodo. 'I see the story come out,' she remembered, 'and my first reaction is: this is not good.' The story was about the Facebook News Feed. Whistle-blowers told Gizmodo that news stories with a conservative slant were routinely suppressed on the 'trending topics' section of the website. Other stories – such as ones about the Black Lives Matter movement – were promoted.[9] The 'trending topics' section was a powerful force in news. It defined what the top news was for Facebook's (then) 167 million users in the US. The stories were supposed to be selected according to how popular they were, how widely they were shared. But the whistle-blowers claimed they were often selected by 'news curators', mostly journalism graduates of elite Ivy League schools: people with the same liberal biases on display at old establishment news organisations like CNN and the *New York Times*.

As soon as she was off air, Katie Harbath jumped in a taxi and made her way through the traffic-clogged streets of Manila. On her way to the airport, she joined a conference call with HQ in California. Being a Republican, she had been hired in part for her contacts in conservative media circles. Now, Facebook's senior leadership wanted to know what to do. 'My phone was already blowing up with different folks messaging me, wanting to know what the heck was going on.' Forget the Philippines; this was an election year in the United States. And not just any election. Trump vs Clinton was shaping up to be the most divisive political contest in a generation. The last thing Mark Zuckerberg wanted was to alienate half the electorate. Time for damage control.

The solution they came up with was to invite a group of conservative 'thought leaders' out to Facebook's campus. By the following week, around a dozen of the most influential figures on the American right were in Palo Alto, including Tucker Carlson and Glenn Beck. *Move fast and put the pieces back together.*

Facebook put on a charm offensive. The guests were met at the entrance and led through to a 'micro-kitchen' next to a glass-walled boardroom – food for those who wanted it. Mark Zuckerberg brought his deputy, Sheryl Sandberg, and Peter Thiel, his trusted mentor and member of Facebook's board.

But perhaps the most significant name in the meeting that day was also the least well known: Joel Kaplan. During the 2000 election, Kaplan had been a lawyer for the Bush campaign. (He was sent down to Miami that November and had been present during the Brooks Brothers riot.) He joined Facebook in 2011, the same year as Katie Harbath. He was Katie's boss in the Washington, DC, office, where he had built a formidable lobbying operation.

Kaplan presented the findings of Facebook's internal investigation into the whistle-blowers' allegations. The company had (perhaps unsurprisingly) concluded there was no conspiracy to suppress conservative content. But Zuckerberg and his fellow execs were keen to show they were in listening mode. The assembled stars of conservative media reeled off a litany of complaints. In the middle of the meeting, the lights went out. Sheryl Sandberg started waving her arms about, trying to activate the automatic light switch. But the lights wouldn't come back on. Nor would the air con. It was a power cut. So Zuckerberg, Sandberg and the other Facebook execs sat there with the temperature rising, taking the heat from their irate guests.

After the meeting, Facebook's senior team had to decide what to do. Joel Kaplan argued that, in order to insulate the company from future allegations of bias (however 'unconscious'), Facebook should eliminate the human element in the News Feed. Not everyone agreed. Some argued that the things that people liked to click on and share weren't always the most reliable. They worried that, without some kind of human quality control, the News Feed would be deluged with toxic falsehoods, as had happened in the Philippines. But it was Kaplan's job to steer the Facebook ship away from political danger lurking in conservative waters. Trump was unpredictable. He had a tendency to lash out. Facebook stood to lose millions of users if a narrative emerged that it was suppressing the kinds of stories his supporters were interested in.

Mark Zuckerberg listened to the arguments. Facebook said that Kaplan's team was just one of many groups consulted on content decisions. In the end, he agreed with Kaplan.

Katie Harbath said she noticed the difference almost immediately: more and more bogus stories started floating to the top of the News Feed. At Facebook, people could see what was happening, but they didn't know what to do about it. 'The company didn't want to be, had no earthly idea how to even begin to think about determining what's false or not,' Harbath said. Facebook's whole business model was based on the idea that it was not a publisher but a neutral platform, a place for other people to air their news and views. They didn't want to be seen to be 'putting a thumb on the scale' in the middle of an election. So, they did nothing.

A month after the Menlo Park meeting came the Brexit referendum in the UK. Again, Facebook came under scrutiny for its role in spreading disinformation. In September, *The Economist* published a picture on its cover of a human silhouette with green eyes and a forked snake's tongue. The headline read: 'Art of the Lie: Post-truth Politics in the Age of Social Media'. Harbath, as head of Facebook's global elections team, remembered thinking, 'this is going to be a big deal'. The problem, she thought, would come in Germany and France. Both countries were due to hold national elections the following year. It didn't occur to Harbath that matters might come to a head sooner than expected, and closer to home.

Going back to her whiteboard, Katie Harbath had another big notch on her timeline: 8 November 2016. 'The night of the 2016 election is when what I call the reckoning-phase began for tech. Overnight.' For most rank-and-file staffers at Facebook, Donald Trump embodied all the evil, the racism, the misogyny that festered in America's past. His election represented a giant leap backwards against the technological tide they were working so hard to harness. Trump himself said that Facebook had been key to his victory. At Facebook HQ people were asking themselves: *Is it our fault?*

All of this was going on beneath the surface when I visited Menlo Park a few days after the election. Facebook staff were in a collective state of shock. Beyond the sun-dappled campus, out in the world, a new reality was taking shape. Yes, Facebook had to be seen to do something about the epidemic of fake news the company appeared to have unleashed. But more importantly, there was going to be a new sheriff in town. And if Facebook was going to continue on its path to world domination, it was going to have to make friends with the new administration. The only person who seemed to have the skills and the contacts to do the job was Joel Kaplan.

Kaplan had grown up in Massachusetts. His parents were Democrats – his father a union lawyer, his mother a college administrator. He studied law at Harvard, where he became involved in Democratic student politics.* But he disagreed with his fellow students' opposition to the first Gulf War. After three years in the Marines and a stint as a law clerk in

---

* On his first day at Harvard he met a sparky young woman from Miami named Sheryl Sandberg. They dated briefly.

Washington, DC, Kaplan joined the Bush campaign in the summer of 2000. And when, on election night, Florida went from the Bush column to the Gore column and back again, settling at 'too close to call', Kaplan was on a flight to Miami, a junior officer in the protracted battle for the White House. On the day of the Brooks Brothers riot, Kaplan was one of two Bush campaign lawyers inside the room on the nineteenth floor, where votes were being recounted. According to Jake Tapper, who witnessed the scene as a young reporter, the spokesman for Miami Dade asked them to go out and calm the protestors. But Kaplan and his colleague stalled.[10]

What lesson did Joel Kaplan take away from the Brooks Brothers riot? Did he learn that day that sometimes, in a crisis, the most powerful thing is to do nothing? Years later, many at Facebook began to feel that way, as Kaplan's power and influence grew in the wake of Donald Trump's victory. The first crisis came before Trump had even taken office.

In the aftermath of the 2016 election, Facebook began compiling lists of all the fake news pages that had become such a contentious issue. They found that most of them originated from anonymous accounts outside the US. They appeared to be motivated by financial gain rather than ideology, but they skewed right in their political orientation. During a conference call in December between staff at Facebook's Silicon Valley HQ and the Washington, DC, office, where Kaplan held sway, senior employees debated what to do. One person on the call suggested they delete all fake news pages without delay. Joel Kaplan argued against it: to do so, he said, would disproportionately affect conservatives. 'They don't believe it to be fake news,' he said.[11]

The result: some of the pages were taken down, but most were left up. When Facebook launched a fact-checking programme, Kaplan pushed for a subsidiary of the right-wing news site the Daily Caller to be included in the list of approved fact-checkers, even though, as some staff pointed out, the website had itself promoted right-wing conspiracy theory sites like *InfoWars*.[12] Facebook also looked at ways to reduce polarisation. A team of engineers and product managers suggested they reduce the reach of angry, hyper-partisan posts, and expose users to alternative points of view. But the initiative fell foul of Joel Kaplan. In review sessions that came to be nicknamed 'Eat Your Veggies', Kaplan would subject the team to a gruelling process of questioning that led inexorably to the conclusion that any changes would have an outsized effect on users on the right of the political spectrum.[13] The initiative never took off.

As Kaplan's deputy, Katie Harbath played a similar role. Katie told me. 'It was our job to give our perspective of what the political landscape looked like and what the repercussions could be for different decisions.' American politics had changed. Mark Zuckerberg understood that. Despite Harbath and Kaplan's efforts to placate the new administration, the attacks from Trump-world kept on coming. Senior Republicans publicly accused Facebook of liberal bias. Donald Trump himself threatened to regulate or even close down social media companies that silenced 'conservative voices'. Harbath and other colleagues of Kaplan said he played an even-handed role in tough circumstances. But one whistle-blower told the tech magazine *Wired*, 'Joel was the stumbling block and the halting mechanism of nearly every chance we had to clean up the platform. He was the guy who stopped it.'[14]

Facebook's failure to inoculate itself against hyper-polarised fake news would have devastating consequences. As the next election approached, Harbath said, she had a sense of foreboding. 'You kind of lived every day trying to do a little bit, but knowing you weren't doing enough, you hadn't done enough, to think through all the bad ways that the platform could be weaponised.'

CHAPTER 9

THE PATRIOT

Donald Trump's first year in office was a roller-coaster ride. A blizzard of lies emanated from the White House podium. Staff were hired and fired with dizzying speed. The president was a loose cannon (and, according to the press, possibly a Russian spy). Every day seemed to produce some unprecedented development, the unsayable said, the unthinkable thought out loud. For a journalist it was exhilarating, but you had to know how to pace yourself. And so it was, on 5 October 2017, that a consequential thing happened, and almost no one noticed.

It was a Thursday evening. The White House press corps was packing up for the day, having been told there would be no more public engagements. But at around 7 p.m. Mr Trump, ever capricious, summoned journalists to the State Dining Room. The president was hosting a dinner for high-ranking military commanders and their spouses. The guests were lined up beneath a pensive-looking portrait of Abraham Lincoln, a few dozen men and women, some in military uniform, some in formal wear. In the middle stood Donald Trump with his wife Melania by his side.

'You guys know what this represents?' he asked, sweeping his arm around in a broad circle. 'Tell us, sir,' one of the journalists responded gamely.

'I don't know,' he mused. 'Maybe it's the calm before the storm.'

'What's the storm?' another journalist asked. The president just repeated the phrase, *calm before the storm*, adding: 'We have the world's greatest military people in this room.'

'What storm, Mr President?' asked a third bemused hack.

'You'll find out,' replied the president, with a half-smile and a twinkle in his eye.

No one, not even his staff, seemed to know what he was talking about.

In my world, these strange remarks generated a few inches of newsprint the following day, a few minutes of half-hearted speculation on cable news, before everyone moved on to the next unprecedented thing. But in the other world, the world of Jack Posobiec and meme warfare, in the second cinema of America's bifurcated reality, Donald Trump's random word-salad would soon take on a whole other meaning. In the dark recesses of the internet, among Trump's troll-fans, someone saw the ball the president had just tossed up into the air for them, and they decided to run with it.

Three weeks later, on 28 October 2017, someone posted a cryptic message on 4chan. 'HRC extradition already in motion effective yesterday with several countries in case of cross border run ... Passport approved to be flagged effective 10/30 @ 12:01am.' In other words, Hillary Rodham Clinton would be prevented from leaving the country (but not for another two days). The post continued: 'Expect massive riots organized in defiance and others fleeing the US to occur. US M's will conduct the operation while NG activated.' Did US M's stand for US Marines, and NG for National Guard? The message ended with a suggestion: 'Proof check: Locate a NG member and ask if activated for duty 10/30 across most major cities.' So, approach a random member of the National Guard and ask them if their leave has been cancelled.

These kinds of messages weren't unusual on 4chan. As with Pizzagate, the site was full of people pretending to be high-level officials with access to secret information. But this poster, whoever they were, didn't just leave it at that. They went on a posting spree. 'Mockingbird. HRC detained, not arrested (yet). Where is Huma? Follow Huma. This has nothing to do w/ Russia (yet). Why does POTUS surround himself w/ generals?' And so it went on.

'Mockingbird' referred to an (at least partially real) CIA programme to infiltrate and control the media and entertainment industry. 'Huma' was Huma Abedin, a long-time aide and confidante of Hillary Clinton. She was the ex-wife of Anthony Weiner, the former senior Democratic Party operative who went to jail after texting sexually explicit images to a 15-year-old girl.* 'Russia' referred to the sprawling Mueller investigation into alleged links between the Trump campaign and Moscow. 'POTUS', of course, stood for 'president of the United States'. Those first few posts contained all the ingredients of what would become QAnon, a mass-delusion about a cabal of Satan-worshipping paedophiles and a Deep State plot to steal the 2020 election.

The anonymous poster claimed to be a high-level US government agent, a 'Patriot' with 'Q clearance', implying access to top-secret information. Over the course of the next few days, in dozens of posts, often framed as rhetorical questions, they sketched out the skeleton of a story about an undercover operation being carried out in real time.

It read like the plot of a Hollywood thriller: a covert group of patriots had installed a renegade outsider in the White House. Their mission: to expose and dismantle an elite cabal of child traffickers and paedophiles, and the good guys were up against powerful forces, a satanic Deep State. For now, the operation was being carried out in secret. But soon, all would become clear, and Donald Trump would reveal the truth, with the words: 'My fellow Americans, the Storm is upon us ...' The current phase of the operation was described as 'the calm before the storm'.

---

* It was an investigation into material on Weiner's computers and phones that led to James Comey, then FBI Director, reopening the investigation into Hillary Clinton's emails in the weeks before the 2016 election.

Was *that* what Trump was on about when he made that remark, standing in a room full of generals? To the feverish hive-mind of 4chan it looked very much like it. They rewatched the video from that evening a few weeks earlier. As the president swept his arm around the room, was he in fact drawing the letter Q in the air? Was Trump sending a secret signal?

Still, even to the most naïve 4chan user, there were obvious signs that whole thing was a game, a hoax dreamed up by someone like them: a geek-nerd steeped in the fantasy world of *Dungeons & Dragons*. Whoever Q was, they kept referring to the good guys as 'wizards and warlocks'. They kept predicting seismic events, a series of high-profile arrests, the imposition of martial law, predictions that kept not coming to pass. And they were posting all this supposedly top-secret information on the same 4chan board that had given birth to Pizzagate a year earlier. Out of this meme-soup now emerged a person calling themselves 'Q Clearance Patriot', spinning the sequel in the franchise.

Before they became known as 'Q', the poster was known as 'LARPer Guy'. This was how the LARP worked: Q pretended to drop clues, crumbs of information about a secret operation against an unholy cabal of paedophiles, and the denizens of 4chan pretended to take it seriously. They would start digging, scouring the internet for 'facts' that would add flesh to the bones of the story. This was fun because the cast of characters in the story – Hillary Clinton and her rogues' gallery from the world of liberal politics – represented everything they feared and despised. And despite Trump's stunning victory in the election a year ago, the establishment was fighting back hard. There was no shortage of material in the sphere of current events that could point to a looming and epic battle between Donald Trump – the trolls' president – and the organs of the state.

The QAnon story was like a distorted mirror image of the real world. It landed just as the Russia investigation was gathering momentum. A day before the first 'Q drop', on 27 October 2017, CNN reported that Robert Mueller, the special prosecutor in charge of the investigation, was preparing to issue the first criminal charges in his probe into possible collusion between the Trump campaign and Moscow during the 2016 election. Citing anonymous sources, the report mentioned sealed indictments, imminent arrests, and fears that suspects might try to flee the country[1] – all elements that made their way directly into the early Q drops. Trump, meanwhile, was Tweeting furiously about how the real target of the investigation should be Hillary Clinton, not him. On 4chan, the mysterious Q and his fellow LARPers were busy constructing an alternate world. QAnon was an inverted piece of fan fiction in which Trump's dream was in fact a reality, and Robert Mueller and his team were actually investigating Hillary Clinton and the cabal, using the Russia probe as cover.

Many on 4chan understood the nature of the game they were playing. But some people were taking Q seriously. Or at least so they said. Less than a week after Q began posting, a citizen journalist and YouTuber called Tracy Beanz uploaded a video entitled 'Q Clearance Anon – Is It #happening???'

She starts with a disclaimer: she wouldn't usually do a video like this, she says. But she has decided to cover the QAnon posts, 'just in case this stuff turns out to be legit. Because, honestly, it kind of seems legit.' She goes on to read through a long list of Q drops, adding bits of her own commentary here and there. 'Do what you will with this information, guys,' she says. 'There's a lot of research to be done. I guess, if nothing happens, then this is the hugest, most detailed, amazing LARP in the history of LARPs. Or … this person really has Q clearance and is really sharing all of this stuff on /pol/ and wants us to let everyone know about it. Make up your own minds. Buckle up, I guess.'

Beanz's videos would typically be watched by a few thousand people at most. But her Q video was a hit. In the first two weeks it racked up more than 150,000 views. So she made more. QAnon was about to get turbocharged, and Beanz would play a key role in helping it jump from the niche world of 4chan onto the mainstream internet.

•   •   •

Beanz's real name is Tracy Diaz. When I met her, in 2021, she was reluctant to talk about Q. She had left all that behind, she said. 'In retrospect, that period was something I'd like to forget ever happened.' Originally from New York, she came across as one of those straight-talking, no-nonsense people the city is famous for. 'If this is all we talk about, I'm going to be angry,' she told me when I pressed her on the subject of QAnon. These days she runs an 'alternative media' platform called UncoverDC. She is a 'truth-seeker.' Her journey into what she called the 'truth community' began in 2001, with the attacks on the World Trade Center, when Diaz was in her early twenties. 'It wasn't specifically because of 9/11,' she told me. 'It was more because of what the government did after 9/11. That kind of woke me up.' She described civil liberties being eroded by the security establishment; the invasion of Iraq based on false claims about weapons of mass destruction. It was her red pill moment. 'When everything that you thought was true about things is shown to be false, you kind of question everything,' she said.

As the internet grew, so did Tracy Diaz. In the early 2000s she started reading government documents online, dissecting the detail, looking for hidden meaning and posting about it on Myspace. Then came Facebook and Twitter. She would organise in-person meet-ups with like-minded sceptics, people who believed that much of the country was effectively brainwashed because the 'legacy media' had 'lied about so much for so long'. Diaz and her fellow truth-seekers aimed to provide an alternative source of information. In 2016, she was volunteering for the Trump campaign. By now, she had found 4chan. When WikiLeaks published the hacked emails from the Clinton campaign, she buried herself in the details. She built a small following online, combing through the messages looking for clues that would help expose what she believed were the secret machinations of the Deep State. Her imagination was deeply enmeshed in the world of the chans, a world in which America was ruled by an amorphous conspiracy involving the FBI and the CIA, the media and Hollywood. When Q came along, the effect was electric. Maybe, she thought, Q was for real. An insider who confirmed all of her suspicions, a person who said: the storm is upon us, the fightback is about to begin.

Diaz decided the Q drops deserved a wider audience. She teamed up with two other early devotees: a 4chan moderator called Coleman Rogers, known online as 'Pamphlet Anon'; and a guy calling himself 'Baruch The Scribe', a South African coder and tech writer from Johannesburg by the name of Paul Furber. Together they curated a thread dedicated to discussion of the Q drops on Reddit. They called the thread CBTS, or Calm Before the Storm. They appeared on 'alternative media' outlets with the explicit aim of spreading the message. In December, Furber and Rogers hit the big time. They went on InfoWars, the conspiracy theory juggernaut. Rogers told the show's host that many older people simply couldn't navigate notoriously toxic and user-unfriendly sites like 4chan. But, he said, the boomers had all sorts of connections. 'A lot of them could be retired intel or military. They are a massive untapped resource,' Rogers said. 'The story behind QAnon is so big that we need to get it out to as many people as possible,' Furber added.

Thanks in large part to Furber, Rogers and Beanz, everything Q posted was spreading to YouTube, Reddit, Twitter and Facebook. And out there, in normieland, on mainstream social media, they didn't know about LARPs and meme warfare and the doctrine of total irony. People who weren't inoculated against the virus of the chans were highly susceptible to infection.

The whole situation was reminiscent of the 1938 adaptation of H.G. Wells's *War of the Worlds*. Structured like a normal evening radio broadcast, Wells's science fiction fantasy was interrupted by increasingly dramatic 'live' news reports. The production by Orson Welles was apparently so realistic it caused panic across America, with police banging on the doors of the studio demanding the broadcast be stopped, and people calling in to radio stations offering to enlist in the fight against the alien invasion.

When Wells and Welles met for the first time in Texas two years later, in 1940, the British author asked the American actor: 'Are you sure there was such a panic in America, or wasn't it your Halloween fun?' Orson Welles responded that the excitement caused by the broadcast was indeed 'the same kind of excitement that we extract from a practical joke in which somebody puts a sheet over his head and says "Boo!" I don't think anybody believes that individual is a ghost, but we do scream and yell and rush down the hall, and that's just about what happened.' In other words, it was a LARP.

This conversation happened at a moment in history when Britain was at war with Germany, but America had not yet entered the conflict. Indeed, there was a strong political current that, under the slogan 'America First', sympathised with the Fascist cause and wanted to keep the United States out of the war. 'You aren't quite serious in America yet,' Wells reflected to Welles. 'You haven't got the war right under your chins. And the consequence is, you can still play with ideas of terror and conflict. It's a natural thing to do until you're right up against it. And then it ceases to be a game.'

In 1938, any misapprehension could be rectified quickly and easily. CBS called a press conference, Orson Welles confirmed it was all a play, no alien invasion had actually occurred, he was terribly sorry. This was duly reported by all outlets, and there the matter ended. It was a different story 80 years later. The first articles debunking QAnon started appearing in the establishment media in late 2017.[2] But these did nothing to stem the flow of Q drops, or the increasingly popular pastime of dissecting the posts on social media. Thanks to the internet, the gatekeepers of information had lost control of the conversation. The articles also did nothing to persuade believers that QAnon was a hoax. In fact, it had the opposite effect. Since the 'mainstream media' was part of the cabal, of course they would do everything they could to dismiss those searching out the truth. The more journalists trashed QAnon and warned about its potentially dangerous consequences, the more its devotees believed the network of Deep State paedophiles and their allies in the media were in a panic about their imminent unmasking. All the more reason to keep digging.

That initial post about Hillary Clinton's imminent arrest, which appeared at the end of October 2017, was the first of nearly 5,000 Q drops. Over the course of the next three years it would evolve from a game on a niche website into a mass movement that threatened the very foundations of American democracy.

The genius of QAnon, the thing that sets it apart from other conspiracy theories, is participation. Believing you know what *really* happened with the Kennedy assassination, or 9/11, can make you feel clever, powerful even, like you have secret knowledge about something huge that happened in the past. But QAnon was about something happening right now, an active 'operation' supposedly unfolding in real time. From the very beginning, Q encouraged his followers to 'do their own research'. 'We all sincerely appreciate the work you do. Keep up the good fight. The flow of information is vital,' he wrote on 1 November 2017. If you were reading Q, you were not just privy to secret information, you were part of the operation, a 'plan to save the world'. And the stakes were high. Because the Deep State was fighting back.

Q repeatedly emphasised the important role 'Anons' could play, if only they decoded his clues correctly. 'We need to get organized,' Q wrote on 5 November 2017. 'Things need to be solved to understand what is about to happen. When big news drops please re-read entire graphic. This is so critical and why information is provided in a certain order,' Q continued, before referencing Hillary Clinton and Saudi Arabia.

And so a growing army of followers took to the internet. When they googled Saudi Arabia, they found that something big had indeed happened there the previous day: 400 of the kingdom's most powerful people – princes, courtiers, tycoons – had been rounded up and imprisoned in a luxury hotel. Something was going on inside the Saudi ruling elite. Was the storm in the House of Saud a prefiguring of what was to come in the United States? Q was leaving 'breadcrumbs' and his followers were supposed to turn them into something coherent, comprehensible. They became known as 'bakers'. A whole industry sprang up, a mixture of grifters and true believers, who read Q's tea leaves, parsed and interpreted them for the masses on blogs and social media, like latter-day apostles. It was all part of the work that true patriots needed to do to help bring about the Great Awakening. QAnon was becoming a vast networked role-play game. But the players, many of them older and less tech-savvy boomers, didn't realise it was a game. They thought that, together with Donald Trump, they were truly involved in a life-and-death struggle for the survival of the American Republic.

In 2018, people began showing up at Trump rallies with Q signs. In June, Matthew Phillip Wright, a 30-year-old unemployed former Marine from Nevada, drove a self-made armoured vehicle onto a bridge over the Colorado River over-looking the Hoover Dam. He parked perpendicular to the road, blocking traffic between Arizona and Nevada. The vehicle had portal openings for guns; on board Wright had two rifles, two handguns and 900 rounds of ammunition. During a standoff with police, Wright held out a sign that read: RELEASE THE OIG REPORT. This was a reference to a report by the Department of Justice (that had in fact already been released) into former FBI director James Comey's investigation into Hillary Clinton's emails. The standoff ended after about an hour and a half. No one was hurt. From jail, Wright sent a letter to the White House, the FBI and the CIA in which he explained he didn't mean anyone any harm, he simply wanted the truth for all Americans. He ended with 'Where We Go One We Go All', a phrase that Q used in his posts. Abbreviated to WWG1WGA, it had become one of the slogans of the movement. QAnon had leapt off the pages of the internet and into real life.

. . .

Diaz's initial excitement about QAnon, she told me, didn't last long. After a few months of analysing the Q drops online, she moved on. 'It was a tiny part of my life,' she said.

But she still believed in QAnon's central tenet: that the Deep State was trying to keep Donald Trump out of power. On the question of whether she thought the US government was run by a cabal of satanic child sex traffickers, she equivocated. 'I think that the politicisation of child sex trafficking is disgusting and that we need to protect our kids,' she said. 'It's a major problem across the world. Anybody who wants to deny that I think is living in an alternate reality. And politicising it in order to then be able to attack people as being conspiracy theorist or crazy, I think does a very big disservice to people that need our help. But do I think that everybody in government is part of a big sex-trafficking ring or something? Absolutely not.'

Linguistic experts analysed the writing style of the Q drops, compared them to Paul Furber's own writing style, and concluded that Furber likely *was* Q, at least in the early days.[3] Furber himself denied this. But then he would. Because if Furber *was* Q, then obviously Q was not a government insider with top-level security clearance; he was an obscure tech geek living in Johannesburg. And that would have been the end of QAnon. I asked Tracy Diaz who she thought Q really was. 'Gosh ...' she replied, as if it had never occurred to her to wonder, 'I've no idea.' Then she added, 'I've been accused of being Q.' For the record, she said, she absolutely was not Q.

I came away from my encounter with Tracy Diaz believing that, on balance, she was probably sincere. The things that Q was saying were so similar to many of her closely held beliefs, they just *felt right* to her. 'It was a puzzle,' she said. 'It was a series of questions, telling people to look for things. And if you were able to find the answer to them, it kind of compiled a story.' I had been in that situation. As a journalist, you live for those moments when a source gives you a glimpse of a story. When someone drops a piece of information in your lap, a tip, a clue, a breadcrumb if you like, that maybe adds a fresh perspective to something you had already been obsessing over, the missing piece of a jigsaw you once puzzled over but had never quite managed to complete. I understood Diaz's frustration.*

Tracy Diaz stopped posting about Q in early 2018. But the reason she moved on was not because she lost faith in what Q was saying, but because of a power struggle behind the scenes for control of the Q account. By that time, Q had moved off 4chan and onto a different message board. Q's new home was 8chan, the site created by Fred Brennan.

---

* Unlike Diaz, however, when I can't find enough hard evidence to back up my story, I don't take to YouTube and just blurt out the accusations online, telling my viewers to 'do what you will' with the information. That is the difference between a citizen journalist and a professional one. At least in theory. It doesn't always work like that. Which was why the Iraq WMD debacle was so corrosive.

CHAPTER 10

THE CALM
BEFORE THE
STORM

The big difference between 4chan and 8chan was control. On 4chan, boards were ultimately controlled by the site's creator, Christopher Poole, the teenage geek turned tyrant who went by the moniker moot. If moot didn't like what was being posted on a particular board, he would simply shut it down. Fred Brennan had designed 8chan so that users could create and run their own boards. *They* were in control.

When Q moved to 8chan, he began posting on a board created by Paul Furber called /cbts/ – calm before the storm. Even if Furber wasn't actually penning the Q drops himself (and writing analysis suggested he was, at least some of the time), he was effectively in control of the Q account. He had access to certain information – such as IP addresses – about who was posting on his board. On

5 January 2018, Q posted: 'Follow the MONEY. Loop Capital Markets. Happy Hunting. BIG NEXT WEEK. Q.'

It was pretty standard QAnon fare: throw out an obscure thread to pull at, promise big developments soon, sign off. But a few hours later, Furber cried foul: 'Not Q,' he wrote. The Q account, he said, had been hacked. This had happened before. Passwords on the chans were notoriously insecure. But instead of slinking off to some even darker corner of the internet to recover from the humiliation of being exposed as an impostor, the new Q came out fighting. 'False,' New-Q replied to Furber. 'Did they get to you? Board compromised. Q.'

Now there were two Qs. Which one was 'real'? On 8chan, there was only one authority above the board owner, and that was the person running the whole site. Once upon a time that had been Fred Brennan. But by early 2018, it was someone else. Someone in the Philippines.

• • •

In 2013, Fred Brennan moved out of his mother's place on the outskirts of Atlantic City and into a sparsely furnished apartment in Brooklyn. For the first time in his life he was living independently. The place was poorly set up for the needs of someone three feet tall whose only way of getting around was an old electric wheelchair. Everyday tasks such as cooking or even opening the front door were fraught with danger, requiring elaborate strategies and large amounts of effort. As well as running 8chan, he was working two jobs as a coder. After rent and tax, he was left with $800 per month. His electric wheelchair was his lifeline. But it was old and kept breaking down. He was saving up for a new one.

By January 2014 he had almost enough money. He went to visit his mother. Not wanting to leave the cash he had saved in his flat in New York, he took the money with him. He was at the New York Port Authority Bus Terminal with nearly $5,000 in his wallet when he was robbed. Police arrested a suspect and Fred went to the station in Greenwich Village to identify the mugger. Afterwards, he asked an officer for a ride home. It was bitterly cold and he worried his old wheelchair would get stuck in the snow. The officer told him they didn't have a van with a chair lift. Instead, he accompanied Fred through the snow to Union Square subway station and left him there. Fred took one subway train, then changed to another, and emerged in Brooklyn where he waited at a bus stop for the final ride home. By now it was nearly midnight, freezing cold and snowing heavily. He waited for an hour. The bus never came. Stranded in the snow, he called 911. He spent the night in hospital being treated for suspected hypothermia.

Life was a constant struggle. Despite the influx of users to 8chan from the Gamergate fracas, his site wasn't doing well. Alongside the torrent of misogynistic abuse generated by Gamergate, there were discussion boards dedicated to paedophilia and anime-style cartoons of child sex abuse. (8chan's only real rule was you couldn't post anything illegal, and it sailed very close to the wind.) When 8chan's web hosts kicked the site off its servers, Fred had to scramble to find new ones. He got into financial difficulty. The site was costing $2,000 a month to run. 'I couldn't just go to the bank and get a loan,' Fred said. 'We had no host and no money.' Fred was getting ready to pack it in. 'Definitely it would not have survived into 2015,' he said. But then he got an email from a stranger: an American expat living in the Philippines named Ron Watkins.

Watkins had an offer for Fred: he and his father, Jim, would host 8chan. Fred would continue to own and run the site, but the Watkinses would take care of all the costs. Plus, they were offering to fly him out to the Philippines and set him up in an apartment in Manila with full-time nursing care.

Fred was sceptical at first. He had never heard of the Watkinses. There wasn't much information online about the son, Ron, but there was quite a lot about the father. After working as a helicopter repair man for the US military, Jim Watkins moved to the Philippines in 2001. There he ran a pig farm and built up a small online business hosting internet porn sites with names like Asian Bikini Bar.[1] In his spare time he made YouTube videos where he indulged his two favourite hobbies: unboxing expensive fountain pens, and spouting conspiracy theories. He had a site called The Goldwater dedicated to discussing topics such as the Clinton Body Count and other mainstays of the American conspiracy theory scene.

None of this impressed Fred. But Ron had a trump card: he said his father owned and ran the Japanese website 2channel. 2channel was the original anonymous message board, the forefather of 4chan and 8chan. Fred asked for proof, so Ron Watkins put a link to 8chan on the 2channel homepage. Now Fred was impressed.

'They basically just rolled out the red carpet,' he remembered. The Watkinses knew that he was struggling, living with his disability on his own in Brooklyn. Fred had split up with his girlfriend, the one who had taken his virginity and helped set him on the path from administrator of an incel forum to wannabe king of the edgelords. She had trashed his apartment, he said. 'My life wasn't going very well. It wasn't that hard for me to say yes.' So he packed up his life and got on an aeroplane. What he didn't know at the time was that the Watkinses had acquired 2channel in a kind of hostile takeover. That was their modus operandi: they would spot something promising and take control of it. They were about to do the same to 8chan, and later to QAnon.

Fred Brennan flew from New York to Hong Kong where he had a layover. Jim Watkins flew out to meet him. His host sported a Hawaiian shirt and a moustache that curled upwards at the tips. 'He looked like a pornographer,' Fred remembered, 'this heavyset man, always smoking a cigarette, hitting on every woman he saw, every stewardess, every waitress: *Thanks honey, thanks baby, you look cute in that uniform.*' Fred was not encouraged. When they landed in Manila, they were met by Ron, who picked them up in a big Jeep. Ron was different. He came across as someone from Fred's world: less brash than his father, a bit nerdy. Immediately Ron and Fred started talking about servers and operating systems. Fred was reassured.

But it didn't last long. 'There were signs that not all was well in Jim's little paradise,' Fred said. He remembered Jim being paranoid. When Google blocked 8chan, he started talking about Silicon Valley as a cabal. After a few months, the Watkinses moved 8chan over to their own domain. Fred began to wonder whether he was being edged out. But in the end he didn't mind too much. 8chan was taking its toll on him. 'It's a hellhole. It's one of the most toxic places on earth and administering it, you age by like ten days in a day because it's just constant.' Fred had fallen out of love with his creation.

Then Q appeared. 'I remember Ron being very excited when Q first dropped on 8chan,' Fred said. Not because Ron believed that Q really was a secret government agent who was about to lift the curtain on the Deep State cabal. Ron was excited because Q was good for business. 'It represented all of these new users.' But Jim *did* seem to believe in Q. 'He would talk about the Q posts as if they were classified information,' Fred remembered. 'I think he believed that Q was somebody in the Trump administration.' Whether they believed in Q or not, Fred said they both understood how powerful the QAnon movement could be.

By January 2018, when Paul Furber claimed the Q account had been hacked, Fred had handed over the keys of 8chan to Ron Watkins. As the new administrator, Ron went by the name 'CodemonkeyZ'. The new 'Q', the one Furber claimed was an imposter, appealed to Ron Watkins: 'Test. CodeMonkeyZ pls log and confirm IDEN'. New Q asked Watkins to set up a new board specifically for the Q posts, and he obliged. He gave the new Q his seal of approval. Henceforth, Q would post exclusively on an 8chan board created and controlled by Ron. Furber was out. Whoever was now posting as Q, they had been captured by the Watkinses.

Fred felt his life, too, had been captured by the erratic Watkins duo. He saw Jim as a bully. Once, when Fred requested time off work, Jim appeared at his apartment. Fred had just got out of the shower; he was naked. Jim took no notice and started shouting at him. Fred felt vulnerable and afraid; memories of his unhappy childhood came flooding back to him. Eventually, he decided he had had enough. He quit working for the Watkinses at the end of 2018. Without a job and disenchanted with the website that was supposed to be his proudest achievement, he wasn't sure what to do with himself. He contemplated suicide. In the end he sought solace in religion. He joined a Baptist church in Manila and married a member of the congregation. He watched from a distance as the toxicity, racism and violence of 8chan began to spill over into the real world. In March 2019, a white supremacist in Christchurch, New Zealand, posted a message on 8chan. 'Well lads,' he wrote, 'it's time to stop shitposting and time to make a real life effort post.' Then he walked into a mosque with a camera strapped to his head and an assault rifle in his hands. He broadcast his killing spree live on Facebook. He was apprehended after attacking a second mosque nearby: 51 people were dead. Trolling had become murder.

Fred began campaigning for 8chan to be shut down. By now, he was also convinced that the person posting as Q – at least some of the time – was Ron Watkins himself, something Watkins has denied. He teamed up with Dale Beran – now a proper journalist – and together they made a convincing case that, from around the start of 2018 until its disappearance at the end of 2020, the QAnon LARP/scam was in effect run by a small-time website administrator and his father living in the Philippines. (The Watkinses have denied this.)

Finding out the identity of the person or persons posting as Q, though, always felt anticlimactic to me. The first time I spoke to Fred, in the chaotic days following the storming of the Capitol, he told me it didn't really matter who started Q, or even was posting as Q. The important thing was who was *using* Q. 'I think that Republican operatives didn't understand where all this stuff was coming from. But they did understand that a lot of it was helpful to them.'

•   •   •

I was going back over all the evidence I could find for the origins of Q when I came across a video on YouTube. It was a news report from 2018, less than a year after QAnon began and long before it impinged in any serious way on the mainstream consciousness. A reporter with the right-wing cable news network One America News Network (OANN) claimed to have uncovered the origins of the movement. He said that, sometime in 2017, before Q began posting, a Twitter user who went by the handle 'Dreamcatcher' contacted him to tell him about an 'op' he was planning. Together with a 'notorious pro-Trump troll' called 'Microchip', they planned to 'plant bits of information on 4chan and act like it was coming from a high-level source inside the administration or the intelligence community'. The reporter claimed to have seen chat logs from August 2017 that confirmed the veracity of the story.

In the report, Microchip is interviewed, his face a shadowy avatar of a man in a baseball cap, his voice distorted. He and his associates had seen what FBIAnon had done with Pizzagate and thought they should do something similar. One day, Microchip says, Dreamcatcher replied to a post on 4chan about Hillary Clinton being arrested. And that was it: QAnon was born. According to Microchip, Dreamcatcher was the original Q. The whole thing was just a prank, he claimed. He and his small group of associates messed around posting as Q and replying to Q's posts for a while. But they soon abandoned the project. Microchip was speaking out now, he said, because he recognised how dangerous QAnon was becoming. 'It wasn't meant to go as far as it has,' he said. 'People are being exploited, they're being used, and I feel terrible about that.'

But there was a big problem with Microchip's credibility. He was not merely a 'notorious pro-Trump troll'; he was a virulent antisemite and racist who posted remarks on social media like 'Hitler 2.0 is coming and it's glorious.'[2] These were classic 'shitposts': statements that probably reflected something of the author's state of mind, but were simultaneously deniable as a 'joke' and designed to drive normies crazy. So anything he said had to be taken in that vein. Microchip's real identity is still unknown.* The identity of Dreamcatcher, however, is known: James Brower, another notorious shitposter who had worked on the MAGA3X project with Mike Cernovich, Jeff Giesea and Jack Posobiec. In 2019, James Brower also went public about his involvement in QAnon.[3] His claims were more modest: he said he had written a small number of early posts on 4chan. On 4 November, he posted on Twitter: 'Hope you've enjoyed the 4chan posts. Q.' Brower said it was an experiment that 'spiralled out of control,' and he bowed out.

---

* Unknown to the public, that is. Microchip appeared – anonymously – in 2023 as the star witness for the prosecution at the trial of Douglass Mackey, a self-styled far-right propagandist. Mackey was accused of election interference in the 2016 election after he spread false information about Hillary Clinton and the campaign. He was convicted in part on the strength of evidence provided to the FBI by Microchip. See Michael Edison Hayden, 'Douglass Mackey Verdict Sinks "Shitposting" Defense', SPLC, 4 April 2023, https://www.splcenter.org/hatewatch/2023/04/04/douglass-mackey-verdict-sinks-shitposting-defense.

In that 2018 piece on OANN, the reporter signs off: 'Hopefully this information will be seen as a helpful reminder to question anonymous sources on the internet and to remain sceptical about claims when events and situations take other directions.' Sound advice from a journalist. But again, there was a problem. The reporter 'debunking' QAnon was Jack Posobiec himself – a shitposter LARPing as a journalist interviewing his shitposting friends.

If what Posobiec was saying was true, then QAnon began as a pro-Trump psy-op, part of the MAGA3X operation Posobiec himself helped create. It's highly possible that Posobiec's OANN report was yet more disinformation. But there's also some evidence there might be some truth to it. In August 2017, two months before QAnon began, a document appeared online that looked to be a manifesto of sorts, a call to arms, a bid to recruit more trolls to the MAGA3X movement. Under the heading 'MAGA3X General Strategy', it offered readers a chance to 'join a fun group [...] and show your loyalty to Emperor Trump'. The document instructs MAGA3X members to form themselves into 'squads' consisting of eight men. (It specifies 'men'.) The squad should then select its own leader, a 'sergeant', who is to communicate with the MAGA3X leadership, which in turn will set overall objectives. The command structure would be light-touch. '[Y]ou can do whatever you want to accomplish the objective – work together, have fun, [...] and understand; if all butterflies flap their wings organized, they will create a hurricane of epic proportions.'

The document looks like a composite. Parts of it had clearly been written after the election. There are graphs demonstrating how, in the final days of the campaign, the MAGA3X troll army got the hashtag #spiritcooking to trend – a reference to Pizzagate. Another table shows a steep rise in Google searches for 'Is Hillary a witch?' It was posted on an obscure website devoted to anime and gaming, which also dabbled in infighting within the alt-right movement. The person who posted the document was the site's administrator, 'Zanting', who liked posting pictures of Hitler photoshopped in with waif-like anime characters. It's not clear whether Zanting himself was ever formally a part of MAGA3X. But in 2017 he was a pro-Trump internet troll with a big reputation in alt-right circles. The document was posted under the headline: 'Peter Thiel's MAGA3X With Jeff Giesea and Mike Cernovich Revealed in Document Leak'.

Was the document genuine, or was it just more shitposting, designed to be picked up by journalists like me and send us off down pointless rabbit holes? Possibly. It seemed possible that the MAGA3X boys were just bragging, like they were at the DeploraBall months earlier, continuing their swagger across the internet with their shitposter-in-chief installed in the White House.

Around the same time that the MAGA3X strategy document was published, Jeff Giesea delivered a talk to a NATO conference in Riga. Giesea had one foot in the murky world of internet trolls. But he was also the businessman protégé of Peter Thiel.

Western governments and their militaries were stuck in the past when it came to cyberwarfare, he told his audience of politicians and military officers. 'Cyberwar is talked about solely in terms of hacking computers and networks. I believe we should be just as concerned about the hacking of hearts and minds, and our democratic systems,' he said. And he had some practical advice: 'Build relationships with internet trolls. There is much to learn from the trolling community.' Giesea concluded that the most important lesson was that excessive hierarchy does not work. Point the trolls in the direction you want, he advised, and then let them loose and see what they come up with. 'The freer the hand of the operator at a tactical level, the more likely it is that that person will find a way to achieve the objectives. Elite trolling, some might say, is a form of art. And memetics is a form of culture creation.' Giesea ended his talk with a quote from Victor Hugo: 'One withstands the invasion of armies; one does not withstand the invasion of ideas.'

In my mind, everything seemed to be falling into place: Posobiec claimed that Brower had contacted him a few months before QAnon began to say he and Microchip and a handful of others were planning an 'op'. Was Brower the 'sergeant' communicating with the MAGA3X leadership? And did Posobiec, following Giesea's principle of minimal intervention, just tell them to get on with it? Let them carry out their operation at arm's length, just as MAGA3X itself operated at arm's length from the Trump campaign?

Jack Posobiec wouldn't speak to me, nor would Mike Cernovich or James Brower. But Jeff Giesea responded to my messages. He told me he had turned his back on the politics of trolling. He and his husband had had a child through surrogacy. 'I kind of had a realisation: that culture war bullshit? I don't want to play into that.' (*Bit late now*, I thought.) Giesea told me he didn't particularly want to revisit this chapter of his life. 'It's super triggering for me,' he said. Nevertheless, he agreed to talk about his tortuous journey into Trump world and back out again.

* * *

It had started with the death of his brother, he said. The Gieseas were a Mormon family. After Stanford, he and Peter Thiel set up an investment fund in Palo Alto. Giesea began moving in the elite circles of Silicon Valley. His brother's life took a very different path. He had mental health problems, and never went to university. In 2015, he went missing in the mountains of southern Oregon. A month later, his body was found. Jeff was the one who got the call. It was a week before his fortieth birthday. 'It was a devastating thing for me,' he said. He was grieving, and he struggled to reconcile the disparity between his brother's fortunes and his own. 'I realised I was sort of billionaire co-opted, and so I became more focused on the forgotten Middle American. Like my brother.' Giesea became curious about the nascent alt-right movement. Its members were mostly younger than him, and they thrived almost exclusively online. With his interest in internet culture and memes, he began to see Donald Trump as a kind of avatar for the grievances of Middle America. He saw Trump's politics, the politics of the alt-right, as a way of honouring his dead brother. He felt a sense of disgust with the Republican Party establishment, which he thought served the 'interests of the billionaire class' and was 'selling out the Middle American'.

Oddly, he found an ally in his old billionaire friend, Peter Thiel. They began exploring this world together, hanging out in circles that included some of its more radical exponents: white nationalists. When Thiel spoke at the Republican National Convention in July 2016, Giesea went along. At the convention, Donald Trump had pledged to protect America's LGBTQ community from violence. (Which sounded nice, except it was really a dig at America's Muslim community. A few weeks earlier, an Afghan American who identified with IS had shot up a gay nightclub in Florida, killing 50 people.) Giesea helped organise the 'Gays for Trump' party. He said the party was intended to be a 'conversation starter about some of these issues – clash of civilisations-type stuff'. But it ended up becoming 'a grab bag of all the – like – trolls …' He corrected himself: 'Not the trolls but, like, yeah … the grassroots people there.' The party was held at a civic centre, 'the kind of place where they have high school proms'. But it didn't feel like a high school prom, he said. 'It felt like your internet feed in person.'

Among the attendees were Milo Yiannopoulos, who liked to flirt with neo-Nazism, and Richard Spencer, a real neo-Nazi who would go on to proclaim 'Heil Trump' at a gathering to celebrate his victory in the presidential election months later.

At this point, Jeff Giesea might have had some misgivings. But he forged on. He teamed up with Posobiec and Cernovich and MAGA3X. 'I viewed myself as like a business organiser behind this,' he told me. The objective was to use the power of memes, the culture of 4chan and of trolling, to get Trump elected. The organisation of MAGA3X, he said, was chaotic, unstructured. 'We formed one cluster. But there were lots of other clusters out there.' It was 'open source', he said. That was part of its strength, but also one of its weaknesses. 'Like Move-On or Occupy, [open-source movements] can be easily co-opted or infiltrated. You have all these people who are weird, toxic even, and you can't say no.' There was always a lot of drama and infighting. That dynamic increased after Trump got elected. A split emerged, between the out-and-out white nationalists like Richard Spencer, and the Trump crowd, like Giesea, who worried that the overt racism would damage their cause. Giesea said he was exhausted, he'd had enough, and began to withdraw.

I asked Giesea about the MAGA3X 'strategy document'. Someone had tried to pass it on to him, he said, but he didn't know who they were. 'I remember being like, what the hell is this? Who is this? What's the agenda here?' As far as he was aware, the document was never used as an organisational manual. 'That implies this military level of organisation that's laughably non-existent here.' When, a few months later, QAnon appeared, Giesea said, it felt 'fucked up'. He claimed he never talked to Jack Posobiec about it. 'It felt like a disinformation project of someone or another. It felt like a herding of Trump voters based on disinformation.'

Something didn't add up. If QAnon was an information operation started by pro-Trump trolls, why were they trying to shoot it down just as the movement was gaining traction? Was it because of the tussle for control of the Q account? Perhaps, as they saw it, the problem started when the MAGA3X boys lost control of their own creation, when Ron and Jim Watkins effectively took control of 8chan in early 2018?

Another piece of the puzzle emerged in a clip from a documentary that came out a few months after the storming of the Capitol. It was recorded in December 2019, when QAnon was becoming a mass movement. The director of the documentary, Cullen Hoback, was making a film about free speech on the internet. He was filming a video call with Ron Watkins, the administrator of 8chan (now rebranded as 8kun), when another person joined the conversation. 'Nice to meet you,' the voice said, 'my name is Jason Sullivan.'

Sullivan called himself the 'Wizard of Oz' of Twitter. Another Roger Stone protégé, he had worked on the Trump campaign in 2016, doing social media. Now he was back, working to get Trump re-elected in 2020. In the clip, Sullivan explains that he has developed software that essentially turns people's Twitter accounts into bots, automatically retweeting other accounts to amplify their message. Ron Watkins doesn't say much. He sounds guarded, suspicious. Sullivan continues, apparently unaware he is being recorded: 'This is not a sales call. This is just an introduction and see if there's any things we can do to help the cause of the Great Awakening ... If Q is trying to utilise or optimise abilities on Twitter we can make them better. We've got proprietary tools that can help recruit their armies and get everyone on the same sheet of music so we're all disseminating together and our splash in the pond is getting bigger and bigger every time we drop something. The bottom line is I want to help the president of the US get his word out.' It looked like Sullivan wanted to recruit Q to team Trump. Or perhaps bring Q back into the fold, if indeed QAnon had started as a MAGA3X 'op', before escaping the lab and running wild out in the real world.

As the 2020 election loomed, the sprawling conspiracy theory was becoming hard to ignore. In August, at a White House press conference, a reporter asked the president about QAnon. 'I don't know much about it,' Donald Trump said. 'But I understand they like me very much.' The reporter wasn't satisfied. 'Mr President,' she persisted, 'part of the theory is this belief that you are saving the world from this satanic cult of paedophiles and cannibals. Does that sound like something you are behind?' Trump seemed to consider this for a moment and then replied: 'Well I haven't heard that, but ... is that supposed to be a bad thing ...?'

•   •   •

We are back where we started: Phoenix, Arizona, November 2020. It's a few days after polling day. I'm standing among the crowd, with their guns and their yellow Gadsden flags. But now I too am armed – with more information. I know now that many of those protestors turned up after a call on Twitter by Mike Cernovich, who had driven seven hours from California to be there. Their chants of *Stop the Steal* didn't just come out of nowhere: they were a continuation of the campaign Roger Stone had set in motion in 2016 (in case Trump lost); they were an echo of his mischief-making in Florida, 20 years earlier, during the Brooks Brothers riot. And the man with the horns and the furs, ranting about paedophiles and a Deep State cabal repre-sented the outgrowth of seeds that were planted in Arkansas three decades earlier by the Clintons' political opponents. As I looked back over my notes and interviews, as I retraced my steps through the contested states, it seemed to me that without realising it, I had witnessed a great confluence of forces, a reck-oning that had been brewing for 30 years. Familiar figures were converging on Washington, DC. At a rally in November, I'd seen an unremarkable-looking woman with a New York accent call me and my ilk in the 'fake news media' the 'enemies of the people'. I hadn't paid her much attention at the time. Now her name had significance: Tracy Diaz, aka Beanz, the woman who had helped early QAnon spread from the chans into the mainstream. At another rally in December, there was Jack Posobiec, the MAGA operative who thought reality was like a movie: 'I think we should all together send a message to the mainstream media,' he said, before leading the crown in a chant of *Turn them off, turn them off!* If you could get people to watch a different movie, he thought, you could turn a fantasy into a political reality. And then there was Mike Flynn, Donald Trump's short-lived national security advisor, who had led that first chant of *Lock her up!* at the Republican National Convention in 2016. He was convicted for lying to the FBI about his contacts with Russian officials and had gone down the QAnon rabbit hole. On 4 July 2020, he had filmed himself taking the QAnon oath: 'Where We Go One We Go All.' Now, in the chill of December in DC, in the perilous no-man's land between election and inauguration, he was riling up the crowd. Introduced as 'the people's general,' he urged Trump supporters to 'fight like a Flynn'. Later he appeared on Newsmax, the cable channel headed by Vince Foster conspiracy theorist Chris Ruddy, and founded with money and support from the Arkansas Project financier Richard Mellon Scaife and the authors of *The Sovereign Individual*. He said Donald Trump should use the military to seize control of the electoral process. He was, in effect, calling for a coup.

Q had been silent since election day. Two weeks after the election, OANN ran a 'report' claiming to lift the lid on how the vote had been stolen. The segment was built around an interview with a man wearing a Stetson hat and a red-chequered shirt. Billed as a 'large systems analyst', he spoke against a featureless white background, claiming he had discovered that machines used to count ballots in many states could be easily hacked to discard votes for Donald Trump, or indeed 'flip' votes from one candidate to another. The machines, the man said, could be set to reject certain ballots, which would then be decided by hand-picked 'adjudicators'. This expert, promoting the idea of a vast conspiracy to falsify the results of the 2020 election, was none other than Ron Watkins.

The report did not mention that their central witness was the same man who had spent the past three years playing host to the QAnon conspiracy theory. Nor was there any evidence to support Watkins's allegations of systematic vote rigging. (OANN settled a defamation lawsuit brought by Dominion Voting Systems in 2023, one of several the company has brought, winning them hundreds of thousands of dollars in damages.) But when Donald Trump tweeted a link to the report to his 88 million followers, MAGA-world merged with QAnon. The convergence was complete. The stage was set.

PART III

DOWN THE RABBIT HOLE

CHAPTER 11

YOU ARE
THE PLAN

By the time I figured out what a mistake I'd made not interviewing the man with the furs and the horns it was too late: Jacob Chansley, aka Jake Angeli, aka the Q Shaman, was in jail.

Some months later I met a friend of his. He called himself Bert. (I had a feeling that wasn't his real name.) Like so many people in this world of conspiracy theories, he was friendly but suspicious. A soft-spoken video blogger, he was with Chansley on January 6th. He said the picture the media had painted of Jake as a violent insurrectionist wasn't accurate. Since I was part of that other world, the world of establishment journalism, it took some time to earn his trust. But after exchanging emails for a couple of months, he agreed to talk to me.

Bert and Jake had joined the Stop the Steal caravan, driving up from Phoenix by van. 'It was kind of a last-second decision,' he said. They arrived in Washington, DC, on the evening of 5 January 2021. The following morning, they got up early, wandered around the city for a bit and then headed towards the Ellipse, where Donald Trump was due to speak. The area around the White House was already crowded; thousands of people with flags and banners were milling around. Bert was filming for his blog. It was cold. In order to operate his camera, he had taken one of his gloves off and wedged it under his armpit. As they were walking towards the stage, the glove fell to the ground. Bert bent down to retrieve it. When he looked up, his friend had vanished. 'There was just a sea of people and Jake was gone.' Bert listened to the speech. Trump told his supporters to walk down Pennsylvania Avenue to the Capitol building and 'fight like hell'. When Trump finished speaking, there was still no sign of Chansley. So Bert headed back to where they had parked the van. He waited. The battery on his phone was dying, and Jake had the keys. To conserve power, Bert said, he stayed off social media, waiting for his friend to call. He was getting annoyed. Then his phone rang – it was his wife. From her he learned what was happening a few blocks away: Trump's supporters were storming the Capitol. Bert grabbed his camera and ran. 'You could just see people all over the Capitol, just red, white and blue specks, like ants. It was pretty wild to see.'

When he finally found Chansley, his friend was exhilarated. He had walked with the crowd towards the Capitol, he said. Amid the chaos, he climbed a ladder to get a better view. From there, he said, he saw people being 'ushered into' the Capitol building by police. And so he joined them. (A slightly selective interpretation of events: video of the scene shows Chansley walking unimpeded through an open door. But that door had earlier been smashed open by other protestors.) Once inside, Bert said, Chansley did his best to stop people vandalising a painting. He remonstrated with a rioter who had broken into a kitchenette and was trying to steal a muffin. Then he made his way to the Senate.

At this point, Chansley was captured on camera by a reporter for the *New Yorker*. 'Fuckin' A, man! Glad to see you guys, you guys are fuckin' patriots,' Chansley says to his fellow protestors as he walks around the hallowed chamber. Moments earlier, senators had fled in fear of their lives. 'Look at this guy,' Chansley says, pointing to an injured protestor. 'He's covered in blood. God bless you.' Bare-chested, tattoos on display, he has a broad grin on his face. He looks relaxed. Like he's meant to be there. There are only about a dozen people in the room, all rioters, apart from the journalist and one lone policeman. Chansley leads a prayer. Then he walks up to the desk of the vice president. He takes out his phone and asks another protestor to take a picture of him. 'Now that you've done that, can I get you guys to walk out of this room, please?' says the cop, gently trying to coax them out. 'Yes, sir, yes, sir ...' say the intruders. They're compliant. It is not a violent scene. But the Shaman wants to do one more thing. He grabs a piece of paper and starts scribbling. When he's finished, he turns the note towards the camera and reads out his message: 'It's only a matter of time. Justice is coming.'

Chansley and the other rioters were escorted out of the building. Congress went back to work. Joe Biden was certified as the winner. The insurrection was over. Jake and Bert drove back to Phoenix. Bert dropped his friend at his mother's home. The next day Chansley surrendered to the FBI. He pleaded guilty to attempting to obstruct Congress in its certification of the results of the 2020 election. By virtue of his eye-catching garb, he had become the face of the insurrection. At his sentencing, the judge acknowledged he had not been violent, but said he had made himself the 'epitome' of the riot and that his actions had been 'horrific'. He sentenced him to three and a half years. The Shaman responded: 'That's a lot of bad juju that I never meant to create.'

Trump was out. The insurrectionists were in jail. It was over. Was that 'The Storm'? The big showdown between good and evil that Q had foretold? To those who'd been swept up in QAnon, it looked like the Great Awakening had ended in a Great Disappointment.

· · ·

A few months later, in the late spring of 2021, I was on a plane heading to Texas. Some of the key figures in what was once the QAnon movement were gathering for a conference. But Q had gone silent. Joe Biden was in the White House. America seemed to be going back to normal. Maybe it was really all over. If so, what was I doing? Chasing the ghost of a movement that had already burned itself out? But then, Michael Flynn was going to be there, the renegade former general.

I checked into my hotel room in downtown Dallas and looked across the street. An innocuous-looking red-brick building stared back at me. It was the infamous Texas School Book Depository, from which Lee Harvey Oswald had fired at John F. Kennedy. Sixty years later, more than two-thirds of Americans still don't believe the official narrative, that Oswald acted alone. Dallas is the ground zero of American paranoia.

But it seemed the QAnon crowd was a bit much even for Dallas. The swanky hotel where the conference was supposed to be happening had cancelled at the last minute. I walked with the delegates across some train tracks and underneath a concrete knot of elevated freeway junctions to a cowboy-themed barn that had agreed to host the event at short notice.

I was nervous. I had come with Lucy Proctor, my BBC producer. We had microphones. As journalists from the established media, many would see us as part of the cabal – the Deep State plot against Donald Trump. We presented ourselves to the organiser, an overwrought-looking man in a Stetson who called himself 'QAnon John'. I told him why we were there: we were searching for the long roots of January 6th. At first, this went down badly. I thought we'd blown it. But the more I explained that, although I'd come with an open mind, I really didn't believe there was any evidence the election had been stolen, let alone by a cabal of Satan-worshipping paedophiles, the more he seemed to relax. In the end he put our names on the list. We were in, but they'd be keeping an eye on us.

It was dark inside. The venue was the size of an aircraft hangar. Near the doors, people were selling MAGA merchandise: badges, flags, Trump T-shirts, baseball caps. Also Hillary Clinton toilet paper. At the back of the hall was a stage with three huge screens playing videos that looked like trailers for action movies. The delegates were mostly middle-aged, they seemed pretty affluent and were almost entirely white. It was the height of the COVID pandemic but there was not a face mask in sight. I kept mine off too and tried to blend in.

The organisers came out on stage: QAnon John and his wife Amy. He seemed stressed; she had a steelier look. No one mentioned Q. But they ended their little intro with the slogan: 'Where We Go One ...' And the crowd responded: '... We Go All.'

And then came the speakers. There seemed to be an endless succession of them. They all riffed on the same themes: they were against Black Lives Matter ('All lives matter!') and Antifa; they were worried about wokeness and Communist infiltration. They were Patriots with a capital 'P'; they loved Freedom and – most of all – they loved Trump. Everyone believed the 2020 election was stolen. In between the speeches there were prayer sessions. There was a lot of talk about how America was a Judaeo-Christian country. Periodically a compere appeared on stage to keep the crowd engaged. Microphones were passed around. Members of the audience stood up and talked about their frustrations and their fears. The whole event staggered uneasily from political-science lecture to church service to group therapy session.

I spotted a familiar face, an older lady with grey hair and large glasses. 'I have a sort of a sad story to tell,' she told the audience. It was Juanita Broaddrick. She was becoming a regular fixture on the MAGA conference circuit. I went up to her after her speech and asked if she was worried that her story was being woven into a fantastical tale about Hillary Clinton and a cabal of satanic paedophiles. Not really, she told me, and smiled. She believed the election was stolen, and that anyone who spoke out against the establishment ended up getting discredited in the media. Just like what happened to her.

Backstage, I came across another tentacle from the 1990s: Joshua Matrisciana, the son of Patrick Matrisciana, the evangelical filmmaker behind *The Clinton Chronicles*. His father had died recently, and Joshua had taken over the family film business. His father's old Clinton film was enjoying a new lease of life, he told me.

Matrisciana was one of a handful of citizen journalists, independent bloggers and conspiratorial podcasters gathered in an area reserved for 'press'. In one corner, a blonde woman in a sky-blue double-breasted pant suit was sitting on a plush leather Chesterfield talking earnestly into a camera, while two fluffy dogs perched on a cowhide footstool. Banks of microphones popped up and were dismantled again as speakers from the auditorium came and went, making the same points for the cameras they had just made on stage. The people behind the cameras did what at first appeared to be a credible impression of being reporters, asking softball questions, downloading their footage, fiddling with their laptops, and filing their stories. Except they weren't sending copy back to a news desk somewhere in New York or London, to be edited before going to print or air; they were splurging their 'content' straight onto the internet, mostly unfiltered and certainly un-fact-checked. Many clearly knew each other from the MAGA conference circuit. They were a mixed bunch, the son of the evangelical conspiracy theorist rubbing shoulders with a disaffected Bernie Sanders supporter from Brooklyn who said he'd recently returned from a stint in northern Syria with the Marxist Kurdish fighters. I chatted with a woman who ran a podcast. She gave me her card. It described her as an 'investigative journalist/demon-slayer'. I wondered a little nervously in which of those capacities she was here.

I was here to find Mike Flynn, the star attraction. There was a frisson of excitement whenever his wiry frame was spotted in the hall. But no one seemed to know when he was going to speak.

I drifted back into the main auditorium. There was a man speaking I'd never seen before. But I knew his voice. 'I had major butterflies before I came on stage,' he said. His tone was not bombastic or angry like some of the other speakers. He sounded quietly confident, like he knew some big secret. It was the first time he'd ever spoken publicly, he said. It was Jason Sullivan, the man who was filmed speaking to Ron Watkins in the run-up to the 2020 election with a proposal for the Trump campaign to join forces with QAnon.

A big man, young-ish, tall and well fed, Sullivan was wearing a smart blue suit and a red tie. As he paced the stage, he hit the buttons that fired up the crowd: *they're coming to censor you, they're taking away your right to vote, they're coming for your guns, your freedoms.* And 'they' were child traffickers. 'We are going to pull them up by the nape of their neck and toss them in that lake of fire,' he said, in a half-hearted attempt to summon a tone of anger. He didn't look like he believed any of it, but the audience cheered anyway. To me, Sullivan looked like he was playing a role – LARPing. At one point he mentioned Hillary Clinton and then, with a smirk, he made a noose sign around his neck.

'I'm going to let you into a little secret,' he said: 'You *are* the plan.' The crowd loved this. Since Q had gone silent, the faithful were desperate for some sign, and perhaps this was one. Because one of the slogans of QAnon was 'trust the plan'. 'We need all of you to help us disseminate real-time intel that actually matters in the moment of influence,' he said. 'Join me tomorrow, we're going to be speaking with General Flynn. Together, we're going to grow our digital army.'

Around the time of the conference, a poll came out in which nearly one-fifth of all Americans said they believed that the US government, media and finance were controlled by a group of Satan-worshipping paedophiles. The same number believed violence might be necessary to 'save the country'.[1] (That view was more prevalent among Republicans than Democrats or independents, but by no means exclusive to Trump support-ers.) How many of them, I wondered, might have got that idea thanks to Jason Sullivan?

He finished his speech and came off stage. I'd told myself I was there to observe, to listen, not to confront people. I wanted to get under the skin of the movement, to see what these people say and do when they're among their own, not on the defen-sive. But Sullivan seemed so cynical. I wanted to ask him, *What the hell are you playing at?* Sullivan told me he was merely 'gaming the system', exploiting the algorithms of social media for maximum influence. The 'proprietary tool' he had offered Ron Watkins to help expand the reach of QAnon was an app he developed, known as Power10. Selected Twitter users were invited to opt in, effectively turning their accounts into bots, automatically retweeting Donald Trump's account, as well as other pro-Trump accounts such as that of Gamergate troll Mike Cernovich and, later, QAnon promoters. 'I got attacked, saying that I created some vast Russian-style disinformation network, which is completely false. We created a programme that fell within their guidelines.' It's not manipulation, Sullivan said, if the Twitter code allows for it. (Twitter later shut the app down.) Did he think his Twitter 'wizardry' had helped get Trump elected in 2016? 'I think that we helped move the needle.'

By his own account, Sullivan wasn't a QAnon 'obsessive', not a true believer. But he said he figured there had to be a reason why people were attracted to it. 'If there are terrible things going on in the world, we need to know about them.' I asked him about the recording in the HBO documentary, where he offered to help Ron Watkins boost QAnon in order to help the Trump campaign. His mood changed. It was a conversation, he said, that was recorded without his knowledge. It was intended to be private.

The central narrative of QAnon was that the United States government was secretly run by a cabal of satanic paedophiles. A claim so horrific, so inflammatory, it might well drive good people to violence. I was trying to avoid confrontation. But the question now became inevitable. When Sullivan decided to use that narrative to help the Trump campaign, did he actually believe it was true?

His answer was not what I expected. I thought he would deny it, say he never used QAnon to help the Trump campaign. Instead, he talked about the world being full of bad people: 'There's people that are involved in the drug trade; there's people that are involved in human trafficking; there's people making money off of wars.' I tried again: as a systemic feature of the US government, did he believe it was run by a cabal of satanic paedophiles? 'You know,' he said, as if considering it for the first time. 'I wouldn't go that far. I would say that there's paedophiles out there and we don't know who they are. I don't subscribe to the view that a bunch of paedophiles are running our government.' So if he didn't believe it was true, did he wrestle with his conscience before deciding to boost that insane narrative to try to win in the 2020 election?

Now he slammed the conversation into reverse gear: 'Well, maybe you're assuming that I did exploit some of those narratives based on that particular topic. I don't believe that that's the case.' It was as if, at the third time of asking, Jason Sullivan suddenly realised the implications of what he was saying. And it didn't look good.

·   ·   ·

I stepped outside for a breather. In the car park, I met Rick and Courtney Worrel, a retired couple originally from North Dakota. They had found QAnon quite recently, around the time Q went silent. 'We haven't heard from Q publicly online, but we're hearing from Q in other more subtle ways,' Rick said. What did he mean? From the other speakers, he said. They're 'helping us to identify what we need to do. You have to be able to pick up on it.' I tried to probe this mysterious method of communication. Could he give me an example of these 'subtle' messages? 'I really can't because there's operational security that we're maintaining. So I'd just rather not go into any more detail.' Fair enough. After all, I might be an agent of the Deep State. 'It's coming,' Courtney said. *What is?* 'There's a storm coming.' *What do you think the storm is?* 'The truth is going to come out. You can see it. The dam is starting to crack and it's going to come out like a flood.'

Rick Worrel later emailed me to say how excited he was to talk to the BBC. He'd been a shortwave radio enthusiast in his youth, and had been a fan of a programme called *London Calling* on the BBC World Service. In fact, someone from BBC HQ had once sent him a postcard, thanking him for a letter he'd sent. It showed a picture of Tower Bridge in the 1970s. Rick had treasured it all these years. Many of the conference-goers were much like the Worrels: not cynical people exploiting others' fears and gullibility, but honest, public-spirited types who had become convinced that everything they're told – by the media, the politicians, the 'establishment' – is a lie. They honestly believed that America was in the grip of evil forces. This movement seemed to give them a chance to take back control, to do something about it.

• • •

Back in the 'press area', the moment everyone had been waiting for. Flynn strode in, compact, lean, intense, wearing jeans and a grey suit jacket over a T-shirt with his own name emblazoned on it. The citizen journalists huddled round. There was a frisson of excitement. Some believed Flynn *was* Q.

The general issued instructions on how to proceed: 'Be brief and to the point. Identify yourself and who you represent.' Then the questions began. Hardly anyone managed to satisfy the general's strict criteria: either they hadn't introduced themselves properly, or their questions were too long. But he gamely answered them all (usually after a stern telling-off). His answers boiled down to this: the 2020 election was stolen. True patriots are engaged in a battle for the soul of America. They are fighting for an 'information beachhead'. An army of 'digital soldiers' can and will prevail against the Deep State and their allies in the establishment media. Every time he got onto that topic he glared at me. Everyone got to ask a question. Even the demon-slayer. (She asked about the use of black magic or satanic rituals to shift the collective consciousness. The general seemed a little stumped by that one.)

The only person who didn't get to ask a question was me. Flynn started moving off. I pushed my way past the podcasters and the YouTubers and tried to block his path. 'I've come all the way from England to speak to you,' I ventured. He wasn't interested. 'I'm done with media nonsense,' he said, and strode off.

I felt deflated. In our collective fantasy of what makes a scoop, journalists think that to truly get to the bottom of a story we must meticulously gather evidence, build a case out of facts that others want to keep hidden. Then, when we're ready, we confront our adversary – look them in the eye and, through a combination of charm, aggression and wily questioning, drag a confession out of them. Gotcha!

Sometimes it does work like that. But sometimes the truth is hiding in plain sight. Sometimes the people who don't want to talk to you are happy to tell others exactly what they've done and what they're planning to do next. And so it was with Michael T. Flynn and Jason Sullivan.

Shortly after the 'press conference', Sullivan and Flynn were back on stage. They wanted to recruit the audience into their digital army. They wanted to talk tactics and battle plans. But some in the hall wanted something a bit spicier than digital warfare. A man at the front stood up, introduced himself as a 'simple Marine', and asked: 'I'm just wondering why what happened in Myanmar can't happen here.' In Myanmar, there had just been a military coup. The pro-democracy leader, Aung Sang Suu Kyi, was under arrest again. There was a beat, a moment of silence, while Flynn considered this. And then he replied: 'No reason. I mean, it should happen here. No reason.'[2]

But Michael Flynn's message wasn't actually for his audience to pick up their guns. 'The battle space that we are on has to do with information,' he said. 'To win the information war, you have to dominate the information domain. Maintain the high ground. Fight on the terrain of your choosing.'

Flynn wanted his digital soldiers to do more than just tweet. 'Get involved in your school boards,' he said. 'Get involved at the local level, parish, town, county.' He wanted to take over the country from the bottom up, to flood American democracy with conspiracy theorists.

Now, Flynn turned his attention to the enemy within: the *fake news media*. 'They've snuck in here,' he said, scanning the hall. 'They're a bunch of snakes.' The crowd started chanting *CNN Sucks, CNN Sucks!* The woman next to me turned and looked suspiciously at my microphone. 'You're not from CNN, are you?' she asked. I shook my head in a way I hoped looked casually dismissive. But I was getting nervous. Flynn was whipping up the crowd. 'Get 'em out!' he shouted. Militiamen were making their way through the hall, looking for infiltrators. *Get Out! Get Out!* the chant went up. As the heavies reached our row, I lowered my microphone and stared straight ahead, pretending – ludicrously – not to notice them. I prepared myself for a confrontation.

But they moved on past us, towards someone several rows in front, a reporter from an American news website. They hauled him out of his seat (accompanied, somewhat disconcertingly, by uniformed police officers) and marched him out of the hall. The crowd cheered. I kept my head down.

'We are in biblical times,' I heard Flynn say. I felt like I'd just witnessed an exorcism.

• • •

Over the course of the next 18 months, a battle played out inside the Republican Party, between the MAGA wing – those who supported Donald Trump and their increasingly unhinged allegations election fraud – and those who believed Biden won a fair contest. If only they could ditch Trump and his 'Big Lie', they believed, American politics might return to its old familiar binary.

Tracy Diaz, the woman who had helped spread QAnon onto the mainstream internet, heeded Gen Flynn's calls to get involved in local politics and got elected to an influential position in the local Republican Party in South Carolina. In that same state I met a woman, a committed Republican, who feared incorporating the QAnon crowd into the fold could mean the 'entrance into fascism for the Republican party'. She would attend MAGA gatherings undercover to gather intelligence on their strategies, to better know the enemy. 'I think competition is a healthy thing,' she told me. 'But when your competitor is insane you don't really have healthy competition.' The MAGA wing, for their part, regarded their opponents inside their own party as an enemy as great as the Democrats.

In the end the MAGA wing prevailed. The Big Lie became Republican party orthodoxy and Trump the candidate for the 2024 election. By that time, I had concluded that party politics no longer mattered.

In the autumn of 2022 I flew to Miami to attend another conference. The event was entitled NatCon 3. 'NatCon' stood for 'National Conservatism'. I was going primarily to hear the headline speaker, Peter Thiel.

An elusive libertarian, Thiel had long been a devotee of eccentric pursuits: sea-steading (founding independent statelets by tying together barges on the high seas) and radical life-extension (he wanted to live for a thousand years). In my head, I had situated him at the centre of a network of obscure far-right online personalities and powerful Silicon Valley players who had ridden the Trump wave all the way to the 2020 election.

Far from being a setback, I now suspected, Donald Trump's loss in 2020 was in fact the whole point: the vehicle they would use to finally kill off faith in America's electoral system, to replace it with a form of anarcho-capitalism, a neo-feudal society in which they would emerge as sovereign individuals in a radically decentralised world. For more than a year I had been burrowing deep into a series of labyrinthine rabbit holes. Now I was in so deep it seemed there was no turning back. The only way out was to keep on digging.

Thiel made for a disappointing arch-villain. His presentation, which included slides with obscure quotes and tables of data, focused largely on the real-estate market in California and the implications for America's squeezed middle class. It was faltering and – frankly – a bit dull. One evening by the hotel pool I got into conversation with a long-haired young Norwegian, Hakon, who whispered to me that he'd come to the conference hoping to meet a blogger known as Mencius Moldbug. *Now we were getting somewhere!* I too wanted to meet Moldbug, the software-engineer-turned-philosopher whose real name was Curtis Yarvin. He was the blogger who had spent election night at Peter Thiel's house, one of the founders of a neo-reactionary movement known as the 'Dark Enlightenment'. He was sometimes described as the intellectual backbone of the MAGA movement, arguing that the American democratic experiment had failed, and that the country needed an American Caesar, a dictator who would cross the Rubicon and seize power from the corrupt functionaries, the sclerotic remnants of the Republic. Yarvin was another reason why I'd come to Miami. But even though people at the conference spoke of him in hushed tones, and his ghost seemed to haunt the corridors of the conference centre, he wasn't actually there.

Back in London, I was scrolling through my Twitter feed, sleepless and red-eyed from the overnight flight, when I came across a strange video. Donald Trump was speaking at a campaign rally in Ohio, in support of J. D. Vance. Vance was the author of *Hillbilly Elegy*, a memoir about growing up poor and white between Appalachian Kentucky and rustbelt Ohio. The book had been well received in the pages of the *New York Times*. Vance had called Trump 'reprehensible', the 'opioid of the masses'. To the *bien-pensant* opinion-formers of the establishment media, his book was an eye-opening window onto a little-seen world. But now Vance was running for the US Senate in the midterms, and he needed Trump's endorsement. As he leaned into the stolen-election narrative, his star was rising in MAGA circles. Polite society disavowed him, but he had received backing from a very powerful player: Peter Thiel.

About an hour and a half into Trump's rambling speech, something odd happened. He uttered the words, 'Now we are a nation in decline,' and as if on cue, music began playing. It was so quiet at first that I couldn't quite make it out, but it wasn't the usual pumping rock fodder of Trump rallies. This was sombre: nostalgic strings, portentous piano. Trump began speaking to the rhythm of the music, his voice halting in odd places, rising to crescendos as if he were performing a piece of spoken-word poetry.

> *We are a nation that has*
> *Weaponised its law enforcement against the opposing*
>   *political party*
> *like never*
> *ever*
> *before*
> *we've got a Federal Bureau of Investigation that won't*
>   *allow bad*
> *election-changing facts to be presented to the public*
> *where Hunter Biden's laptop*
> *was Russian disinformation when they knew it wasn't*
> *and a Department of Justice that refuses to investigate*
> *egregious acts of voting irregularities and fraud*

and we have a president who is cognitively impaired
and in no condition to lead our country which may
end up
in World

War

Three ...

I was mesmerised. The music, it turned out, was from a song entitled 'WWG1WGA' (Where We Go One We Go All). As Donald Trump riffed on how American democracy had been stolen, some in the crowd held up their index fingers, pointing towards the heavens. They looked like members of a cult.

In the run-up to the midterms, Donald Trump had been working to try to resurrect the QAnon movement, which had proved such a powerful support base in his efforts to over-turn the 2020 election. A week before the Ohio rally, he had posted a picture of himself wearing a Q lapel badge beneath the slogan 'The Storm Is Coming'. 'The Storm' was a central plank of the QAnon conspiracy theory: an apocalyptic moment in which, adherents believed, the members of the satanic cabal would be arrested, tried and executed, perhaps live on TV. This was no longer a niche position. In a poll conducted less than six months previously, a majority of Americans said they believed their government was corrupt and rigged, and more than a quarter believed it might soon be necessary to take up arms against it.

Meanwhile, less high profile but possibly more significant preparations were being made to wrest control of the democratic process. In Nevada, a Las Vegas businessman by the name of Jim Marchant was running for elected office. Marchant had run for Congress in 2020 but had been defeated – fraudulently, he claimed. The day after the election, as the Stop the Steal movement was taking shape, which would culminate in the storming of the Capitol, a prominent QAnon influencer came to see him. The man went by the alias Juan O Savin, a play on the numbers 1-0-7 – 'Q' being the 17th letter of the alphabet. Marchant, a strong promoter of Donald Trump's stolen-election narrative, was planning to run for Congress again in 2022, but Savin told him he had a better plan: run for the position of secretary of state instead. Part of the job of the secretary of state is to oversee elections. If elected in 2022, by 2024 Marchant would have the power to refuse to count certain segments of the vote, claiming they had been tainted by fraud, leading potentially to a different electoral outcome from the one voted for by the people. Marchant himself was open about what he wanted to achieve. And Marchant wasn't the only one. At Savin's urging, he had put together a coalition of election-denying candidates for secretaries of state in key states around the country who, if elected, could – effectively – pick the next president of the United States. 'When I'm secretary of state of Nevada, we are going to fix it,' he said at a MAGA rally. 'And when my coalition of secretary of state candidates around the country get elected we're going to fix the whole country, and President Trump is going to be president again in 2024.'

Perhaps I had spent too much time down the rabbit hole. But, fresh from Miami, I had a theory: the reason all this was happening was not so that Donald Trump might be reinstalled in the White House in 2024. Underlying all the political manoeuvring, I believed, behind all the crazy conspiracy theories and all the madness, was an attempt to radically alter the power balance in America. I believed that at the nexus of politics and new technology a small group of people were plotting to overthrow the Republic. They were preparing the ground for a period of epochal change, leading to a dark and fundamentally undemocratic future. Was this the real conspiracy? If so, it was the biggest of them all.

CHAPTER 12

EVERYTHING IS CONNECTED

Around the time I began seriously delving into QAnon, a container ship became stuck in the Suez Canal. The *Ever Given* was 1,300 feet long, a 220,000-tonne cargo vessel, one of the largest on the ocean. It was on its way from Malaysia to Rotterdam, loaded with $3 billion worth of cargo. As it traversed the canal on its way into the Mediterranean it was buffeted by a storm and ran aground, blocking the busiest trade route in the world. It was a huge story, making front-page news around the world. But in the darker recesses of the online universe, people saw not a huge maritime traffic jam, but something more sinister.

Q had been silent for months, leaving a community of internet conspiracy sleuths bereft. They were hungry for clues, and now they had found one. The *Ever Given* was run by a shipping company based in Taiwan called Evergreen. That name was emblazoned in large letters on the side of the ship, and across thousands of the containers piled on board. In the world of QAnon, the word 'Evergreen' was laden with significance. It was Hillary Clinton's Secret Service code name.

All US presidents, their spouses and close family members are given a code name by the Secret Service. Donald Trump was 'Mogul', Barack Obama was 'Renegade', Michelle Obama was 'Renaissance', Bill Clinton was 'Eagle'. As First Lady, Hillary was 'Evergreen', and she retained that name when she ran for president in 2016. It was an ideal clue for QAnon's army of out-of-work armchair detectives – shrouded in mystique by virtue of its association with the Secret Service, but not actually a secret, discoverable with a simple Google search.

If this huge container ship had the word 'Evergreen' painted on the side, then in the minds of QAnon believers, it had to have something to do with Hillary Clinton. And there was more. The ship's international call sign, its unique identifier used in all radio communications, was H3RC, almost identical to the abbreviation Q often used to refer to Hillary Rodham Clinton, HRC.

In the world of QAnon, there is no such thing as coincidence, so they got to work. They searched back through the old Q drops for references to 'Evergreen'. One post, from 2018, read, in part: 'The right people have the information. GOOD people are acting on the information. [...] Define Evergreen. When do you call a plumber?'

A *plumber*? To unblock a waterway, perhaps? Had Q *predicted* this event?

The QAnon community was abuzz with theories: the containers were full of trafficked children, being transported across the world by Hillary to feed the depraved appetites of her international cabal of satanic paedophiles. The good guys, the 'white hats' fighting with Trump to expose the cabal, knew all about the operation and had somehow arranged for the ship to run aground, so they could save the children. A tussle was going on behind the scenes, with the agents of the cabal, who were fighting to keep the true nature of the cargo secret. If the good guys prevailed, the whole plot would be blown open. The Great Awakening.

It took six days to dislodge the *Ever Given*. When the ship finally resumed its voyage, it continued on to Rotterdam, where it unloaded its varied cargo which included IKEA furniture and barbecues, microchips and vibrators. (An erotic wholesaler in the Netherlands lamented the delay of 20 containers full of dildoes and other adult equipment, saying the company might struggle to recover in time for the following year's Valentine's Day rush.) In short, that ship was carrying pretty much anything you could imagine, except what the QAnonners believed. There were no trafficked children.

I chuckled to myself about the silliness of all this. Child trafficking is of course a serious problem. But if Hillary Clinton *were* the leader of a global cabal of paedophiles, and if she *were* transporting children halfway around the world to supply her evil co-conspirators, how dumb would she have to be paint her name on the side of the boat? QAnon people were clutching at straws. What need did this conspiracy-theorising fulfil, this desperate desire to see connections everywhere? Perhaps, during periods of great change, the feeling of being in possession of secret knowledge – a key that unlocked the meaning of baffling events – conferred a sense of agency? Was the conspiracy theory an anchor in an uncertain world? But why did this tendency seem so much more prevalent on the right of the political spectrum, among Trump supporters in particular?

Or was it? I thought back to the Russia story, and the Steele dossier, the 'intelligence' file compiled by a former MI6 spy that was leaked to the press days before Donald Trump's inauguration in 2016. The file suggested that the man who was about to become president of the United States might in fact be a Russian agent; that the Russians had 'kompromat' on Trump – compromising information that the Kremlin could use to control him.

At the heart of the dossier was an allegation so sensational, so salacious, it might have come straight off the pages of a bad spy thriller. The story was that Donald Trump had supposedly had an encounter with some prostitutes in a Moscow hotel room. The prostitutes were engaged in an unusual sex act: urinating on the bed. According to the dossier, there was a video.

The 'pee tape', as it became known, was, supposedly, the kompromat the Kremlin had on Trump. It wasn't the most serious allegation in the dossier. But it was the most dramatic, the most outrageous. Among journalists of my ilk, the hunt was on – for the tape, or indeed to verify any of the detail in the dossier.

Together with a small group of colleagues at the BBC, we set up a secret unit: select reporters and editors with contacts either in Russia or the US intelligence community. We met in an anonymous-looking building behind Oxford Street, near the BBC's London headquarters. The room was in the basement of a company that supplied security equipment to journalists flying out to war zones around the world. We'd ring the buzzer, the door would open, and we would walk past the flak jackets and gas masks, down a flight of stairs. It was all a bit dingy. We called it the Flea Circus, an ironic homage to John le Carré's fictional spy HQ, the Circus.

We were paranoid about our security. Were the Russians on to us? Or the Americans? We thought people might be listening to us through our mobile phones. So we'd zip them up in a specially designed pouch that was supposed to block low-frequency electromagnetic waves. For good measure, we stashed the pouch in a locker outside the room. We really had very little clue about security: we were playing at being spies, and for the most part we were relying on the le Carré novels we'd read for our 'tradecraft'.

I travelled to Kyiv to meet contacts, former spies, Ukrainian agents, a Russian arms dealer. A colleague flew to Istanbul to meet a man who claimed to have actually seen the pee tape. None of them delivered. I also began meeting Christopher Steele, the former British spy who had compiled the dossier, off the record and in secret. He acknowledged that, in the intelligence business, you could never be 100 per cent sure. Nevertheless, he was confident in his sources. But no evidence of the pee tape ever emerged. Other key elements of the dossier remained stubbornly resistant to verification. Eventually we quietly disbanded our secret little unit in the basement behind Oxford Street. We moved on to other stories. But the American media did not.

The Russia story dominated the headlines for almost the entire Trump presidency. Journalists pored over every aspect of Donald Trump's connections to Russia, financial or otherwise. They uncovered some interesting links. But never the smoking gun (or the soggy sheets). There were investigations by the FBI and Special Counsel Robert Mueller III. After two years, Mueller concluded that, yes, there had been contacts between Russian officials and the Trump campaign, and that the Kremlin had sought to harm Hillary Clinton's chances by helping Trump, but Mueller said he had found no evidence that the Trump campaign had 'conspired or coordinated' with the Kremlin. In other words, Donald Trump was not a Russian agent.*

---

* Mueller stopped short of *collusion*, though he added, confusingly, 'If we had confidence that the president clearly did not commit a crime, we would have said so. We did not, however, make a determination as to whether the president did commit a crime.'

From the very beginning, Donald Trump – and many of his supporters – had said the whole Russia story was a hoax. Steele's dossier, they argued, was a work of fantasy, part of a Deep State plot dreamed up by a cabal of establishment figures, from politics, the media and the intelligence services, designed to delegitimise Donald Trump as president, and perhaps unseat him from office. That was a conspiracy theory. But then so was the Trump-as-Russian-agent story. It was, in Naomi Klein's phrase, the 'doppelgänger' of QAnon – its shadow opposite, a fantastical tale dreamed up by people to explain how something apparently inexplicable had happened: Donald Trump becoming president.

It was a conspiracy theory I believed in for a time.

Was I making the same mistake again, I wondered, as I searched for the origins of what I had come to believe was a plot against American democracy? Just as I was digging deeper, I came across someone who was already well advanced down my own rabbit hole.

•   •   •

Dave Troy was hard to pin down. He got into crypto early, he said, before deciding crypto was a bad thing and dedicating his time to warning the world why. He described himself as a researcher on disinformation networks, but also a conceptual artist. When I spoke to him, he told me he was 'trained in the liberal arts'. What did that mean? A karate black belt for the liberal order?

The reason I'd contacted Dave Troy was because we had a shared interest: *The Sovereign Individual* by James Dale Davidson and William Rees-Mogg. Troy had written a series of essays entitled 'The Big History Behind January 6th'. QAnon, he wrote, was just one facet in a series of 'interlocking plays' that would 'ultimately result in the destruction of the state and the rise of the sovereign individual'. The events at the Capitol that day were, in his view, part of a set of carefully calculated moves designed to bring into being the world that *The Sovereign Individual* had foreseen.

The plot Troy outlined had all the hallmarks of a conspiracy theory. He brought together such disparate phenomena as the rise of cryptocurrencies, the anti-capitalist Occupy movement and the Russian disinformation campaign during the 2016 election into one sweeping narrative. The trouble was, I couldn't find anything that appeared obviously bogus or made up. Troy was essentially doing what I was trying to do: pulling at the long roots of January 6th. There seemed to me two possibilities: either Troy was a conspiracy theorist, and by implication I was becoming one too. Or we had both stumbled upon a real conspiracy to bring down democracy. There was only one thing to do: I had to dive into the detail of Troy's tale.

I had begun my investigation by digging into the 1990s and the conspiracy theories surrounding the Clintons in Arkansas. But in Troy's telling, it all began much longer ago, in the 1930s, with a former major general in the Marines by the name of Smedley Butler.

Butler was a legend in his own lifetime. Nicknamed 'Old Gimlet Eye', he had fought in the First World War, as well as in many of America's less glorious entanglements around the world in the early twentieth century. In Panama and Haiti, Nicaragua and Honduras, China, the Philippines and elsewhere, Butler had helped forge the American empire, seizing territory, helping carry out coups, and propping up friendly regimes. He was highly decorated for his exploits, twice awarded the Medal of Honor; Theodore Roosevelt was said to have called him the 'ideal American soldier'. But he became uneasy about the role he had played. He came to believe his exploits had been in service not of the national interest, but of a small number of wealthy businesses. 'I spent 33 years and 4 months in active service as a member of our country's most agile military force – the Marine Corps,' he wrote. 'And during that period I spent most of my time being a high-class muscle man for Big Business, for Wall Street and for the bankers. In short, I was a racketeer for capitalism.'

After retiring from the military in 1931, he became a popular public speaker with a large following, especially among unemployed veterans. When the Great Depression hit, thousands of ex-soldiers marched on Washington, DC, demanding payment of a 'veterans' bonus'. Butler campaigned on their behalf, and the men revered him. When they camped out in front of Congress, Butler was among them, urging them to stay until their demands were met. (President Hoover eventually deployed the army under General Douglas MacArthur to disperse them.)

That was 1932. Then came Franklin Delano Roosevelt and his radical programme to reemploy America: the New Deal. Dave Troy called that moment a 'fork in the universe'. To help pay for the New Deal, FDR suspended the gold standard, enabling the Federal Reserve to print more dollars. What came as blessed relief to the mass of unemployed people struggling to survive was a nasty shock to some industrialists and bankers. They saw the gold standard as a bulwark against inflation – its removal opened the door to the erosion of their wealth. Roosevelt's policies concentrated power in the hands of the federal government. That government now appeared bent on redistribution. To some, that smacked of socialism.

Not long after FDR's inauguration, an employee at one of Wall Street's top brokerage firms began insistently courting Butler. Gerald MacGuire, himself a navy veteran, went to see Butler at his converted farmhouse in Philadelphia; he turned up at a hotel where Butler was staying with a wad of cash; he sent postcards from Italy and Germany, where he regaled the former general with tales of Fascist Europe. Butler wasn't sure what the man was after, but MacGuire eventually revealed his purpose: he wanted Butler to gather an army of half a million veterans and march on Washington. This show of force, he hoped, would persuade Roosevelt to reverse his New Deal policies. If FDR acceded to their demands, he would be allowed to remain as president, in a largely ceremonial role. A new minister – a 'secretary of general affairs' – would in effect run the country. If FDR resisted, he would be removed, 'to preserve his health'.

'You know, the American people will swallow that,' MacGuire told Butler. 'We have got the newspapers. We will start a campaign that the President's health is failing. Everybody can tell that by looking at him, and the dumb American people will fall for it in a second.'

(*A campaign that the president's health is failing*, I thought. Wasn't that exactly what was happening to Joe Biden as he faced Donald Trump in 2024? The same had happened to Hillary Clinton in 2016. The rumours about her failing health had started on 4chan.)

Unfortunately for MacGuire, he had picked the wrong Marine. Smedley Butler was appalled. But he pretended to go along with the scheme in order to find out who was behind it. MacGuire didn't mention any names but said he and his fellow plotters had $3 million to start with, and could get $300 million more. Where was the money coming from? Butler wanted to know. 'You watch,' MacGuire told him. 'In about two or three weeks you will see it come out in the paper. There will be big fellows in it.' The group, Maguire said, would promote itself as a society concerned with the preservation of the Constitution.

As if on cue, a few weeks later, the front page of the *New York Times* announced the creation of a new organisation. As MacGuire had promised, the American Liberty League claimed to be a non-partisan group whose aim was to 'combat radicalism, preserve property rights, uphold and maintain the Constitution'. Among its founders and backers were some of the biggest names in American industry and banking: Irénée du Pont, former president of the DuPont chemical company; Alfred P. Sloan, head of General Motors; and executives from General Foods, Sun Oil and Phillips Petroleum. Also on the board was John W. Davis, a former Democratic presidential candidate who had represented J. P. Morgan; and MacGuire's boss at the Wall Street brokerage firm, Grayson Murphy.

What MacGuire didn't know was that Smedley Butler was setting him up. Fearing no one would believe him if he came forward on his own, he confided in a journalist, Paul Comly French, who conducted his own investigation that backed up Butler's claims. On 20 November 1934, the *New York Post* ran the story. It alleged that a group of New York brokers were plotting to install a Fascist dictatorship in America.

Butler and French were called to testify in Congress.[1] French told a Congressional committee that MacGuire had continually discussed 'the need of a man on a white horse [...] a dictator who would come galloping in [...] to save the capitalistic system'. There was, apparently, some disagreement as to who that man should be. According to Butler, MacGuire told him that 'his group' were in favour of having Butler lead the rebellion. But 'the Morgan interests', presumably a group connected with the banking house J. P. Morgan, thought Butler was not to be trusted. They believed he was 'too radical [...] too much on the side of the little fellow'. Their preference was for another general: Douglas MacArthur, the man who had dispersed the veterans in Washington, DC.

Butler told the committee that MacGuire had been inspired by an incident in France earlier that year, when a group called the Croix-de-Feu (Cross of Fire) had taken part in an assault on the French legislature. The insurrection failed. But it led to the toppling of the left-wing coalition and the installation of a conservative government in its place.

MacGuire denied being involved in any plot. But the Congressional committee concluded that there was indeed a genuine attempt to establish a Fascist organisation in the United States. 'There is no question that these attempts were discussed, were planned, and might have been placed in execution when and if the financial backers deemed it expedient,' they wrote in their final report in February 1935. However, the names Butler had mentioned, those titans of industry and Wall Street, were absent from the report. The members of the American Liberty League were never called to testify, their alleged involvement, the committee decided, was mere 'hearsay'.

The significance of the 'Business Plot', as it became known, was much downplayed in the press at the time. The *New York Times* wrote that Smedley Butler had been the victim of a 'gigantic hoax'. The plot against FDR was quietly forgotten. But Dave Troy believed this stillborn rebellion was more than just a sinister echo of January 6th. The vision of the future that animated the plotters, he said, has never gone away. At play was an 'overarching conflict [...] over whether the world should seek to pursue democratic or so-called "neofeudal" forms of governance. Advocates of neofeudalism believe that departure from the gold standard was a mistake, and that scarcity of wealth provides a mechanism for keeping score and assignment of value. People with more gold are thus more valuable.'[2]

Troy picks up again some decades later, with another renegade general, John K. Singlaub. Jack Singlaub was in many ways similar to Smedley Butler. A legendary officer who had led guerrilla efforts behind enemy lines in the Second World War, he helped found the CIA. But while for Butler in the 1930s, fascism was enemy number one, for Singlaub in the post-war years, the chief threat came from Communism. In 1977, Singlaub was chief of staff of the US armed forces in South Korea. When President Carter announced his intention to withdraw American troops from the Korean Peninsula, Singlaub publicly disagreed. He was promptly fired – the first time a president had sacked a general since 1951, when President Truman fired General Douglas MacArthur (also over disagreements about US military policy in Korea).

Forced into early retirement, Singlaub continued his battle against the Communist threat, in a freelance capacity. He teamed up with a Democratic Congressman from Georgia by the name of Larry McDonald. Politically however, McDonald was far to the right of many Republicans.

At this point in the story, a small historical detour becomes necessary. Larry McDonald was a leading light in the John Birch Society, an anti-Communist group founded in the late 1950s by a man named Robert Welch. Welch had made his money selling caramel lollypops called Sugar Daddies. By 1958 he was rich and retired, and refocused his efforts on battling what he saw as a grand Communist conspiracy.

In December that year, Welch invited 11 like-minded men to a secret meeting in Indianapolis. Over two days, he outlined to his audience the situation in America as he saw it. 'The truth I bring you is simple, incontrovertible and deadly,' he said. 'Unless we can reverse forces which now seem inexorable in their movement, you have only a few more years before the country in which you live will become four separate provinces in a world-wide dominion ruled by police-state methods from the Kremlin.'[3] Welch was an anti-Communist, but he and his fellow Birchers believed in a wider conspiracy. He drew a direct line from the Illuminati – a secret society founded in Bavaria in 1776 dedicated to promoting enlightenment rationalism – through the French Revolution, the writings of Karl Marx, the Russian Revolution of 1917 and the rise of Soviet Communism, to FDR, the New Deal and the rise of the post-war welfare state. All of these historical developments, he believed, were steps on the road to a sinister and oppressive 'New World Order'. The overt Communists in Moscow were not the ones pulling the strings. Nor were the politicians in Washington, whose supposed goal was to fight Communism. Both of these were 'but two hands of one body, controlled by one brain'.[4] The political and military leaders you could see on the news, on your television screen, were but puppets, often unwittingly so, in the hands of a shadowy group Welch called the 'insiders'. This cabal had secured control not only of the levers of political power, but the economic, media and educational establishments too.

One of their most powerful weapons in the United States, Welch said, was the federal reserve system, the establishment of central banking and the imposition of income tax, which combined gave these 'insiders' 'the control of credit, the control of the money supply and the ability to spend with increasing profligacy and the means to steal continuously from the people by the debasement of our currency on the part of the federal government'.[5] The group's goal was nothing less than total global control. Democracy itself was a tool in their satanic scheme. Democracy, Welch believed, was 'not only the worst of all forms of government, but was the last direct step of any nation and any people on the road to an unbridled, mobocratic dictatorship'.[6]

Welch was a crank, a marginal figure of the mid-twentieth century. His ideas had little traction among those with any real power in Washington. But his grand conspiracy theory gained followers in suburban America, in no small measure thanks to Larry McDonald, the Congressman from Georgia. In the 1960s, before he ran for Congress, McDonald developed his local chapter of the John Birch Society in Atlanta into one of the largest in America. He held meetings at his home once or twice a week, often going on late into the night.[7] His first wife, Anna, estimated he had hosted 10,000 people in his living room, according to Zach Dorfman, a researcher who has written about the Congressman's strange life and even stranger death.[8]

In 1972, McDonald ran for Congress and lost. In 1974 he ran again and won. With the civil rights movement in full swing, he seemed ill at ease in the Democratic Party. He collected guns and went around wearing a bulletproof vest; he stocked up on purified drinking water and dried rations; he exchanged dollars for silver. The Communist plot had infiltrated every level of American society, he believed. The threat was everywhere.

Larry McDonald took his seat in Congress in January 1975, representing Georgia's 7th district.* At the time, Congress was investigating abuses of power carried out by US intelligence agencies supposedly in furtherance of the fight against Communism. The revelations of the Church Committee would shock America: MK-Ultra, the drugging of American citizens for purposes of mind-control; mass surveillance and infiltration of political and civil rights organisations; the CIA's covert programme to assassinate foreign leaders. By the end of the decade, the FBI, the CIA and the NSA had had their wings clipped, their ability to conduct covert operations against Communist sympathisers curtailed, both at home and abroad.

---

* The same district won in 2020 by QAnon-believing congresswoman Marjorie Taylor Greene.

Into this void stepped McDonald. He hired former FBI and military intelligence officers to continue their work on leftist individuals and organisations. They worked out of an office next to his on Capitol Hill. In 1979, with the help of newly retired former CIA legend General John Singlaub, he set up an organisation called Western Goals. Western Goals served as a 'massive intelligence clearing house,' according to Zach Dorfman. The aim was to 'launder' intelligence about potential subversives. 'Individuals working for local or federal law enforcement would provide Western Goals with derogatory – and potentially illegally acquired – intelligence information about perceived radicals or groups,' Dorfman writes. Western Goals would then publish this information in a newsletter, whereupon Larry McDonald would enter it into the Congressional Record where it would sit in the public domain, immune from libel prosecution.

In 1983, scandal erupted when the *LA Times* reported that a Los Angeles Police Department (LAPD) intelligence officer had been entering vast amounts of data – information from surveillance files that weren't supposed to exist – into a state-of-the-art computer owned by Western Goals. The files, according to the newspaper, had come from a variety of sources, including ones 'generated by military intelligence agencies'. The LAPD launched an internal investigation; the American Civil Liberties Union filed a lawsuit, and the LA County district attorney began a criminal investigation. But just as the net was tightening around Larry McDonald's rogue intelligence gathering scheme, a scarcely believable twist of fate saved him from accountability. Albeit at the cost of his life.

On 1 September 1983, in the early hours of the morning, Korean Airlines flight 007 from New York bound for Seoul disappeared off radar. Initial reports suggested the Soviet military had forced the aeroplane to land after straying off course and into Soviet airspace in the Russian far east. In reality, the passenger airliner had been shot down by a MiG fighter jet. The Soviets had mistaken it for a spy plane. All 269 passengers and crew were killed, including Larry McDonald, who was on his way to a conference in South Korea.

The Soviets initially denied involvement, then said the plane had not responded to its requests to land. President Reagan, fresh from his 'evil empire' speech, called it a barbaric and terrorist act that provided yet more evidence of the contempt in which the Soviet Union held the sanctity of human life. For a brief moment, on both sides of the Atlantic, people worried about escalation. But the danger passed, subsumed into the general tensions of the Cold War. The Soviets' actions may have been precipitous, incompetent, callous even. But the Reagan administration appeared to accept that they had genuinely believed they were firing on a spy plane, not a civilian airliner.

Not so the Birchers. Earlier that year, Larry McDonald had been appointed chairman of the John Birch Society. Now, one of America's fiercest anti-Communist crusaders, a man who had lived his life as if in the crosshairs of a terrifying conspiracy of civilisational proportions, had been killed by a Communist missile. Larry McDonald's friends and supporters didn't believe in coincidences.

Jack Singlaub said he himself had narrowly escaped McDonald's fate. The Congressman had invited him to accompany him on his trip to Seoul, but the general had declined, having only recently returned from South Korea. In 1991 he wrote, 'Even under the supposed openness of Glasnost, it's never been revealed whether the Soviet pilot knew the Boeing 747 was a civilian airliner or if he mistook it for an American RC-135 electronic intelligence aircraft that had been flying in international air space well offshore that same morning. In either case, the cruelty of the act underscored the fundamental brutality of the Soviet system.'

McDonald was gone, but Singlaub continued his work. In 1981, he had helped set up a new American chapter of the World Anti-Communist League (WACL). In the 1970s, the American branch of the WACL had been headed by a notorious antisemite and white supremacist by the name of Roger Pearson. Singlaub himself had noticed the tendency of right-wing extremists and 'anti-democratic fanatics' to gravitate towards anti-Communist groups such as the WACL. Young fanatics, he wrote, 'would telephone my office with "vital intelligence", which inevitably boiled down to their paranoid theories that the world was being dominated by an unholy alliance of Jewish bankers, the British royal family (who "controlled" global drug traffic), and their Soviet subordinates.'[9] Singlaub was determined that the new chapter he headed, called the United States Council for World Freedom (USCWF), would be free of such characters. He wanted to focus on what he saw as the real threat: the proliferation of leftist regimes around the world.

During the 1980s, as Congress progressively constrained the Reagan administration's efforts to fund the overthrow of such regimes, Singlaub acted as a conduit, funnelling money and weapons to anti-communist insurgents, particularly the Nicaraguan Contras. Singlaub was good at networking. He solicited donations from sympathetic wealthy benefactors, people connected to the John Birch Society. But in the wake of the Iran–Contra scandal, fundraising got harder. So in 1986, General Singlaub went digging for gold.

Legend had it that, towards the end of the Second World War, the retreating Japanese military had taken billions of dollars' worth of treasure, looted from across Southeast Asia, and buried it in the Philippines. The hoard was known as 'Yamashita's gold', after the Japanese general who supposedly oversaw its concealment. In 1986, Singlaub joined an effort to recover the treasure. 'Normally, I would not have been interested in buried-treasure schemes,' Singlaub wrote in his autobiography. But the company behind the effort, Nippon Star, had promised to donate several percent of the eventual profit directly to his anti-Communist organisation, the USCWF.

By Singlaub's own account, efforts to recover the treasure were haphazard and plagued by difficulties. The Japanese had carefully concealed the gold in hundreds of booby-trapped sites dotted around the Philippines. The treasure hunters first concentrated their efforts on an underwater site beneath a coral reef in Calatagan Bay, south of Manila. But the concrete cover to the shaft was apparently too hard for their drilling equipment, and treacherous tides and currents kept washing away their drilling platform.

Singlaub described how he studied old Japanese war maps, partially decoded their ledgers, and decided the most promising prospects were to be found beneath the kitchen of a modern house in the southern suburbs of Manila. They started digging but hit a Japanese booby trap. 'The men digging were almost drowned in liquid mud,' he wrote. Singlaub and his team had to contend with extortion attempts by the local cavitano Mafia, 'who controlled everything form the colorfully painted jitney busses to the cockfights of the sugarcane workers', and death threats from Communist insurgents. He 'began to move about cautiously, using real tradecraft, not the James Bond movie nonsense' previous crews had employed.

If Jack Singlaub ever recovered any gold in the Philippines, he does not mention it in his autobiography. According to one highly detailed (but possibly fanciful) account, Singlaub was only the latest in a long succession of American treasure hunters attempting to dig up Yamashita's gold. In their book,

Gold Warriors: How America Secretly Recovered Yamashita's Gold, authors Sterling and Peggy Seagrave claimed that General MacArthur and the US government knew about the treasure and had secretly recovered parts of it after the war. The US administration had, they write, used the money to shape and control post-war Japanese politics, and to fund covert anti-Communist actions throughout East and South-East Asia. But, according to the Seagraves, much of the gold remained where it had been buried by the retreating Japanese army, in those secret booby-trapped tunnels scattered across the Philippines. By the time Singlaub came on the scene, the Seagraves write, 'a group of senior U.S. Government officials and Pentagon generals hoped to use [the] treasure to create a new private FBI and a military-industrial complex controlled by them, in partnership with the John Birch Society, the Moonies, and far-right tycoons.'[10]

The Seagraves' book is a swash-buckling tale full of secret treasure maps and improbable characters: rogue spies and Japanese princes; Filipino torturers; a Swedish psychic named Olof Jonson, whose efforts to locate the loot were considered indispensable to the Nippon Star team. Many of their claims are hard to verify. Indeed, some historians have questioned the very existence of Yamashita's gold.

But Singlaub and others certainly *believed* it existed and acted accordingly. And, for Dave Troy, that was the point.

Troy believed that Singlaub's aim in the Philippines was not just to help the cause of freedom by funding anti-Communist insurgents around the world. A secondary aim, Troy said, was to secure enough gold to make returning the US to the gold standard a viable proposition.

In 1933, FDR had ended the practice whereby Americans could trade their paper dollars for government gold. In 1971, President Nixon went a step further: he severed all links between the US dollar and gold. The 'Nixon shock' effectively ended the post-war economic order, the system devised at a meeting in the New Hampshire resort of Bretton Woods in 1944. Troy believed Singlaub's treasure hunt was part of a continuing effort to reduce the power of the federal government by returning power over the money supply to a group of individuals rich in gold and other assets. It was carried out by people outside of – but with close affiliation to – government and state institutions. They were, Troy believed, continuing what the Business Plotters started in the 1930s. Only now they were doing so in a kind of hybrid pubic-private partnership, an off-the-books collaboration with elements of the American State. And the vehicle for this collaboration, Troy writes, was a secretive organisation called the Council for National Policy.

•   •   •

The CNP was founded in 1981 by a group of wealthy conservative businessmen (as well as the occasional woman) together with a handful of Southern Baptists. One was a pastor by the name of Tim LaHaye. LaHaye was an associate of Jerry Falwell, who would go on to help fund and distribute *The Clinton Chronicles*, and had been a prominent supporter of Larry McDonald. I had come across LaHaye during my research because of a series of books he had written called *Left Behind*.

The series is perhaps the most successful example of a literary sub-genre known as Christian apocalyptic fiction. The plot starts with an airline pilot who notices, mid-flight, that some of his passengers are missing. And it's not just on board his aeroplane – all around the world, millions have vanished. The pilot realises that what has happened is the Rapture: the righteous have been taken up to heaven, while sinners remain on earth. The pilot understands why he was left behind: he did not *truly* believe in the Lord. He converts and forms an underground group of rebels, fighting an evil new world order involving bankers, the United Nations and the Antichrist (masquerading as a Romanian politician). The plot is based on the biblical Book of Revelation in which a seven-year period of turbulence, known as the Great Tribulation, is followed by a Great Awakening. (The structural narrative links to QAnon were practically screaming in my face.)

LaHaye's books were a publishing phenomenon in evangelical circles, selling tens of millions of copies worldwide. Troy wasn't interested in LaHaye's apocalyptic fiction, though, but in his organisation, the Council for National Policy. Tim LaHaye founded the CNP after the election of Ronald Reagan as an umbrella for various conservative, Christian and right-wing groups. Over the years it grew into one of the most influential but least known forces on the American right. CNP membership is supposed to be a secret, but lists of members have occasionally leaked out. Early members included Singlaub and some of the wealthy Bircherers he was tapping up for money. Some of the names are more well known in political circles today: Steve Bannon; Kellyanne Conway; and the DeVos family, whose extended members include Trump's former education secretary Betsy, and her brother Erik Prince, founder of Blackwater, the notorious private military company. They worked together with the Koch brothers, heirs to an oil fortune who channelled their wealth into politics. This group of individuals and organisations has been described as a 'shadow network' that has secretly shaped and driven American conservative politics for the past four decades.[11]

One of its long-time members was the anti-feminist activist Phyllis Schlafly. Schlafly set up a conservative interest group called the Eagle Forum in 1972. Throughout the 1970s, her main focus was opposition to the Equal Rights Amendment (a clause that would give men and women equal rights under the law, which has still not been adopted into the US Constitution). But Schlafly also swam in Bircherist conspiracy waters. In 2016 she endorsed Donald Trump for president. She died in September that year, two months before Trump was elected. After her death, Schlafly's movement split, between pro- and anti-Trump factions.

And here is where Dave Troy brings his conspiracy (theory?) full circle. The pro-Trump faction, calling itself the Phyllis Schlafly Eagles, began attracting conspiracy theorists to its annual gatherings. Speakers railed against 'cultural Marxism' (a supposed plot by Democrats to turn the United States into a Communist dystopia by adopting 'woke' ideology). In 2018, in association with another of Schlafly's organisations, the America's Future Foundation, they inaugurated a new award: the Gen. Jack Singlaub Award for Service to America. Singlaub himself, then aged 97 and chairman of the Foundation, was not at the ceremony. But the man receiving the award was someone well known to me – another renegade former general, Michael T. Flynn.

'I spoke to General Singlaub this week about serving America and what it means for both of us,' he said, as he accepted the award. 'The future of this country depends on each one of you in this room tonight [...] You cannot and must not be silent or take for granted that our great nation will not fall to the many threats that we face around the world, and some right here at home [...] For those who oppose our fundamental principles could take us down in the snap of a finger.'[12]

This was more than two years before the 2020 election and the events of January 6th. Flynn had already been forced to resign as Donald Trump's national security advisor and had pleaded guilty to lying to the FBI over his contact with Russian officials. But he had not yet descended into the morass of QAnon. Still, according to Dave Troy, 'the network behind January 6th' was already coalescing. He points to a photograph taken that evening. In addition to Mike Flynn, the recipient of the inaugural Singlaub Award, there were two other faces that were familiar to me: Jack Posobiec and Mike Cernovich. At the same event the following year, another key figure in the events of January 6th appeared: Ali Alexander. Alexander was a former CNP member and an associate of Roger Stone. In November 2020, the day after the election, he registered a site under the name StopTheSteal.us. 'Proud to be working with these patriots to Save the Election,' he tweeted, naming more than a dozen other Twitter users, including Ed Martin, president of the Phyllis Schlafly Eagles organisation, the man who had given Flynn the Singlaub award, as well as Posobiec and Cernovich.[13] The following day he sent off another tweet urging people to gather at their local state capitols. This time he included Tracy Diaz, aka Beanz, who had been so instrumental in promoting QAnon in the early days.

From there it was but a few frenzied weeks to the storming of the Capitol in Washington, DC. Anne Nelson, an author and journalist who investigated the CNP networks of power, wrote, 'The CNP's affiliates were by no means acting alone in attempting to overturn the results of the election,' but concluded it was 'irrefutable [...] that members of the CNP and their inner circle exerted their influence and manipulated their followers to support Trump's lies about the stolen election and his efforts to derail the electoral process. Many of these people emerged as key players in the efforts to disrupt America's 220-year-old tradition of the peaceful transfer of power.'[14]

Dave Troy had arrived at the same destination as I had, but by a different route. We had followed different tributaries into the same great river that flowed inexorably toward a single conclusion: January 6th appeared to be a spontaneous outburst of fury by a disorganised rabble led by a narcissistic opportunist. But in fact, behind these events lay a carefully planned operation, hatched over decades, perhaps nearly a century, by people whose aims went far beyond keeping Donald Trump in the White House. They wanted to fundamentally alter the basis upon which American democracy had functioned for the past century, clawing back power from the federal government and returning it to private hands.

If that indeed was the case, two further conclusions followed: one – January 6th had failed; and, therefore, two – another attempt would likely be made around the next election in 2024.

CHAPTER 13

THE BLACK PILL

As polling day neared, events seemed to speed up: time appeared compressed. Donald Trump, by now the presumptive nominee for the Republican party, was on trial in New York. At issue was the question of whether he had paid hush money to a porn star. (There was, for me, a neat circularity in the case: the porn star in question, Stormy Daniels, was a self-identified witch. I had begun my journey with a story about witches, I had followed that thread down numerous rabbit holes, heard Donald Trump describe the cases against him as 'the greatest witch-hunt in American history'. Now a witch was exacting her revenge.) Additionally, Trump was facing trial in three other cases. He was accused variously of using the January 6th riot to obstruct the peaceful transfer of power, conspiring to overturn his narrow election defeat in Georgia, and taking classified documents from the White House and storing them at his home in Mar-a-Lago.

It was uncharted territory. Never before had an American president been charged with criminal activity. His opponents said it was enough to disqualify him from standing again. Trump himself denied all the charges, which he said were politically motivated and designed to keep him out of the White House. In the space of eight frantic years, fanciful chants of *Lock her up* had become a campaign to lock *him* up, and now it looked like it could actually happen.

Amid this fevered atmosphere, a cavalcade of increasingly convoluted conspiracy theories paraded through the right-wing media. Taylor Swift was a 'Pentagon psy-op asset' – the singer's romance with an American football player was all part of an elaborate psychological operation to rig the Super Bowl and hypnotise American women into voting for Biden. (Predictably, Jack Posobiec's fingerprints were all over this obviously bogus story.)

Trump alleged that the instruments of justice had been weaponised against him, and by extension, his tens of millions of supporters. And they agreed with him. They saw the cases against him as nakedly political. America was supposed to be the 'greatest nation on earth'. But now they saw the Biden administration apparently using the law to prosecute its opponents in a way more commonly associated with tin-pot dictatorships.

At NatCon, the conference of nationalists and conservatives in Miami, people referred to the Biden administration as 'the Regime'. They pointed to the trials and convictions of those involved in the storming of the Capitol on January 6th. These people, they believed, were being persecuted for their political beliefs, given lengthy jail sentences for what they saw as a minor misdemeanour: trespassing on Capitol grounds. Many mentioned a speech Joe Biden had made in September 2022, ahead of the midterm elections.

The setting was Philadelphia, Independence Hall. It was here, in 1776, that the Founding Fathers articulated a set of truths that they held to be 'self-evident'. This was the birthplace of those most vaunted of American principles: freedom, equality, democracy. 'As I stand here tonight,' Biden said, 'equality and democracy are under assault. Donald Trump and the MAGA Republicans represent an extremism that threatens the very foundations of our republic.' Even though Trump lost in 2020, 75 million Americans had still voted for him. This movement, Biden was saying, went beyond legitimate opposition in the rough and tumble of democratic politics. 'History tells us that blind loyalty to a single leader, and a willingness to engage in political violence, is fatal to democracy.'

Biden did not define exactly what period of history he was referring to. He never used the word 'fascism'. But many of my liberal American friends heard exactly that. They were heartened to hear their president speaking so plainly. Trump, they believed, was an existential threat that had to be confronted.

But there was something slightly unsettling about the backdrop to his speech. It was nighttime, and in the darkness, the edifice of Independence Hall was lit up in blood red. As he spoke, Biden was flanked by two uniformed marines. It looked dramatic, theatrical, with a whiff of the 1930s. Many Trump supporters watched that speech and saw the opposite of what was intended. They thought it was Biden who represented the spectre of fascism in America, a president who used a speech against a spectacular setting to paint his opponents as illegitimate, un-American. They believed the Biden administration had politicised the instruments of the state – the military, the Justice Department, the intelligence agencies – and was using them to stay in power at any cost.

By way of proof, one story came up again and again: Hunter Biden's laptop.

•   •   •

The first time I heard mention of Joe Biden's son's computer was back in 2020, in the aftermath of the election. In Atlanta, I had met a woman standing on the steps of the Georgia state capitol building holding up a Q sign. 'How much do you know about Hunter Biden's laptop?' she asked me. This device, she said, contained evidence about the 'Biden crime family'. I was beginning my hunt for the origins of QAnon. Another conspiracy theory designed to befuddle the electorate, I thought. I ignored it.

But at that conference in Miami, I met a man who cheerfully admitted he was behind this story.

Vish Burra described himself as a 'MAGA-jihadist, one of the top mullahs in the "MAGAhideen"'. He was a New Yorker, born in Brooklyn, raised in Staten Island, the child of Indian immigrants. He did well at school. When he was 13, he won an award for a presentation he gave about how real reality TV was. (The example he used was Donald Trump in *The Apprentice*.) But in high school he got bored and dropped out. By his early 20s, he was dealing drugs. 'I was the weed kingpin on Staten Island,' he boasted. When he got busted, he pleaded guilty and avoided prison. But the way the local newspaper covered his arrest really rankled with him. 'The story that they wrote was that I got caught with two and a half pounds of weed and *one thousand milligrams* of psilocybin.' That translated, Vish said, to one gramme of magic mushrooms. 'Nobody can trip on that,' he said. 'They wrote it as one thousand milligrams to make it seem as if I had a lot.' That incident, he said, made him realise that the American media was dishonest. Or, as he put it, 'so full of it'.

Vish never forgot that lesson. And perhaps that's why, many years later, he wound up working for Steve Bannon. Bannon had a particular view of the world. He was drawn to Traditionalist philosophies that obsessed about the collapse of Western civilisation. His praise for Julius Evola, an Italian fascist thinker, had drawn much flack (Bannon explicitly disavowed Evola's views on race); he saw Muslim immigration as a 'civilizational jihad' that had to be fought. He viewed the media as the 'opposition' and believed 'the way to deal with them is to flood the zone with shit'. After his chaotic stint running the Trump White House, he reverted to what he did best: propaganda. He hosted a podcast called *War Room*, in which he bombarded his listeners with his insurgent spirit ('What you're seeing in the United States today *is* the French revolution'), interviewing conspiracy theorists and other assorted oddballs. He hired Vish Burra as a producer. And it was in that capacity that Vish ended up shepherding Hunter Biden's laptop into the public consciousness.

Unlike many in Bannon's world, so often hostile toward the establishment media, Vish was charming, and seemed disarmingly honest. 'Flooding the zone with shit is a brilliant tactic,' he laughed. 'That is the game, baby. I still use it to this day.' So, with that warning, almost two years after it first appeared, I dived into the laptop story.

It begins in a computer repair shop in Wilmington, Delaware, with a man called John Paul Mac Isaac. One Friday evening in April 2019, JP, as he is generally known, was getting ready to go home for the night, when a customer walked into his shop with three broken laptops. The man was intoxicated, his speech a little slurred, JP thought. He took a look at the computers. They'd all had some kind of liquid spilled on them. The first was beyond repair. The second just needed a new keyboard. The third was badly damaged. But JP told the man he thought he might be able to recover the files on the hard drive.

JP asked the customer for his first name. 'Hunter', he replied. Then he asked for his surname. 'And he goes, "Biden", kinda sarcastically, like I should have known who he was.'[1] Perhaps JP should have known. Delaware is Joe Biden's home state. The Bidens have been the dominant political family there for decades.

JP got to work, transferring the files from the damaged laptop onto an external hard drive. A lot of the material, he said, was pornography. But JP had been dealing with other people's computers for years – he'd seen a lot of stuff in his time. He figured the porn wasn't his business. When he finished the job, JP said he messaged Hunter to say the drive was ready for collection. But Hunter never showed up.

At the time, Hunter Biden's life was in chaos. His brother Beau had died of brain cancer a few years earlier. Hunter was struggling with addiction. By the time he dropped off his laptop at JP's shop, his marriage had fallen apart; his life was spiralling out of control.

Two weeks later, his father, Joe, announced he was running for president.

Now JP started getting nervous about this drive sitting in a drawer in his shop. Not so much because of the porn, but because of other material he had seen on the laptop: emails and documents relating to Hunter Biden's business activities, and his links to Ukraine. The laptop, he realised, was political dynamite; the Bidens, he reasoned, were powerful. JP wanted rid of it.

'I made a copy to give to my father so he could give it to the FBI,' he said. 'I made another copy to give to a friend of mine should something happen to me. That way, if I disappeared, if the FBI threw me in a hole somewhere, my friend would reach out with a copy of the drive.'

JP was getting paranoid. The FBI did not 'throw him in a hole'. They did pay him a visit, and took the laptop away with them. But JP still had the two copies.

* * *

By the start of 2020, Donald Trump's first impeachment trial was underway. The case centred on Ukraine. Specifically, whether Trump had tried to get Ukraine's president, Volodymyr Zelensky, to investigate the Bidens – in other words, whether the president of the United States had pressured another head of state to go after his political opponent. JP, who was a Trump supporter, thought the documents he had seen on the laptop could exonerate Trump. And he figured, since the FBI had the laptop, that material was bound to come out.

He watched the hearings in the Senate, but no laptop was ever mentioned. JP became suspicious: was the FBI involved in a cover-up? He sent a copy of the drive to Rudy Giuliani, the former mayor of New York, who was working for Donald Trump. Giuliani had become obsessed with trying to find dirt on the Bidens in Ukraine. The laptop was a treasure trove. But by now Trump's impeachment was over and an election was approaching. Giuliani wanted to weaponise the laptop in the court of public opinion. So he passed a copy of the drive to Steve Bannon. And Bannon gave the drive to Vish Burra.

Vish had no qualms about invading Hunter Biden's privacy. 'Obviously, me being who I am, the first thing I hit is the photos.' There were thousands of pictures. 'You start seeing enough skin and you're like: "Oh, there's *good* stuff on here."' He chuckled. It wasn't just any old porn, Vish said. It was homemade stuff, starring Hunter Biden himself.

But Giuliani and Bannon weren't after embarrassing pictures of Hunter. They wanted dirt on his father. By now, the election was just weeks away. They needed to work fast. There were so many emails on the drive, it was hard to know where to start looking. Vish focused on the one story that was already very much in the public consciousness: Ukraine.

• • •

In 2014, while his father was vice president, Hunter Biden had joined the board of a Ukrainian gas company, Burisma. At the time, the company was embroiled in corruption allegations. Donald Trump alleged that Joe Biden had used his position as vice president to pressure the Ukrainian government to shield the company from investigation. Biden had always maintained that there was a firewall between his job and his son's business activities. But when Vish searched the emails on the drive for the word 'Burisma', he struck gold.

There was an email, dated April 2015, from an executive at the gas company. It read: 'Dear Hunter, thank you for inviting me to DC and giving an opportunity to meet your father and spent [sic] some time together.' It looked like there wasn't a fire-wall after all. On the contrary, it looked like Hunter Biden had helped arrange a meeting between his Ukrainian gas contact and his dad, the vice president of the United States.

Now Vish and his friends needed to get the story out. Bannon's podcast, *War Room*, wasn't going to have the reach they wanted – practically all their listeners were Trump voters anyway. Vish said they tried to pass the story to various outlets, including Mail Online and Fox News. Both were suspicious and turned it down. But eventually someone bit.

The *New York Post* published the story on 14 October 2020. It was a Wednesday, a warm sunny day in New York City. Vish woke up early to go and get his copy of the newspaper from the local deli. 'Biden Secret E-mails', screamed the headline. He was thrilled. Three weeks from the presidential election, it was the perfect October surprise – a tabloid bombshell that could change everything.

But something didn't seem quite right. Vish couldn't under-stand why there wasn't more reaction on the morning TV shows or social media. Later that morning he got a message, saying: 'Hey – I just tried to share the *New York Post* story through Facebook Messenger, and it literally won't go through.' On Twitter people were experiencing the same problem. Facebook announced it was 'reducing distribution' while they fact-checked the story. Twitter blocked its users from posting it altogether, and locked the *New York Post* out of its account.

When the TV news shows picked up the story, they were sceptical. Fox News (which had rejected the story initially but, like the *New York Post*, was owned by Rupert Murdoch) poured cold water on its authenticity, calling it 'sketchy'. Five days later came the killer: a public letter, signed by 51 former national security officials. The emails, they wrote, had 'all the classic earmarks of a Russian information operation'.[2] The letter was signed by the former director of National Intelligence, three former heads of the CIA and 47 other senior ex-intelligence officers.

Now the media had an easier story to report – not dubiously sourced suggestions of corruption against a presidential candidate, but something more familiar: election meddling by the Kremlin. It made sense. The Russians had, after all, interfered in the last election to try to help get Trump elected. Now they were at it again.

Joe Biden dismissed the story out of hand. It was a 'last-ditch effort in a desperate campaign to smear' him and his family; there was no basis to the story at all, he said.

But Vish saw it differently. 'That's when my eyes opened and I was like, *Oh my gosh the Regime is coming down on this.*' He had always suspected the media were against him. But now he thought big tech, the FBI and the CIA were all involved in a cover-up. To Vish, it wasn't the Russians who were meddling in the election, it was the Deep State. 'How scary is it that these folks actively coordinated to bury the story on so many different levels, all the way to the intelligence agencies in our government? It's insane.'

After the election, Vish Burra, Steve Bannon and Rudy Giuliani refocused their efforts, trying to convince the American public their democracy had been stolen. Wild tales of rigged voting machines, ballot dumps in the middle of the night, magic pens that couldn't be read – there was no credible evidence for any of it, but it worked: the zone was well and truly deluged with shit. But Vish never gave up on the laptop story. In the months and years that followed, he continued to distribute copies of the laptop, mostly to journalists on the right of America's polarised media ecosystem. So while the liberal establishment media largely ignored the story, on the right, Hunter Biden's laptop became a byword for corruption at the very top, proof that America had been captured by a Deep State determined to hang on to power at all costs. 'We never stopped,' he told me. 'We're still continuing to inject copies of the laptop into the system everywhere we can.'

Injecting the story into the system. I was struck by his choice of words. It was the same phrase David Brock had used when he was spreading conspiracy theories about the Clintons in Arkansas in the 1990s. When Vish offered to show me a copy of the laptop, was he flooding *my* zone with shit? There was only one way to find out.

And so it was with some trepidation that I found myself in New York one late summer evening, climbing the stairs of an old Manhattan apartment block, to pick up what Vish said was a copy of Hunter Biden's laptop. 'You know what still hasn't come out?' he asked me, as the files slowly transferred onto a small blue hard drive. 'The *Staten Island Advance*, that wrote that story about me getting convicted, my house raided, they've never written how this guy from Staten Island is now in the centre of one of the largest scandals in political history. And because they haven't, I am now a MAGAhideen.'

Transfer complete, Vish handed me the drive. I dropped it into my bag and headed back out into the New York night. I felt like I was transporting some kind of virus, a toxic agent.

Back in London, I plugged the drive into a computer. It was supposed to be a clone of Hunter Biden's laptop as it appeared in 2019. But immediately it was clear someone else had been moving things around. On the desktop was a group of folders. One was entitled 'salacious pics package'. Vish said he had created the folders when he first opened the drive in 2020, grouping together certain files and pictures by theme. That didn't mean the files weren't genuine. But it was worth noting that the contents had been messed around with, by people whose explicit aim was to damage the Bidens.

There was a lot of material on the drive. The most obvious place to start seemed to be that email exchange on Ukraine which, according to the *New York Post*, suggested that Hunter had arranged for his father to drop in on a dinner for his clients at a restaurant in Washington, DC.

The message was indeed on the drive. Of course, it could have been faked. But taking it at face value for the moment, and reading through the email chain, it seemed the *New York Post* had reported on it accurately and fairly, neither adding extraneous detail nor leaving out important context.

There were other interesting emails too, which the *Post* had also featured in the run-up to the election. One referred to a business deal Hunter was involved in with a Chinese company with links to the government in Beijing. In this email, one of Hunter's business partners seems to outline how the equity in the venture would be divided up among the partners. The *New York Post* had zeroed in on a phrase at the end of that email: '10 held by H for the big guy?' 'H', the paper said, stood for 'Hunter', and 'the big guy' was his father, Joe Biden.

Again, the email was on the drive. The details were as the *New York Post* had reported them. The exchange was from 2017, so Joe Biden was at that point not in office; he was a private citizen. That particular deal collapsed the following year, the joint venture with its division of equity never materialised. But Hunter Biden and his uncle, Jim Biden (Joe's brother) had in the meantime made $4.8 million out of their Chinese business deals. There was no evidence on the drive that I could find that suggested that Joe Biden made any money out them, or even knew about them.

The emails on the laptop suggested Hunter Biden was leveraging his family name and his father's position to pursue business deals and make money. That might be distasteful to many, but it was not illegal. The question was: was his father in on it too? I could not find a clear answer to that on the drive.

There were pictures of Hunter Biden aboard Air Force Two, the official vice-presidential plane, hitching a ride to China to pursue his business deals. But I also saw emails in which Hunter appeared to suggest he could *not* influence his father. There was no smoking gun. But there was certainly enough material to warrant asking some questions. *If the material was real.*

The *New York Post* had satisfied itself that the messages they reported were genuine, in part, by checking with other people on the email chains. They spoke to one of Hunter's former business partners, Tony Bobulinski, who confirmed he had also received the 'big guy' email and said there was no doubt in his mind that the phrase referred to Joe Biden. In fact, he said, Hunter frequently referred to his father as 'the big guy' or 'my chairman'.

So why hadn't other news outlets done the same? In fact, they had tried. The *Washington Post* and others had asked for a copy of the drive before the election, but Guiliani and Bannon declined to provide one. Without the source material, no responsible journalist could have run the story. But after the election, other news outlets *did* get hold of the drive. They had it checked by a number of forensic experts. They eventually concluded that the material on the drive had been handled by different people at different times and, in some places, its contents had been altered (Vish's 'salacious pics' folders). But they authenticated thousands of emails, using forensic analysis and cross checking with other recipients, prosecutors and other public documents. They found no evidence of fake messages planted among the real ones. More than a year after the story originally appeared, the *Washington Post* and others acknowledged that the material on the laptop appeared genuine. But by then, Joe Biden was in the White House.

What looked to Vish Burra like a cover-up by the mainstream media appeared to me more like journalistic due diligence. Sure, when it appeared the laptop wasn't fake news, journalists of the establishment didn't cover the story with quite the same vigour they had lavished on stories about Donald Trump's business links to Moscow (some of which were of equally dubious provenance). That might suggest bias – it didn't look like conspiracy.

But what about Twitter and Facebook? In August 2022, Mark Zuckerberg made a startling admission. The FBI had approached Facebook in the weeks before the election. Zuckerberg said agents had reminded the company about the Russian disinformation fiasco of 2016, and added: 'We have it on notice there's about to be some kind of dump that's similar to that, so just be vigilant.' That would help explain why Facebook had prevented users from sharing the story when it first came out. Zuckerberg was a little vague about the details: when did the FBI approach them? How specific were they about the nature of this 'dump'? Katie Harbath, a Facebook executive at the time, told me she thought the FBI had not cited a specific story about a laptop in their initial warning. 'It was just to be on the lookout for potential interference from the Russians, to be on heightened alert. And then when this story broke a lot of [people] were like, "Well maybe this is it."' Katie was in charge of elections at Facebook in 2016. Social media companies had been 'absolutely skewered', she said, 'for not catching this stuff early enough, for not having safeguards in place to stop it, and for contributing to the spread of mis- and disinformation.' Harbath said that, in 2020, Facebook and other social media companies wanted to show that they 'had a handle' on the problem. Perhaps that had led to instances of overzealousness.

But where did that leave the FBI? They had been in possession of the laptop itself since 2019, when they had taken it from JP Mac Isaac. They could have told Facebook and Twitter that the laptop *wasn't* Russian disinformation. Perhaps the FBI hadn't got around to verifying its contents, so they thought it was a Kremlin plant. But that didn't gel with other reporting, which suggested that the IRS had examined the laptop as part of an investigation into Hunter Biden's tax affairs. If they thought the laptop was fake, why would they bother? Perhaps the laptop got lost in the giant bureaucracy of the FBI, and the agents who warned Facebook didn't know anything about the laptop. That was plausible.* But in the absence of a satisfactory

---

* In 2023, an FBI agent told a Congressional committee that the FBI knew the laptop was real in October 2020 but stuck to a policy of 'no comment' when asked about it by social media companies. https://judiciary.house. gov/media/press-releases/testimony-reveals-fbi-employees-who-warned-social-media-companies-about-hack#:~:text=After%20the%20New%20 York%20Post,sharing%20up%20to%20that%20time.

explanation, it became all too easy to assume the worst: that the FBI was trying to shield a presidential candidate from a possibly embarrassing news story.

Unlike Vish Burra, at the BBC we were reluctant to 'hit the pictures'. I would have left them well alone, were it not for the fact that there were suggestions on the internet that among the photos on Hunter Biden's laptop, among the homemade porn videos and pictures of him taking drugs, there was also child pornography. The *New York Post* had not reported that. And Vish Burra hadn't said so explicitly. But he did try to steer me in that direction. 'A fifty-year-old man should not be having this kind of content anywhere near him,' he told me, 'and it's on his laptop.'

These allegations appeared online almost as soon as the laptop story emerged. They were then amplified on right-wing TV news. 'They find a hard drive,' a guest told Tucker Carlson on Fox News in April 2021, referring to FBI investigators, 'and they are told that the hard drive has on it evidence of child pornography or worse.' Carlson himself then appeared to reinforce the allegation, saying: 'That's such a great point. "By the way, there's kiddy porn on the hard drive." "No, not interested, we're just the FBI."'

So, I had to take a look. The photo library was a strange collection: pictures of Hunter Biden in various states of undress, taking drugs and having sex, mixed in with family snaps. In among what appear to be Hunter's pictures, there are hundreds of selfies of a teenage girl. In some she is wearing a bikini; in some she is striking what could be described as flirtatious poses. It looked like these pictures had been uploaded to Hunter Biden's laptop from someone else's phone, which might happen if, say, a friend or relative plugged their phone into the laptop to charge it.

These pictures looked like the kind of photos any teenager might take of themselves. By no stretch of the imagination did they constitute child pornography – not even close. Nor could we find any such images on the laptop. That part of the story was pure invention.

The bald facts about the laptop were this: in the weeks before the 2020 election, a potentially consequential story appeared. The sources for the story were deeply suspect – self-confessed peddlers of effluence. The media shunned it; the FBI warned social media companies to suppress it; and the nation's top intelligence agents branded it Russian disinformation.

But it turned out the FBI knew it was real all along.

What to make of this? I was reluctant to believe in a conspiracy. There was no evidence of criminal wrongdoing by Joe Biden on the laptop. But if the story had got more coverage in the weeks leading up to the election, might it have made a difference to the outcome? That is impossible to say. But it's worth noting that Hillary Clinton believed the saga surrounding her emails (another October surprise) cost her the 2016 election.

At the very least, the laptop provided a rare insight into how networks of power and money intersect at the top of American society: an insight the establishment media didn't seem terribly interested in covering.

I remembered what Ambrose Evans-Pritchard had said about the 1990s: that the journalists from the *New York Times* and the *Washington Post* were so *uncurious*. They tried to avoid investigating any potentially damaging stories about the Clintons for fear of being associated with conspiracy theorists. And when the 'big boys', as Ambrose called them, ignored those stories, they metastasised, multiplying and morphing beneath the surface into baroque fantasies. The laptop was an echo of Arkansas.

* * *

Now, in MAGA world, in the second cinema of America's bifurcated reality, a scary film was playing, one in which 'the Regime' swung into action to subvert democracy. In Miami, at NatCon, that story was animating a nihilistic mood.

One evening in the main conference hall, I sat down with other delegates to watch a screening of *The Wind and the Lion*, directed by John Milius. The film was introduced by Milius's daughter, Amanda. She described it as 'both al-Qaeda's and Newt Gingrich's favourite movie', an epic adventure from 1975 set in Morocco at the turn of the twentieth century. A director herself (she'd made a film about the whole Russia saga), Amanda was a minor celebrity at NatCon, bestriding the corridors of the conference dressed in black with a double string of pearls and a diamante tiara. Her father had made his name as a screenwriter, penning some of the most memorable lines in the history of Hollywood ('I love the smell of napalm in the morning' – *Apocalypse Now*).

John Milius is almost as famous for his eyebrow-raising lines off-screen. 'I respect our democratic institutions,' he told an interviewer in 1985. 'But if Douglas MacArthur had returned in 1951 and crossed the Mississippi like Caesar crossed the Rubicon and proclaimed himself Emperor Douglas the First, it might not have been bad for this country.'[3]

Amanda Milius's father had been into the idea of an American Caesar decades before Curtis Yarvin, whose ideas some saw as the intellectual backbone of the MAGA movement. Amanda herself dismissed it as a joke. But she, like many others, believes there is something rotten at the heart of the American Republic. 'I would like it if our institutions were not utterly and irreparably corrupt,' she told me. 'That's why I am black-pilled.'

The black pill. It was a phrase I heard more than once at the conference. I was by now familiar enough with the red pill – the secret knowledge that lifted the veil and revealed the truth. (QAnon, to its adherents, was the ultimate red pill.)

Amanda Milius had moved beyond the red pill. She never bought into QAnon. But through making her documentary she had come to believe the Deep State had conspired to try to delegitimise – perhaps even remove – a sitting president by concocting a bogus story about Donald Trump being a Russian agent. Now Hunter Biden's laptop suggested to her they were at it again. Was America's fabled democracy nothing more than a façade, a box of nutrition-free popcorn consumed by unthinking 'sheeple' beguiled by the movies they were watching on their screens?

'I go back and forth on it every day,' Amanda said. 'Is the country saveable? I don't know. That's a very scary place to be.'

The red pill allowed you to see reality clearly so you could *do something about it*, be the hero of your own movie and maybe save the world. But now nothing was real and there was nothing to be done. That was the black pill.

• • •

By the time I returned to America in the spring of 2024, the black pill was everywhere. It wasn't just the laptop anymore. And it wasn't just conspiracy theorists like General Flynn and his acolytes, drawing spider diagrams linking 'Russiagate' to January 6th. According to a poll conducted at the end of 2023, trust in America's institutions was at an all-time low: 41 per cent believed that a secret cabal controlled events and ruled the world together, no matter who was officially in charge; 29 per cent believed that voting machines had been programmed to rig the 2020 election; the same number believed many top Democrats were involved in child-sex-trafficking rings. Only slightly fewer, 25 per cent, believed that many top Republicans were involved in the same horrible trade.[4]

At a political rally in Long Island, I met an elementary school teacher. When she taught her fourth grade class about American government, she told me, she felt ashamed: the reality of it had become so far removed from the pieties in her lessons. She wasn't the only one at that event who believed the COVID pandemic had been either exploited or even engineered so that big pharma could make billions from vaccines. Many were convinced those vaccines were killing people. They were wrong about the last part – the vaccines were saving lives (though valid questions about adverse side effects and 'vaccine harms' were often dismissed as 'misinformation'). Nor was there any evidence that the pandemic had been deliberately engineered (though people who asked questions about the origins of the virus had been dismissed as conspiracy theorists). They were right, of course, that pharmaceutical companies had made vast sums of money from the vaccines, with the help of governments mandating their use. Small grains of truth were morphing into monstrous narratives.

Up on the stage stood Robert F. Kennedy Jr, running for president as an independent. A vaccine-sceptic, RFK Jr had accused Anthony Fauci, the veteran public health official who led America's response to the COVID pandemic, of helping to orchestrate 'a historic *coup d'état* against Western democracy'. Kennedy had spent much of his career as a lawyer and activist, fighting big chemical companies who denied they were polluting America's waterways. (They were.) He was nine years old in 1963 when his uncle, President John F. Kennedy, was shot and killed in Dallas. Five years later, when he was 14, his father was gunned down. Kennedy believed the full truth about both assassinations had been withheld.* (It had.) Little wonder that such a man would be primed to believe in conspiracy theories.

Kennedy talked about ending America's 'forever wars', which allowed arms manufacturers and private military contractors to profit from death and destruction under the guise of spreading freedom and democracy. Like Trump, he promised to end the Biden administration's support for the Ukrainian military in the face of the Russian invasion. He told his audience they risked becoming enslaved by big tech and new AI technology. The audience lapped it up.

I wanted to talk to Kennedy – perhaps, I thought, beneath the outlandish claims about COVID and Fauci and his *'coup d'état'*, this scion of a great American political dynasty had hit upon a deeper truth about the relationship between money, power and the state. But he bristled at the first mention of conspiracy theories and that was the end of our conversation.

I left the Kennedy rally and travelled west – to Colorado and Utah, Idaho and Arizona, and then to California and the Pacific coast. In towns and cities, in taxis and diners, in parks and living rooms I found people converting real-life events into

---

* There was 'overwhelming evidence that the CIA was involved' in President Kennedy's murder, he said in 2023; as for his father, Kennedy was convinced that the man convicted of his killing was not the only one involved.

grand conspiracies: sex and gender education in schools was evidence of a Marxist plot to 'groom' young children both sexually and politically; a newly released list of names connected to the financier and paedophile Jeffrey Epstein was proof that QAnon's cabal of satanic child sex traffickers was real. (It wasn't. But court cases and dogged reporting by reputable newspapers like the *Wall Street Journal* did reveal how Epstein leveraged his connections among the rich and powerful to continue sexually exploiting vulnerable young women long after his conviction for having sex with a minor was widely known.) The bigger the story, the more the conspiracy theory expanded, until sometimes it merged with another conspiracy theory altogether.

This happened with COVID and the war in Ukraine. Like Pizzagate and QAnon, this fantastical story had begun on social media. On 24 February 2022, hours after Russia began its full-scale invasion, an obscure Twitter account posted a thread, complete with maps, claiming that Russian missile strikes were aimed not at Ukrainian military installations but at US-run biolabs in Ukraine. 'China and Russia indirectly (and correctly) blamed the US for the C19 outbreak, and are fearful that the US/allies have more viruses (bioweapons) to let out,' the poster wrote, concluding: 'get the hashtag going and see if we can trend it …#USBiolabs.'

The poster turned out to be a former restaurant manager and National Guard veteran from Virginia. Similar to the way QAnon spread, his story was picked up by conspiracy sites like

InfoWars, and was further boosted by Russian media and officials, who enthusiastically repeated the claims.

On 12 March 2022, the Russian foreign ministry posted a picture of a middle-aged woman with glasses and long blonde curly hair. A caption read: 'Ulyana Suprun, (neé Jurkiw) US National, Acting Minister of Health of Ukraine, nicknamed by Ukrainians – Dr. Death.'

•   •   •

Ms Suprun (whose first name is actually Ulana) was on a train from Lviv back to her home in Kyiv that day, she told me. The first she knew about this sinister moniker was when a colleague of her husband sent him a screenshot of the Russian post. But neither of them was surprised. Her husband specialised in studying and countering Russian propaganda, and Ulana had been at the receiving end of Russian conspiracy theories before.

Ms Suprun, the post claimed, was an American, 'born and raised in the US', who had been 'sent' to Ukraine by the Obama administration in the summer of 2016, where she became health minister. This was partly true. Ulana was born in Michigan to Ukrainian parents who had fled Soviet rule. She did indeed become Ukraine's acting minister of health in 2016, but not after having been sent there by Obama; she had moved there in 2013 of her own volition and got involved in the Maidan protests that would overthrow the pro-Russian president.

The post continued that her father was a retired senior executive at an American defence corporation (true), and that her grandfather, Ivan Jurkiw, was a 'Nazi collaborator and "polizei"' (false). The accompanying picture showed a man in German military uniform. 'I don't know who that person is,' Ulana said. 'I have never seen that picture before and I don't have any relatives named Ivan Jurkiw.'

The thrust of the post was clear: Ukraine's biological laboratories were under the control of the ministry of health; Suprun, as an American, was controlling these biolabs, a puppet master for the United States. The labs were making biological weapons. Oh, and they were all Nazis. The case illustrated, the post concluded, 'how demilitarization is connected to denazification'.

But the conspiracy theory peddled by the Russians paled in comparison to the story the Americans were telling themselves. Less than two weeks after the start of the invasion, a State Department official called Victoria Nuland was testifying before the Senate. Marco Rubio, a Republican senator from Florida, picked up on the biolabs story and asked: 'Does Ukraine have biological or chemical weapons?' His tone suggested he expected Ms Nuland to laugh the idea off. But she didn't. She paused, briefly, before not quite answering the question. 'Ukraine has, ah ... biological *research* facilities,' she said, adding that the US was concerned Russian forces might be trying to gain control of those facilities.

This was an odd thing to say, because it was well known that Ukraine had such facilities. As Ulana Suprun told me, 'Every country has biological laboratories to test for pathogens and do research.' It was also easily discoverable, through a simple search of the State Department website, that the United States was funding some of those laboratories, and in some cases advising on how those facilities could be run more efficiently and safely.* The awkward nature of Victoria Nuland's response caught the eye of Tucker Carlson (him again).

The following day, on his show on Fox News, Tucker ran a 15-minute monologue on the story. 'If you had told us just four days ago that the Biden administration was funding secret biolabs in Ukraine of all places, we would not have believed you,' he began. That was, he said, until he saw Victoria Nuland testify in the Senate.

To the average American, Nuland may have been an obscure State Department official. But in Russia she was well known as the bogeywoman who, according to state propaganda, instigated a CIA-backed coup in Ukraine in 2014.† (Fact check: the

---

* This had been going on since the 1990s. The Soviet Union had maintained a biological and chemical weapons programme. After the collapse of the USSR, the United States was concerned about chemical and biological agents falling into the wrong hands in former Soviet states that were often plagued by instability and corruption. The programme was managed through the Department of Defense.
† At the time of the Maidan protests, Nuland was assistant secretary of state for Europe. She was photographed visiting protestors on the square, handing out bread from a plastic bag – hardly the work of an undercover CIA coup plotter. Later, a recording of a phone conversation between her and the US ambassador to Kyiv was leaked, in which the two are heard discussing which of the opposition figures the US should favour in negotiations with then President Yanukovych.

revolution on Maidan was not a coup – I was there.*) Tucker
repeated the Russian coup claim, and went further: Nuland,
he said, was one of the people who 'brought us the Iraq war'.
(Fact check: in 2003, Victoria Nuland was an advisor to the
then vice president, Dick Cheney, who was one of the archi-
tects of the Iraq war.)

Tucker Carlson watched Nuland in the Senate and interpreted
her words as an admission of guilt. 'Nuland just confirmed that
the Russian disinformation they've been telling us for days is a
lie and a conspiracy theory and crazy and immoral to believe,
is in fact, totally and completely true.' Ukraine, he said, was
developing pathogens as bioweapons and the US was funding it.
Furthermore, he said, the US had failed to secure these biolabs
ahead of the Russian invasion, and then lied about it all.

And then he turned the corner into COVID.

'We've just spent the last two years living with a pathogen
that began in another foreign biolab funded by the United States
government, secretly.'† Carlson was saying that all the pain
and suffering of COVID had come about because of a secret

---

* There remain unanswered questions about the identity and allegiance of
gunmen who shot into the crowd (and at me and my BBC colleagues) from
the upper floors of the Hotel Ukraine that cold and bloody February day.
But it was not a coup.

† This was a reference to the fact that the US National Institutes of Health
(one part of which Dr Anthony Fauci once headed) had funded research at
the Wuhan Institute of Virology, which is located near the wet market in
China where COVID was first detected. If COVID escaped from that lab, it
was possible the virus might have been 'created' using US funding.

US-funded biolab in China; now the Washington swamp was at it again, playing Russian roulette with the lives and health of everyone in the world while attempting to instigate yet another change of regime.

'When it turns out the people who represent us and run our government are lying to us and never apologise for it and doing horrific things in our names, then you have to open your mind a little bit,' he intoned solemnly, before uncritically playing a clip from the Russian defence ministry.

Less than a month later, a poll suggested around a quarter of all Americans believed the US was developing bioweapons in Ukraine.[5] In 2023, Robert F. Kennedy Jr went on Tucker Carlson's new show (he had by now been fired from Fox and was broadcasting on Twitter/X) to claim that the America's National Institute of Allergy and Infectious Diseases, which conducted research into defence against biological and chemical terrorist threats, was in fact doing the exact opposite.

'You take an infectious microbe and you make it jump species,' he said. 'So it may kill monkeys – now you make it kill humans. And then you make it immune to antibiotics and to therapeutic drugs and to other therapies.' In order to deploy these weapons, he said, you needed to vaccinate your own side. So vaccines were in fact part of a biological weapons programme. And the man in charge of these sinister and lethal efforts? Dr Anthony Fauci (who, by the way, was paid more than the president of the United States).

Kennedy and Carlson threaded their conspiracy theories with verifiable facts: Fauci was one of the highest-paid government officials, on more than $400,000 per year; his institute did study deadly pathogens and fund research in laboratories around the world. But none of this was a secret and there was no evidence they were doing so with any other aim than the one stated publicly on the institute's website: 'NIAID supports research and early development of medical countermeasures against terrorist threats from infectious diseases, radiation exposure and chemical threats to the civilian population.'

Such nuances carried little weight with an electorate high on a cocktail of red and black pills. In the months leading up to the 2024 presidential election, America was becoming unmoored from any common frame of reference. Nothing was as it appeared and no one was to be trusted. In such circumstances, anything seemed possible.

CHAPTER 14

WHATEVER
IT TAKES

In early May 2024, I found myself in the small town of Blackfoot, Idaho. I'd driven down from Boise, the sleepy state capital, through the vast lava fields on the Snake River plain, a scorched landscape of craters and open rift cracks where the earth's crust had been pulled apart; I took a detour past Shoshone Falls – the 'Niagara of the West' – where the water thundered over a horseshoe-shaped cliff down into the river below. These monumental geological formations looked like they might have been there for ever, marking out the contours of this epic country for millions of years. But they were in fact no more than a few millennia old, born out of cataclysmic floods and eruptions that took place between 14,000 and 2,000 years ago, at a time when humans already roamed the plains of North America.

I had come to Idaho because I'd heard that the John Birch Society was making a quiet comeback here, infiltrating the local Republican Party with its conspiratorial paranoia about a secret cabal ruling the world. Ginette Manwaring had been involved in local Republican politics for decades. She welcomed me into her living room, a grand piano standing prominently at its centre. And after an impressive performance of a country ballad entitled 'In This Life', we sat down to talk.

She knew a Bircher when she saw one: her grandfather had been a member. She remembered him going to meetings, writing articles and pamphlets. This was the 1950s and '60s, and Ginette's grandfather believed there was a global conspiracy to destroy America as he knew it. 'He was fearful. He said there was going to be one world government, one monetary system,' Ginette said. He believed he was trying to protect his family, his way of life. 'In our family, we loved and honoured him for that.' But it was not how Ginette saw the world. Politically, she came of age under Ronald Reagan; it was morning in America, and the John Birch Society was a spent force, the fringe conspiracy theorists had been purged from the party. Or so she thought.

•   •   •

Lately, in Idaho, things had been getting weird. It had started with their own 'pizzagate'. Not the strange tale of Hillary Clinton's campaign manager and the non-existent basement in the Washington, DC pizza parlour – the Idaho iteration of this conspiracy was more mundane.

In 2022, the Idaho Republican Party held elections to senior leadership positions. The incumbent Party chair was a man called Tom Luna. Running against him was an Idaho state representative by the name of Dorothy Moon. Perhaps, given the unusual juxtaposition of surnames in the race, some sort of strange cosmic collision was to be expected. Luna, hoping for re-election, was holding a campaign event at a hotel in the town of Twin Falls, a few miles from the Shoshone waterfall. He had sent out fliers to GOP delegates advertising 'Pizza & Patriots with Tom Luna'. When the event began, he was surprised when a child walked in asking whether he was in the right place for his free dinner. Then more people started arriving, all looking for the same thing. It turned out *someone* had been distributing alternative fliers at a homeless shelter in town: 'Pizza for the Hungry: Join Tom Luna, Idaho GOP Chair', the leaflet proclaimed. Luna and his campaign took things in their stride and ordered pizza for everyone. It was hardly the work of a satanic cabal. But Ginette saw the hand of Moon's supporters in this devious bit of political trickery. Dorothy Moon denounced the stunt as a 'dirty trick'; the director of the homeless shelter pointed the finger of blame at one of her supporters, an alt-right internet provocateur.

Originally from Kansas City, Dorothy Moon moved to Idaho in the 1990s, working as a schoolteacher before going into politics. Together with her husband, Darr Moon, she also ran mining operations in the gold fields of central Idaho. Mr Moon also just so happened to be president of the Idaho chapter of the John Birch Society.

Over two terms as Idaho state representative, Dorothy had earned herself a reputation as a hard right-winger – she had campaigned on behalf of Eric Parker, a militia leader known as the 'Bundy Ranch Sniper'. In 2022, she won her campaign against Luna and became leader of the state party. Ginette was worried. Were the Birchers back? It certainly looked like Dorothy Moon was trying to purge the party of mainstream Republicans and stuff it with her supporters.

When the Republicans in Ginette's local county replaced their central committee chairman in 2023, they elected Matt Thompson by a large margin. Matt was a softly spoken man who had been on the committee for more than a decade. He knew everyone there – they were all friends. But after his appointment he got an email from Moon's office in Boise. There had been an anonymous complaint about election procedure, she said. It was unclear what exactly the problem was, or who had filed the complaint, but Matt was happy to do what needed to be done to fix it. But when he contacted Moon, he was told the deadline had passed; the chairwoman was going to come down and re-run the election herself.

Matt became suspicious. 'I started learning about other places in the state where the same script has played out,' he said. Incensed, he applied for a legal injunction against Moon, preventing her from entering Bingham County and taking over their meetings. 'I don't know whether she's the Wicked Witch or Dorothy,' he said, 'but it's time for her to click her heels and wind back up in Kansas, or wherever she's from.'

But Dorothy did not go back to Kansas. Moon denied Thompson's claims and the dispute is ongoing. In the meantime, under her leadership, the Party passed a new rule that allowed local committees – the kind that Tom had been elected to chair – to summon Republican officials to a 'tribunal'. If found wanting in their commitment to 'conservative values', they could be censured and barred from standing as a Republican. But who defined those values? Ginette Manwaring certainly thought of herself as a conservative. So did Matt Thompson. In fact, I never met a single person in Idaho who didn't see themselves as conservative. So who was setting the agenda? Ginette and others all thought they knew the answer to that: a group called the Idaho Freedom Foundation (IFF), a think tank whose stated aim was to 'defeat Marxism'. (There was, as far as I could tell, very little evidence of Marxism in Idaho, one of the most conservative states in the country.)

According to Ginette and her allies, the IFF was essentially the John Birch Society under another name, and it now effectively controlled the Idaho Republican Party. The group rated each bill that came before the state legislature, according to its own set of 'conservative values'. It then produced a 'Freedom Index', which rated legislators based on how they voted. If a legislator's score fell too low, they would be labelled a 'RINO' ('Republican in Name Only') and could expect the powerful IFF to lobby against them. Soon, many legislators, Ginette and others felt, simply voted the way they were told.

I wanted to talk to the IFF, to ask them what exactly their ratings were based on, and what they were trying to achieve. It turned out, perhaps unsurprisingly, they didn't have much time for people like me. 'The Idaho Freedom Foundation has found most of the legacy news media to be agenda-driven propagandists working to shift public opinion toward socialist ideas,' their website says. 'The IFF will not help legitimize biased, unfair pseudo-journalism by responding to requests for comment.'

But a bit more digging revealed that the IFF's legislative ratings were based almost entirely on the opinions of one man: Parrish Miller. His profiles on social media showed a man with a huge beard who described himself as a web designer and political consultant. He had some pretty radical views. He called the US government a 'curse', adding: 'I eagerly await the news of its eradication.' In another blog post he wrote: 'If anyone – including an employee of a criminal gang calling itself a government – attempts to initiate force against an innocent individual, it is perfectly justifiable for that individual [...] to use defensive force (up to and including lethal force).' Miller appeared to be referring to police or other law-enforcement bodies, or as he described them, 'thugs who are better armed and better organized.' The answer to this problem, Miller added ominously, was perhaps 'to change the odds in terms of arms and organization.'

Was Miller saying what he appeared to be saying? That the organs of the state, the instruments of justice, had no moral or legal authority? And was he proposing that citizens form a militia in order to be better armed? He did not respond to my emails. Nor did Dorothy Moon.

But someone else did: Eric Parker, the Bundy Ranch Sniper.

In 2018, Dorothy Moon had welcomed him to the state capitol in Boise. He had just walked free after 19 months in jail, having beaten felony charges related to an armed standoff at a ranch in Nevada. The FBI considered Parker a 'domestic terrorist'. These days he led a militia group called the Real Idaho Three Percenters. Moon and her allies in Boise consulted him on policy matters and legislation, and he was a regular at events organised by the John Birch Society and the IFF.

Parker agreed to meet me and Lucy Proctor in his home-town of Haley. Lucy had spoken to him over the phone – he had been alternately accessible and elusive, open and mistrustful. He made one thing clear: he did not like being called a militia leader. As we drove deeper into the epic landscape of Idaho, wondering what to expect, we dug into the details of the event that turned him – overnight – from an unknown Idaho electrician into one of the most well-known faces of America's burgeoning anti-government militia movement.

• • •

The Bundy ranch standoff, also known as the 'Battle of Bunkerville', began in 2014 when federal rangers threatened to confiscate cattle from a rancher in southern Nevada. Cliven Bundy was a Mormon patriarch whose family had been grazing these lands for generations, going back to the late 1800s when they settled out in the West. Much of the land in Nevada was owned by the federal government, and for decades the Bundys and other ranchers had paid the federal Bureau of Land Management annual fees, allowing their cattle to roam the land outside the confines of the ranch. The arrangement worked well, until the ranchers came into conflict with another inhabitant of this arid landscape, one that had been there for a lot longer than the Bundys and other pioneers of the old West (or even the Native Americans they presumably displaced): the desert tortoise.

The desert tortoise was an endangered species, and in the early 1990s the government designated hundreds of thousands of acres of southern Nevada a conservation area. In the years that followed, the authorities persuaded other ranchers to sell their grazing rights back to the federal government. Bundy refused, and he stopped paying. By 2014, he was the last remaining holdout, the last cattleman in southern Nevada; the government said he owed them a million dollars in unpaid fees.

Bundy saw conservation merely as a pretext to wrest control of public lands his family had lived on for generations, a plot to kill off his way of life. And he believed he had the law on his side. Like a cowboy from some latter-day Western, Bundy didn't recognise the writ of the federal government in his back yard. He went further: he didn't recognise the United States, its courts and its law enforcement agencies, as an authority at all. He saw himself as a citizen of the 'sovereign state of Nevada'. If he recognised any authority other than God, it was the United States Constitution. His rights as a 'sovereign citizen', an authority unto himself, he believed, were enshrined in that document. As far as he was concerned, the power to enforce the law was vested in the local sheriff, whose job it was to protect him from the tyranny of central government.

In 2014, the government had finally had enough of Cliven Bundy. They sent in armed federal agents, with horses and helicopters, and began rounding up his cattle. Bundy responded by declaring a 'range war'. He called on his supporters to gather at his ranch in a show of force; hundreds came, some of them heavily armed militia members. It was during this standoff that a Reuters photographer snapped a picture that would become the iconic image of that event, a rallying cry for people who – like Bundy – had a strong dislike of government. The picture showed a man wearing sunglasses and black baseball cap, flak jacket over a plaid shirt, lying prone on an interstate overpass, squinting down the barrel of his rifle trained on the Feds below. That man was Eric Parker.

We arrived in Haley early. It seemed an oddly genteel little town, with upmarket delis selling overpriced pesto and fine wines. Parker wasn't keen to invite us to his home and, given his reputation, I didn't want to meet him in a busy public space, so we found a quiet spot by a wood on the outskirts of town. We waited under a small wooden shelter as the temperature dropped and a light, unseasonable snow began to fall. Eventually, Parker appeared in a giant pickup truck.

'I'm always armed,' he said, in response to a question I hadn't asked. I didn't do what perhaps he'd expected me to do and ask to see it. Instead, I asked him to tell me about his tattoos. On his forearm, he had the logo of the 1980s punk rock band Black Flag. Parker's anti-authoritarian streak came from punk, he said, which was closely linked with anti-fascism. He once beat up a Nazi at a gig, he told me with pride. 'That's where I was coming from when I was young – probably not your standard approach to where I am now.' There was another tattoo with a Latin inscription: '*Quicquid capit*' – 'Whatever it takes.'

· · ·

One day, in April 2014, Eric Parker got home from work and logged on to the internet. What he saw disturbed him: heavily armed federal rangers in Nevada facing off against protestors. He'd seen reports of government snipers taking up positions on the hills surrounding Cliven Bundy's ranch. 'Bringing snipers against a family over taxes is problematic in my opinion.' One of Bundy's sons had been tasered after kicking a police dog. At one point, Parker said, an officer body-slammed an elderly woman, tossing her to the ground. 'These federal officers were heavy handed. They were assaulting people.'

Parker was, at that time, not a member of any militia. Nor did he have any special affinity for ranchers. He was an electrician, he said, not a cowboy. But, like Bundy and many others in the 'patriot movement', he was very into the United States Constitution. The First Amendment to that document guarantees the right not only to free speech, but also to peaceably assemble and to 'petition the Government for a redress of grievances'. That right, he believed, was being violated in Bunkerville. So he decided to go down there. Partly to see with his own eyes what was really happening. And partly to protect the Constitution.

As he was getting ready to leave, a friend sent him another video – a local official on TV warning that anyone thinking of coming down to support the Bundys had 'better have funeral plans'. Now Parker was angry. 'I wasn't going to be intimidated into not exercising my First Amendment,' he told me. 'So I brought my Second Amendment.'*

Parker threw his rifle and his camping gear into his truck, picked up a couple of friends, and drove down to Nevada. They arrived at the ranch late at night and set up camp. The following morning he made his way to the area where the protesters were

---

* The Second Amendment is so often invoked it's perhaps worth quoting in full: 'A well regulated Militia, being necessary to the security of a free State, the right of the people to keep and bear Arms, shall not be infringed.'

gathered. It was a mixed bunch, he said. 'I think you had a lot of different people there for a lot of different reasons.' There were members of various militia groups, but also people from the online hacktivist collective Anonymous. So, not all gun-toting right-wingers. 'The militarisation of law enforcement was definitely a reason a lot of people were there,' he said, 'which at the time probably wasn't a very right-wing talking point.'

When he got to the place where the Bundys and their supporters had gathered, Parker saw Cliven Bundy talking to the local sheriff. The federal officers had apparently made the decision to stand down. 'So we figured it was over – drove all that way for nothing. We were going to go to Vegas, get a cheeseburger, and head home.' But first, they figured, they'd better check. Bundy told his ranch hands to go see if the rangers had indeed left. The cowboys rode off into the desert and Parker and his mates followed the line of protestors along the highway.

Soon they saw the federal officers. They were still there. Parker said it didn't look like they were getting ready to leave at all. The officers were gathered in a 'wash', or dry gully. Up on the mesa, Parker saw people moving about. He assumed they were government snipers. Suddenly, he said, 'a lady came running down the highway saying the Feds were pointing guns and threatening to shoot protestors in the wash'. Parker and the others walked back up the highway in the direction from which the woman had come, until they got to an overpass over the dry riverbed. 'I borrowed a pair of binoculars from a guy who was standing there, and I saw a lot of men in camouflage, body armour. I started noticing all the positions they had taken, noticing all the rifles pointing at us, guys looking through scopes.' Then he saw a group of Bundy's supporters starting to move up the riverbed – cowboys on horseback, protestors on foot. Parker stayed put, observing. The cops were making announcements over a loudspeaker, telling the protestors not to come any closer, to disperse. From where Parker was standing, he said, the sound was kind of muffled. But he heard the words 'authorised to use force'.

The officers were from the Bureau of Land Management, the agency responsible for administering federal lands. But to Eric Parker they didn't look like harmless bureaucrats. 'It looked like something out of Fallujah,' he said. 'We're talking multi-cam, body armour, rifles, helmets. It looked like a standing army to me.' That's when Parker decided to get down on his front and take up what he called a 'defensive position', pointing his rifle towards the standoff down below; and a Reuters photographer took a picture that would change his life.

The protestors were converging on the officers at a point about 200 yards from where Parker was lying. 'I legitimately thought they were going to shoot them,' he said. He watched the climax of the standoff from a distance, looking down the barrel of his rifle. He saw protestors approach the officers in the wash; then he saw some sheriff's deputies come in and talk to the protestors. 'And then a short time after that I watched the guys with the guns in the camouflage all back out. And then they left. And that was that.' In an armed standoff with ranchers and their supporters in the militia, the government had just backed down.

To the federal agents, things had looked a little different from what Eric Parker saw. They felt outnumbered and outgunned by the protestors. Years later, when they indicted Cliven Bundy, they described the incident as a 'massive armed assault'. In the end, no one was shot. By retreating, the government had successfully de-escalated the situation. But it was a humiliating defeat.

Eric Parker went home; he had been in Nevada for less than 48 hours. Meanwhile, the picture of him lying on the highway, his rifle trained on the feds, had gone viral. 'My aunt called me and said, "Do you have a shamrock tattooed on your finger?" I said, "Yeah, why?" She said: "You're on the cover of Fox News." That's when I realised, I'll probably be answering some questions about this eventually.'

The weird thing was, no one called. Not for a while anyway. It was as if the media (which had lavished coverage on the standoff) and the FBI (which had announced it had launched an investigation) had collectively decided to forget about the incident.

But in right-wing chatrooms and anti-government social media groups, the internet was ablaze. Eric Parker had become a hero to some; to others, he was suspect. A friend pointed him to a Facebook page where people were calling him a 'provocateur', an FBI plant who had infiltrated the protestors and pointed his gun at the Feds with the aim of discrediting the movement and providing the government with legal ammunition to go after its members. That Facebook page was run by the Three Percent movement, the same group as that of the sake-drinking militia-man I'd met in Georgia shortly after the 2020 election, people who believe it only takes a small minority, highly determined and well armed, to build a revolution. Parker engaged with his accusers online, seeking to persuade them he really was just an electrician from Idaho. Eventually he went to meet them in person. And that's how Eric Parker ended up joining the militia.

Later that summer, the media did come knocking. A documentary company called Longbow Productions contacted Parker, saying they were making a film about the standoff at the Bundy ranch. At first he was hesitant, but since no one had asked him for his version of the story, he saw it as an opportunity to speak his truth. He figured the FBI would eventually get to see the results. But so what? As far as he was concerned, he'd done nothing wrong, and so he had nothing to hide. The documentary makers seemed professional, there was a crew of five or six people, multiple cameras, lights. But almost as soon as they started filming, Parker got the feeling something was not right. It felt less like an interview, more like an interrogation, the same questions over and over, phrased slightly differently: *Are you in a militia? Do you train with a militia? Do you know anybody in a militia?*

A year and a half later, the FBI finally made their move. They arrested Cliven Bundy in Portland – he'd flown to Oregon to support two of his sons, Ryan and Ammon, who would be acquitted of their involvement in another armed standoff at a wildlife reserve. (This time it had not ended peacefully – one of the Bundys' associates was shot dead by police.) Parker figured it was only a matter of time before they came for him.

Parker went to see his local sheriff – with a wife and young kids at home, he didn't want the FBI kicking down his door with guns drawn. 'I told him, "I'll turn myself in right now,"' he said. The sheriff told him there was no warrant out for his arrest, no need to worry. But a few days later, on his way to work in the morning, he looked in his rear-view mirror and saw three vehicles pull out behind him. 'By the time I had pulled in, they had all come up to the window, guns out, .45 calibre to the face. One agent said, "Don't move or I'll shoot you." So I put my hands up.' The officer asked Parker whether he was armed. When Parker confirmed that he had a pistol in his waistband, the officer told him to put his truck in park. Now Parker had a problem. If he moved toward the gearstick, it might look like he was going for his gun; if he didn't, he would be obstructing an officer who had a gun pointed at his head.

'Honestly, I think he would have shot me if I'd moved,' Parker said. Eventually another cop stepped in, reached into the car and put it in park, and pulled Parker out.

Eric Parker spent the next 19 months in jail, 6 months of it in solitary confinement. When they let him out of solitary, he said, they offered him a plea deal: take the felony and do ten years.

Parker said he told them: 'I don't negotiate with terrorists.' So the case went to trial. Parker was facing decades in prison. But in court it emerged that Longbow Productions, the documentary company, was in fact an FBI front. The jury was not impressed, especially when it turned out they had plied another defendant with alcohol during their fake interview – agents posing as journalists were trying to get people who had not yet been charged with any crime to incriminate themselves under false pretences.

The jury acquitted Parker on charges of conspiracy to plot with the Bundys to form a militia to resist the enforcement of court orders. (He'd never even spoken to Bundy until he met him in a jail cell, he said.) But they couldn't reach a verdict on the other charges: illegal possession of weapons, and assaulting and threatening federal officers. So the judge ordered a retrial.

In the retrial, Parker's defence attorneys wanted to call witnesses, but the judge disallowed them. She also restricted what Parker could talk about on the stand. He could not explain his motivations for travelling to Bunkerville, he said, because he wasn't permitted to talk about those clauses in the Constitution he believed he was defending. Nor was he allowed to talk about alleged misconduct or excessive force by law enforcement. At one point Parker wanted to explain about the government snipers he believed he had seen up on the mesa, but he was barred from using the word 'sniper'. In the end, the judge struck his entire testimony from the record.[1] The case ended in another mistrial, another hung jury, but the government's case against him had essentially collapsed. Rather than face a third trial, Eric Parker pleaded guilty to a misdemeanour charge of obstructing a court order. After over a year and a half behind bars, he walked free.*

The case against the Bundys themselves, who were tried separately from Parker, was dismissed. The judge found that the prosecution and the FBI had engaged in 'flagrant misconduct', withholding evidence during trial. Those government snipers Parker thought he had seen, which he wasn't allowed to talk about in his defence – it turned out they *were* there. The evidence was found in a tactical operations log which the FBI 'inexplicably placed' or 'perhaps hid' on a thumb drive for three years.[2] At the Bundys' trial in Oregon, prosecutors showed footage of the gunmen firing their weapons during the standoff, apparently training for a possible shootout with police. It emerged that the gunman leading that exercise was in fact a paid informant for the FBI, one of at least nine government 'confidential human sources' present at various times during the 41-day standoff.

What to make of all this? Were Eric Parker and the Bundys heroes, little Davids who had stood up to a tyrannical Goliath and, against all the odds, beaten a system that had done its best

---

* I was surprised to learn that a defendant can be restricted in what they are allowed to say in testimony. It turns out it's not unusual if, say, the judge decides the defence – or the prosecution – is bamboozling the jury with irrelevant information. Fair enough. But here's the thing: the federal courts in the United States have a conviction rate of more than 90 per cent. Acquittal is vanishingly rare – only 0.4 per cent of cases in 2022. Two of Parker's co-defendants were convicted.

to entrap them and lock them away? Or were they right-wing anti-government extremists who had got away with acts of domestic terrorism because of mistakes by incompetent prosecutors and law enforcement officers? What if the answer was: a bit of both?

Parker emerged from his brush with the US justice system believing it had been 'usurped, undermined, manipulated – intentionally – by people within the government: prosecutors, the DOJ, among others'. Nevertheless, he apparently had not lost faith in America, in the institutions of the state. He ran unsuccessfully for the Idaho State Senate in 2020 and again in 2022. Still, he was working with elected representatives – people like Dorothy Moon – to help craft legislation.

But if people like Parker have a hand in making the law, how are they shaping it? He acknowledged that organisations like the one he now leads – the Real Three Percenters of Idaho (a militia by most people's definition) – attract their fair share of racists and white supremacists. He said he has had to chuck people out. 'We just make sure that they know they're not welcome,' he said. 'We don't condone any ideology that would take due process away from any American citizen for any reason, including religious, racial or sexual.' Not all of these organisations are as scrupulous.

Others in this movement were also trying to affect change by engaging in the democratic process. Ryan Bundy, son of Cliven who said he didn't recognise the authority of the US government, had run for governor of Nevada in 2018 (he too was unsuccessful); and his brother Ammon ran for governor of Idaho (unsuccessful again, though he got nearly as many votes as his Democratic rival – not bad for an independent candidate from out of state.) Were these signs of hope? That even anti-government militia leaders still preferred to settle their grievances through the system? Or were we witnessing an attempted take-over of government by people who didn't believe in government?

That's what Ginette Manwaring believed. She and her allies saw what happened in the Idaho Republican party as a 'hostile takeover' by the IFF, who were the modern-day incarnation of the John Birch Society. 'They have been able to control the narra-tive – the anger and disruption in our county – through social media,' she said. 'They think they are on God's errand: they're right and you're wrong. There is no discussion. It is completely contrary to democracy.' It was, she said, un-American.

In her magisterial seven-part audio documentary about the history of the Bundys, the Oregon journalist Leah Sottile probes the complex nuances of this one family's battles with the US government. She traces the Bundys' Mormon roots, noting how they – like many other members of the Church of Latter Day Saints – moved west in the nineteenth century to avoid persecu-tion. (The founder of the church, Joseph Smith, was murdered by a mob in Illinois in 1844.) She investigates Bundy's claims to the land in southern Nevada, concluding his rights can only be argued through the practices of polygamy – including child brides and incest – that American society has collectively decided should not be condoned. She also documents Cliven's racist beliefs* and the violence carried out by some of some of his supporters. She sits in the living room at the Bundy ranch and listens to Cliven (benevolent patriarch with more than sixty grandchildren) outline his selective interpretation of the Constitution which, according to a disputed Mormon prophecy, now 'hangs by a thread'.

In Sottile's telling, the Bundys believe their fight with the government is part of a messianic mission to save America. But their quest is also self-interested. The Bundys want to recreate 'a life out West that they just barely missed out on: a life on the just-settled frontier, ripe with possibility, where the rules are yet to be made.' And their motto is the same as the one inked in Latin on Eric Parker's forearm: *whatever it takes.* That credo, Sottile says, is dangerous – it incites people to violence; it justifies any action.

I emerged from my meeting with Eric Parker wondering whether the US government was not also guilty of operating according to the same maxim. The fake FBI film crew that tried to get Parker to incriminate himself on camera without a lawyer

---

* Around the time of the Bunkerville standoff, he alienated some supporters when he wondered aloud whether 'the negro' had been better off under slavery. 'They abort their young children,' he said, 'they put their young men in jail, because they never learned how to pick cotton. And I've often wondered, are they better off as slaves, picking cotton and having a family life and doing things, or are they better off under government subsidy? They didn't get no more freedom. They got less freedom.'

present? Concealing evidence that might exculpate defendants at trial? FBI informants running weapons training for militants during an armed standoff? *Whatever it takes.*

In such circumstances, was it any wonder that Jan-sixers like Derrick Evans, the state representative I met in West Virginia who served time for his role in the riot at the Capitol, believed they had been set up, that their prosecutions were illegitimate, the charges against them politically motivated? Were they part of a mob that wanted to obstruct the certification of the results of the 2020 presidential election? Yes, they were. But many of those serving lengthy jail sentences had also not committed any acts of violence. They had been sent to the Capitol by a president who told them their democracy was being stolen, and that it was their patriotic duty to defend it. And the government had come down on them in the heaviest way possible. There was no convincing evidence to support the idea that the FBI had a hand in fomenting the events of January 6th, let alone that they were part of a vast conspiracy to subvert the election. But, like QAnon, the *facts* didn't need to be plausible for the *narrative* to be believable.

The narrative was this: the state, sensing an existential threat to its existence, had gone rogue. Now, its targets were not just a handful of cowboys out West, but 75 million Americans who had voted for Donald Trump, members of the MAGA movement who, in Biden's words, had 'held a dagger to the throat of democracy'. What would they do to keep it all from falling apart?

• • •

In 1970, the German-born economist Albert Hirschman wrote a treatise entitled *Exit, Voice, and Loyalty: Responses to Decline in Firms, Organizations and States*. Hirschman was Jewish; he had fought with anti-fascist forces in Spain and worked with the French Resistance to help thousands escape the Nazis (among them Hannah Arendt, the political theorist who wrote the definitive work on the roots of fascism). In his book, Hirschman described the three different ways people might respond to a negative environment. First: *loyalty* – you can grin and bear it; second: *voice* – you can act to try to change your circumstances. At one end of this spectrum lies democratic engagement, and at the other – revolt. *Voice* was the option chosen by the Founding Fathers, when they first petitioned the British Crown, and then took up arms against it in a revolutionary war that birthed the American Republic. The third choice, wrote Hirschman, is *exit* – you can leave, remove yourself from an intolerable situation in order to start afresh elsewhere. This was the option chosen by the Puritans who boarded the *Mayflower* in 1620 and sailed from England to the New World.

The story of America can be told through the lens of a constant tension between *voice* and *exit*: a people who left from many different countries for many different reasons and congregated on a new continent. There they raised their voices in the hope of creating a more perfect society. It didn't always work out. The Bundys' ancestors chose *exit* twice – first when they came to America, and then when they moved out West. But as the modern Bundys found, the frontier has been tamed. *Exit* was no longer an option – there were no more lands to conquer.

At least until another realm opened up: cyberspace.

CHAPTER 15

AMONG
THE GODS

In the spring of 2024, while I was doing my final research for this book, I received an intriguing invite. I had spotted a notice online: 'Praxis magazine launch. Tomorrow night. Photocopy your favourite pages.' That was it. No time. No location. Just a link where you could apply to attend. I applied. I waited.

Praxis was a tech start-up that advertised itself as a new nation. Its founders, a couple of crypto bros, said they were building a city from scratch; they were in talks to acquire a chunk of land somewhere on the Mediterranean coast, but they were a little cagey about the details. For now, Praxis existed mainly on the internet. 'We embody the culture of the pioneer,' the company proclaimed on Twitter/X. They posted edgy slogans and eye-catching artwork in the style of propaganda posters. 'Manifest Your Destiny' read one post, with a nod to the nineteenth-century belief in the 'manifest destiny' of European settlers to expand westward in a holy mission to spread the values of American exceptionalism across the continent (wiping out the indigenous population as they went). It was accompanied by a picture of a half-nude woman, alabaster white, her arms outstretched across an epic American landscape that looked uncannily like those waterfalls I'd driven past in Idaho. The moon loomed large over a canyon; flying saucers zoomed across the sky – a retro-futuristic fever dream.

Praxis was on my radar because of Peter Thiel. He was the most high-profile investor in a small but growing number of ventures known collectively as 'network states'. If Thiel was the concept's best-known financial backer, its principal evangelist was Balaji Srinivasan. A computer scientist and venture capitalist, Balaji (who mostly goes by just his first name) made his money in biotech before going into crypto. At some point he picked up a book that radically reshaped his view of the world: *Exit, Voice, and Loyalty* by Albert Hirschman. The United States, he believed, was destined to become 'the Microsoft of nations' – a once vital force for change and innovation that he said had become bloated, outdated and obsolete. Democracy, or *voice*, wasn't working any more, at least not in the form it was practiced in America. The solution was *exit*, and in a crowded world of 8 billion people, Silicon Valley was uniquely positioned to challenge the power of Washington, DC, and drive a new wave of explorers and pioneers setting out boldly into the unknown.

Starting a new country, he said, would be just like starting a new company. And the best thing was that the naysayers and the Luddites, the people desperately clinging to their old way of doing things, would be excluded from this new world – or rather they would exclude themselves. 'The people who think this is weird, the people who sneer at the frontier, the people who hate technology, they won't follow you out there.'[1] They might, he acknowledged, try to stop you from leaving. But technology provided the answer: cryptocurrencies would ensure the state could not seize your money; property rights would be enforced by smart contracts on the blockchain; 3D printing would circumvent regulation so you could manufacture your own medical devices, drones, and guns. 'Warfare is going to become software, laws are going to become code.'

He told a compelling story: once upon a time, a small group of industries controlled America – banking, law, politics, Hollywood, TV, newspapers – call it a cabal if you will. But now, tech was seizing the means of production: entertainment was being swallowed up by Netflix, the music industry by Spotify; the news industry was being replaced by social media; even space travel was no longer the kind of thing that only big governments could do. There was nothing the state and its backers in the corporate establishment did that tech couldn't do better.

In late 2023, Balaji hosted a Network State conference in Amsterdam – a gathering of this specific subset of tech entrepreneurs pitching visions for their various start-up societies.

It was there that I'd met Dryden Brown, the co-founder of Praxis. Dressed in a grey hoodie, he wandered around the stage talking up his project in a strangely uninspiring monotone. He grew up in Santa Barbara, California, he said, being home schooled so he could spend most of his time surfing. He had an early interest in American colonial history. 'My family came to America from Ireland, they fought in the revolutionary war, they participated in the Pennsylvania constitutional convention.' He wanted, he said, to build a new city, based around the idea of 'vitality'. He promised the first 10,000 residents would be able to move to the as-yet-unnamed location on the Mediterranean in 2026. He fumbled with a little remote in his hand, flashing up slides that suggested Praxis was backed by funds controlling hundreds of billions of dollars of capital. The Praxis community already consisted of tens of thousands of people, he said, who 'met up all around the world and hosted events with one another, made memes, messed around on the internet.' (He flashed up a slide showing a bunch of Pepe the frog memes.)

Brown came across as a surfer dude who'd spent too much time on 4chan. But then Praxis had raised a considerable amount of money – not the billions the slides suggested, but somewhere in the region of $19 million – from people like Balaji and venture capital funds whose investors included Thiel and Sam Altman, the CEO of OpenAI, one of the world's top developers of artificial intelligence. Praxis had a reputation for hosting opulent parties in Manhattan's Lower East Side. People spoke of candle-lit soirees in giant loft spaces where nerdy coders mixed with edgy scenesters discussing Nietzsche while a string quartet played in the background. Journalists were not welcome and attendees were made to sign NDAs.

I went up to Dryden after his talk. He seemed suspicious and a little cold. I figured that, like Balaji, he had no great love for the traditional media. After all, who needed to watch TV or read a newspaper when you had YouTube and Twitter/X. I represented the sneering Luddite class, another 'barrier to exit'. But when I asked for a contact, he gave me his phone number. And then, six months later, when I spotted the announcement for the Praxis magazine launch party and got no response to my application to attend, I messaged him.

His reply was short: 'Ella Funt at 10pm'.

The party was tonight. Ella Funt turned out to be a night-club in the East Village. Luckily, I happened to be in America at the time; less fortunately, I was in Utah, 2,000 miles from New York. If I was going to make it, I had to leave. Now.

• • •

I was actually the first to arrive. The Praxis guys were still setting up, laying copies of their magazine on tables around the bar. It encouraged readers to 'rip pages out and stick them on your walls. Photocopy pages and paste them around your town.' A Xerox machine had been wheeled in for that very purpose.

The place had once been a legendary spot on the New York queer scene. Back in the 1950s and '60s, when this part of lower Manhattan was still truly edgy, celebrities like Liberace and Tennessee Williams would come to Club 82 to drink cocktails served by lesbians in slick tuxedos, and watch drag queens on stage in the basement club. In the 1970s, it morphed into a punk venue – David Bowie and Lou Reed performed there. Club 82 had closed in 2019 and was now re-opened as Ella Funt. It felt like it was trying to recreate those wild days, when anyone could be whatever they wanted to be, where anything seemed possible. Except now the clientele were the kind of people who might need to put in 14 hours of work the next day at a law firm or a hedge fund. Or sit behind their computer terminals writing code and 'buying the dip'.

I hadn't been there long when a group of young men walked in, some wearing cowboy boots, all with the cocksure swagger of the insecure. They sat down at one of the tables, ordered some cocktails (the drinks were on Praxis) and drank a toast: 'To health, good living, and beauty. Amen!'

I got talking to one of them – not the most beautiful of men, it should be noted – who introduced himself as Zac, from Milton Keynes, the co-founder of a crypto start-up. He was wearing a leather Stetson and said he liked to think of himself as a crypto-cowboy. 'If you're not working in crypto you're not working on the frontier.' He thought the whole global economy would eventually end up on the blockchain. In the interim, he said, he was gambling on 'memecoins'.

Memecoins? One of his friends chipped in: they were a 'New Testament of a financial protest to the old system'. Crypto was a challenge to the old dollar system, he explained, and memecoins were a challenge to the big cryptocurrencies backed by venture capital. Tech was moving fast, and I was struggling to keep up. 'All memecoins that are successful have a cult following,' another guy said. 'Pepe has been the most successful.' Pepe: the lurid green frog (sometimes with a mop of yellow Trump hair) that had hopped out of the chatrooms of the internet during the 2016 election campaign and become an alt-right meme. *Pepe was a currency now?* The guys were giggling like schoolboys into their cocktails, trolling the 'newfag' at the table. But, like the denizens of 4chan, their jokes were also deadly serious.

'What crypto really represents is the hyper-financialisation of everything,' Zac explained earnestly. The whole sector was inherently chaotic, he explained. 'We can create and destroy within fractions of seconds.' A memecoin, he said, was an idea that had been hyper-financialised. Thanks to crypto, they could hyper-financialise science, or really anything. Was that a *good* thing, I wondered? It was, he assured me – it represented capitalism in its purest form.

By now there was a DJ playing. The music was pretty loud and not conducive to conversation. I went and got myself a cocktail and began leafing through a copy of the Praxis magazine. It was big and yellow and printed on heavy paper. There were lots of ads. I suspected most of them were not there because companies had bought advertising space. Most seemed to have been included by the editors as a 4chan-style plausibly deniable nod to white supremacy: a Chicago-based power-washing company featuring a guy standing in front of a pristine whitewashed wall with his thumbs up; another for a Comme des Garçons perfume called White ('like white boys'?); another for just milk. There were lots of ads for different types of guns and companies that promised to 3D print guns. There was a QR code that, when scanned, led to a short film on YouTube. It was a twenty-minute polemic against modern life, the degradation of human vitality by a soulless entertainment industry, a lament for a vanished world of moral certainties, of hierarchies and heroism.

'World War Three isn't found on a battlefield,' the narrator intoned. 'It's in the algorithms making you hate yourself and your own civilisation. And if you do anything to take a stance against this degradation, from this bloodbath of morality, then you are a fascist.' This line was accompanied by a shot of an animated figure pointing a pistol straight at the camera.

The cover story was a photoshoot, a riff on the 1991 Hollywood film *Point Break* in which a bunch of California surfers don rubber masks, dress up as former US presidents and rob banks. The Praxis guys had found an empty bank and recreated scenes from the film, pointing their shotguns at their mates dressed as bank tellers, chucking bundles of $100 bills around.

The photos were interspersed with quotes. The first that caught my eye was from *Gone with the Wind*: 'I told you once before that there were two times for making big money, one in the up-building of a country and the other in its destruction. Slow money on the up-building, fast money in the crack-up.' That figured, I thought. Chaos as opportunity. The hyper-financialisation of everything. But then I came across another quote, which sent me straight back down my own rabbit hole.

'All nation-states face bankruptcy and the rapid erosion of their authority. The age of individual economic sovereignty is coming.' It was from *The Sovereign Individual*, the prophetic handbook on how to prosper from chaos in the digital age. There was more:

> Cybermoney controlled by private markets will supersede fiat money issued by governments. As income tax becomes uncollectable, older and more arbitrary extortion methods will resurface. Governments will violate human rights, censor the free flow of information, sabotage useful technologies, and worse. [...] Western governments will seek to suppress the crypto-economy by totalitarian means.

Davidson and Rees-Mogg had foreseen Silicon Valley's challenge to the power of government, and predicted it would fight back.

Over the din of the DJ, I got talking to another young guy. He introduced himself as Azi. I asked his surname. 'Uh … Mandias', he said. It was only when I repeated it back to him that the joke landed: Ozymandias, King of Kings. I remembered another passage from the book: 'Sovereign Individuals will compete and interact on terms that echo the relations among the gods in Greek myth. The elusive Mount Olympus of the next millennium will be in cyberspace.' Mr Mandias seemed to have internalised the message of *The Sovereign Individual*. The printing press destroyed the Church's control over knowledge 500 years ago, he said. Now crypto was going to kill the state's control over money. Current levels of income inequality were blaring signs, he said, that something was very wrong with the American system. And things were only going to get worse. He foresaw a new Luddite revolution, a revolt from people who were losing their once well-paid jobs to AI, while watching capital being siphoned away into 'black boxes', corporate entities that would 'hoover up all the value'. As well as losing their control over money, he said, governments were losing their monopoly on truth. A world in which top-down journalists disseminated a single narrative that society more-or-less agreed upon was being replaced by what he called a 'fractional truth system'. In such a world, governments were going to have a hard time controlling internal strife. Democracies, he said, were going to die.

But Azi wasn't a doomer. Quite the opposite. He was pumped. That's why he had come to Ella Funt tonight, to mingle and chat with other like-minded people. 'I'm just excited to be on the precipice of what I think is the next renaissance.' *Precipice?* 'Yeah. I do believe that the transition period from where we are now to the next stage is going to be very Darwinist and actually quite violent.'

Azi had been born in Bangladesh; he'd moved to America when he was three. In fact, there were lots of Asian and Black people at the event. In that sense, it was significantly more diverse than many journalism awards or literary festivals I'd attended in my life – overwhelmingly liberal spaces where white people proclaimed that Black Lives Matter and clutched their pearls at the mere mention of Pepe the frog. It struck me that the nods to fascism and white supremacy in the magazine were more about a *cultural* supremacy: a vision of America that was born out of the idea of whiteness as a tribe and the oppression of others based on race, but which was now trying to broaden its appeal. This new tribe still fetishised power, strength and vitality, and it was still comfortable with violence as a political tool. But it had neither ethnicity nor nationality; its homeland was cyber, the internet its blood and soil.

There also were members of a different tribe present that night: denizens of the hip world of the downtown New York club scene. At the bar, I got talking to two young women who looked like they were in their early twenties. Ezra said she was the manager of another nightclub, an exclusive underground spot. 'What is Praxis?' I asked her. 'I have no fucking idea,' she giggled. 'I'm just living my life and having some drinks.' Her friend Dylan, a student, chimed in: 'I think it's pretty dumb. All I heard was that they were building a city, which could never work.' Once they got rid of the government, who was going to staff the hospitals, the schools, she wanted to know? Good question.

'This is some dystopian-ass shit,' Ezra said. 'We're just here because we got invited. We just wanted to see what a real cult meeting was like.' Who is the cult leader, I wondered? Just then Dryden Brown appeared at the bar. 'This man has serious Napoleon syndrome,' Ezra said, attempting to speak sotto voce over the music, 'because he's fucking tiny and he thinks he's going to start a new world. He's fucking not.' She laughed again.

I caught up with Dryden when he popped outside for a cigarette. He seemed exhausted by it all, drained of his vitality. He fiddled with his lighter and mumbled something about developing a new aesthetic in pursuit of heroic virtue, building a culture of the frontier. I sincerely doubted he would last very long in a covered wagon out on the prairie. I wanted to ask him some hard questions about Praxis: how exactly was it going to work? Who would be the citizens that would build this new world, and – Dylan's question – who would staff the hospitals? But this did not seem like the right moment. Back inside, the night was getting wilder. Ezra and some of her friends had climbed on top of the Xerox machine and were photocopying not pages from the magazine but bits of their bodies; the bar was still flowing freely and the people in the long queue for the toilets were not, I suspected, just there to empty their bladders. It felt like the last days of Weimar.

• • •

Dryden Brown had invited me to come and see him the following day at the 'Praxis Embassy', housed in a giant loft on Broadway. I turned up, a little hungover from the night before, and was unsurprised to find that Dryden wasn't there yet. A bearded guy called Joseph showed me around the space. There was a kitchen area on one side and a couple of glass-walled offices at both ends, whiteboards and conference tables, the Praxis flag hanging on the wall, a dark blue sun radiating grey lines, like a de-saturated Japanese Second World War-era imperial banner. Another office was dominated by a camp bed piled with clothes. The rest of the space was open, dotted with pictures and sculptures, the walls lined with books (I spotted several biographies of Napoleon, and a volume entitled *The Dictator's Handbook*).

Joseph gave me the tour. Praxis was very focused on the visual, he said, on artwork that 'draws on historic sources of beauty across antiquity and, like, the roots of Western civilisation'. I pointed to a bust of a female head. Who was it, I wondered? Joseph had no idea. 'Hey, Charlie,' he said, turning to a guy making himself an espresso in the kitchenette. 'Do you know who this bust is of?' Charlie didn't know either. (He turned out to be Charlie Callinan, a twenty-something-year-old former college football player and Praxis's other co-founder.) I started to wonder whether they bought their artworks – and their books – by the kilo. My guide talked excitedly about the folklorist and writer Joseph Campbell, whose theory of the hero's journey had been the inspiration for *Star Wars*. Praxis, he told me, was imbued with Campbell's interpretation of the 'Faustian spirit', a yearning for the creative drive, a hyper-masculine will to power. Was Praxis a pact with the devil, I asked? 'Absolutely,' said Joseph, apparently delighted that I'd understood. Faust, he said, took a risk and created a new world. 'That's who we are. That's what we do.'

I hung around for another hour, But Dryden never showed. These guys, I concluded, were not serious. The books, the memes, the 3D-printed guns – they were LARPing as insurgents, as crypto-fascist pioneers. But as I'd learned from the kids on 4chan, a LARP could become a reality. And perhaps that's why these apparently unprepossessing young men at Praxis had managed to persuade some of the biggest players in Silicon Valley to bet on them.

I left the Praxis Embassy and walked south towards the site where the Twin Towers once stood. As the grid-lined streets dipped down towards the tip of Manhattan, they unfurled a vista of the financial district, the Statue of Liberty and the confluence of the Hudson and East Rivers beyond. Now I could see a through-line in the story – from the Clinton conspiracy theories of the 1990s, via 4chan and QAnon, to 'Stop the Steal' and the collapse of faith in democracy. The mantra of Silicon Valley was 'disruption'. According to this worldview, technology would bring chaos, and chaos was exciting; even more importantly – it was profitable. That was the insight of *The Sovereign Individual*; that was why Thiel backed Trump, why Balaji and others in this world railed against government, the newspapers, Hollywood, the Federal Reserve. These were people who were waiting for it all to implode, so that these old institutions could be replaced by their apps; they were waiting for the dollar to collapse so that crypto would become the new gold standard; betting on the death of democracy, so that their start-up societies might become the nation states of the future. It wasn't a conspiracy, there were no meetings in smoky back rooms. It was alignment of interests: *slow money on the up-building, fast money in the crack-up.*

And maybe they were right: maybe the system really wasn't working any more. San Francisco, the city born out of a nineteenth-century gold rush that had a renaissance as the home of the '90s tech boom, had turned into a hellscape: a place where drug addled zombies camped out in tent-cities in front of rows of multi-million-dollar apartments that had been left empty by the tech professionals fleeing the city. All that capital, all that innovation, all that drive: it was eating itself, like a rabid dog feasting on its own festering limbs. And the more the tech guys left, taking their tax-and-latte-dollars with them, the worse things got. And the worse things got, the more it seemed to them that Ayn Rand's prophecy was coming true: like John Galt, the energetic and the productive were simply withdrawing their dynamism, their industry, leaving the rest of us to our slow sclerotic decline.

For now, Silicon Valley's *exit* meant moving to places like Idaho or Utah, Texas or Florida, states where government regulation was lighter, more suited to their dreams. The bigger fish – like Thiel – were buying up tracts of land in New Zealand: bolt holes in case of societal or climate breakdown. But soon, they believed, a hyper-financialised, deregulated healthcare sector would make rapid advances in the field of longevity. Mortality was just another problem tech could solve. And then it would be time to board one of Elon Musk's rockets and build a new society on Mars. (Investors seemed to regard Musk's project to colonise space as a more bankable prospect than Praxis's relatively modest plans to build a small town somewhere on the Mediterranean coast.)

But wait! Surely there was still everything to play for here on earth? There was an election coming up, and Democrats believed that if Trump won, it might be America's last. After all, hadn't he said as much? When a court in Manhattan found him guilty on 34 felony charges, Trump responded: 'The real verdict is going to be November 5th.' In other words – this election would be a contest between the rule of law and the raw political power of Trump. And if he did win, there would be judicial retribution: he promised to use the Justice Department to go after his political enemies. To millions of Americans, that smelled like fascism, pure and simple.

But millions of Trump supporters were equally sincere in their belief that the Biden administration was already using the Justice Department for political ends, that tyranny and fascism had already arrived in America. They believed their opponents had already stolen one election, and if they got away with it again, that government of the people by the people for the people would indeed perish from this earth.

If there was one thing supporters of Biden and Trump agreed on, it was that democracy was on the ballot: each saw in the other an existential threat to the great American experiment. And they were ready to fight for their right to choose those who would exercise power on their behalf. As scary as that prospect seemed, surely that meant that *voice* was not yet dead?

Perhaps.

But in November 2023, with almost exactly a year to go before the election, an apparently small thing happened that lifted the curtain on something big. So big, perhaps, it would make the Trump vs Biden rematch look like a pointless side show.

A company fired its CEO. Five days later, the CEO was reinstated. Members of the board who had plotted to oust the CEO were themselves removed. The company moved on. This would normally be the kind of boardroom intrigue relegated to the inside pages of the *Financial Times*. Except in this case the company was OpenAI, the CEO was Sam Altman, and the kerfuffle had to do with how far the company and its leader were pushing the boundaries of artificial intelligence.

The move seemed to come out of nowhere. Amid a dearth of verifiable information about what actually went down at OpenAI over that weekend in November, Reuters published a scoop: Sam Altman had been fired after researchers at the company warned the board about a powerful new discovery that 'could threaten humanity'.[2] According to Reuters, the new piece of technology was called Q* and some at the company believed it was a breakthrough in the search for artificial general intelligence, or AGI.

OpenAI defined artificial general intelligence as 'AI systems that are generally smarter than humans'.[3] The fear with such systems was that they might decide to destroy humanity, if they thought it was in the interest of the machines. And, since they were smarter than us, we would have no way of stopping them.

OpenAI had begun in 2015 as an open-source, not-for-profit venture, with money from Peter Thiel, Elon Musk and Sam Altman himself, among others. The company's founding mission was to 'advance digital intelligence in the way that is most likely to benefit humanity as a whole, unconstrained by a need to generate financial return.'[4] But by 2023, it had transitioned into a profit-making behemoth valued at over $100 billion and, in partnership with Microsoft, had become one of the world-leaders in AI technology, rivalling companies like Google. Its code was no longer open source. OpenAI had become ClosedAI.

According to the version of the story put forward by Reuters and picked up by others, OpenAI was about to unleash AGI upon the world – the machine that might exterminate the human race – and Sam Altman had hidden this fact from the board, lest they try to stop him. So the board had fired Sam Altman – to save humanity. But when Altman threatened to join Microsoft and take nearly the entire staff of OpenAI with him, the coup was reversed, Altman was reinstated and the advocates of human non-extinction were purged.

No one from the company was talking. The media and the internet went wild with speculation, as people waited for the super-intelligent machine to emerge and do whatever it was going to do. Perhaps inevitably, 4chan helped fan the flames of panic, when an anonymous user uploaded a supposedly leaked document that suggested Q* was a joint project between OpenAI and the NSA that could crack all encryption. (Internet sleuths and citizen journalists quickly got to work trying to verify or debunk the letter. It looked quite technical and convincing – surely no 4chan troll could fake expertise like that? Ironically, they probably could, in a matter of minutes, using OpenAI's chatbot, ChatGPT.)

At the time of writing, humanity still survives and no machine has yet emerged to surpass human intelligence. On tech-Twitter/X, accelerationists mocked 'doomers' and their apocalyptic predictions. But what if the real threat was less eye-catching but more insidious? What if the real threat from AI was already here?

For six months, none of the board members who had mounted the unsuccessful coup said anything in public. Then in May 2024, one of them broke the silence.[5] Helen Toner said that, even though OpenAI was by now a profit-making enterprise, the remit of the board was still to ensure that the company prioritised its founding mission of the public good over profits and the interests of investors. 'For years, Sam had made it really difficult for the board to actually do that job,' she said, 'by withholding information, misrepresenting things that were happening at the company, in some cases outright lying to the board.' As an example she cited ChatGPT, an AI programme that could produce books, essays, computer code and much more – things that might take humans weeks or even years to create, ChatGPT could do in seconds. When OpenAI released the programme in 2022, she said, the board only found out about it on Twitter. 'On multiple occasions he gave us inaccurate information about the small number of safety processes in place,' she added, meaning that the board really had no idea how safe – or dangerous – the company's AI technology really was.

But OpenAI had not achieved AGI, had not invented a super-intelligent machine bent on destroying its creator. Or at least, if it had, Toner either didn't know about it or wasn't telling. Even the experts didn't really know what the actual risks from AI were, Toner said. But listening to her speak, it was clear she didn't think the machines were going to come and kill us all.

Her dystopian vision of the future was that the dysfunction and bad decisions we live with every day in a democracy – from the person who gets wrongly deported by an overzealous official in some government ministry, to the hundreds of thousands of soldiers who get sent to war over fake intelligence – those decisions would be made by automated systems.

This is in fact already happening. A study from 2020 found that nearly half of all federal agencies in the US were using or experimenting with AI,[6] in areas such as law enforcement, the judicial system, public benefits, health and housing. Decisions made by large public bureaucracies can often feel arbitrary and unaccountable. But decisions made by machines, according to code known only to the companies that own them, are essentially made inside a black box – you cannot question them, challenge them or even understand them. The machine becomes God. And you can't get rid of God at the ballot box.

The thing that kept Helen Toner awake at night was not the AI-apocalypse, but what she called the 'Wall-E future'. 'The people in that movie, they just sit in their soft roll-around wheelchairs all day and have content and food and whatever to keep them happy.' AI, Toner said, would be commercially incentivised to perfect the art of feeding humans with junk food for the soul. 'We then end up with this really meaningless, shallow, superficial world, and potentially one where most of the consequential decisions are being made by machines that have no concept of what it means to lead a meaningful life.'

In other words: we would end up living in the Matrix – a place where the media we consumed would become so realistic it would replace reality. And all of our energy would go into serving the algorithm, working for the machine. In such a situation, who would really run the world, I wondered? Not the politicians we'd voted for at the last election, or even the ones we'd voted against. They would be mere simulacra, representations of a system of government that had once existed but was no longer there. The real rulers would be those who controlled the algorithms, who coded the AI. In such a world, the tech titans and their financial backers truly would become sovereign individuals whose power would rival those of the gods in Greek mythology.

In his preface to the 2020 edition of *The Sovereign Individual*, Peter Thiel writes that the future will be decided by the interplay of two great technological advances – AI and crypto. 'AI could theoretically make it possible to centrally control an entire economy,' he writes. 'Strong cryptography, at the other pole, holds out the prospect of a decentralized and individualized world. If AI is communist, crypto is libertarian.' Thiel of course had invested in both technologies, hedging his bets as ever. He had advocated for *more* disinformation to counterbalance what he saw as orthodoxies over climate change and vaccines promoted by governments and the mainstream media.

I think we would be in a much healthier society if we had somewhat more scepticism, somewhat more

misinformation, somewhat more crazy conspiracy
theories, all that would be such a healthy corrective to
the sort of centralised totalitarian one-world state. I'll
take all the QAnon and Pizzagate conspiracy theories
every day versus the ministry of truth.[7]

That was decentralised Thiel, crypto Thiel. But there was also the
other Thiel: 'I have a single idée fixe that I'm completely obsessed
with, which is that if you're starting a company you always
want to aim for a monopoly. Competition is for losers.'[8] That
was totalitarian Thiel, AI Thiel. (He was speaking to students
at Stanford University in 2014, introduced by Sam Altman.) And
then there was Thiel on the subject of tech and democracy: voting
is 'really an inefficient way of going about doing things,' he told
an audience of students in 2012. 'One of the things I like about
technology is that, when technology is unregulated, you can go
about changing the world without getting approval from other
people. At its best it is not subject to democratic control.'[9]

How then to understand this perilous moment for America,
and for the world? Was Trump an existential threat to democracy? When I started out on this project, I probably would have
said that he was. Then, at various points on my journey, I did
wonder whether Biden and his allies, in their earnest attempt
to save the system, might in fact be the authors of their own
demise. But now I've come to the end of the rabbit hole. And
what I think I've learned is this: it's neither.

No system lasts for ever: just as the printing press overturned the old feudal order, so the new technology will overturn that which replaced it – a system that slowly edged towards the values of the Enlightenment, of individual liberty, human rights and universal suffrage. There were some pretty bumpy patches along the road; some might argue we never quite got there. The ship has sailed; the party is over.

We don't know what is coming next, any more than the feudal peasants who moved to towns and cities at the end of the fifteenth century could have predicted the American Revolution or the internet. Who knows, it may be better than what we have now. Or it may be worse. Whatever the case, it seems that Q was right about one thing: there is a storm coming. In the words of Tracy Diaz aka Beanz, conspiracy theorist, truth-seeker and early QAnon apostle: 'Buckle up, I guess.'

NOTES

PROLOGUE

1   Dana Priest and Greg Miller, 'He was one of the most respected intel officers of his generation. Now he's leading "Lock her up" chants', *Washington Post*, 15 August 2016, https://www.washingtonpost.com/world/national-security/nearly-the-entire-national-security-establishment-has-rejected-trumpexcept-for-this-man/2016/08/15/d5072d96-5e4b-11e6-8e45-477372e89d78_story.html.

CHAPTER 1: THE ENEMY WITHIN

1   Benedict Anderson, *Imagined Communities* (London: Verso, 2016).
2   Rev. Montague Summers, Introduction to the English translation in *Malleus Maleficarum* (London: J. Rodker, 1928).
3   Ibid.

CHAPTER 2: LIGHTING THE MATCH

1   In my research on the Vince Foster case I have relied on numerous sources, including David von Drehle's excellent August 1993 account in the *Washington Post* (https://www.washingtonpost.com/archive/politics/1993/08/15/the-crumbling-of-a-pillar-in-washington/58dc8cd8-c737-48ed-852c-4980c82634fe/) and season two, episode two of Leon Neyfakh's *Slow Burn* podcast.
2   e.g. Robert O'Harrow Jr and Michael Kranish, 'After investigating Clinton White House and Vincent Foster's death, Brett Kavanaugh had a change of heart', *Washington Post*, 2 August 2018, https://www.washingtonpost.com/investigations/after-investigating-clinton-white-house-and-vincent-fosters-death-brett-kavanaugh-had-change-of-heart/2018/08/02/66ee2b2c-91f5-11e8-9b0d-749fb254bc3d_story.html.

3 'Once Upon a Time in Arkansas', PBS, https://www.pbs.org/wgbh/
   pages/frontline/shows/arkansas/etc/friends.html.

4 Hillary Clinton, *Living History* (New York: Simon & Schuster, 2003),
   pp. 171–172.

5 'Once Upon a Time in Arkansas', PBS, https://www.pbs.org/wgbh/
   pages/frontline/shows/arkansas/etc/foster.html. Ironically, that inquiry
   was led by another White House lawyer by the name of John Podesta,
   whose hacked emails during Hillary Clinton's 2016 presidential
   campaign would help feed the QAnon conspiracy theory.

6 Elaine Sciolino and Don Van Natta Jr, 'Linda Tripp: The Keeper of
   Secrets – Her Own', *New York Times*, 15 March 1998, https://archive.
   nytimes.com/www.nytimes.com/library/politics/031598clinton-tripp.
   html.

7 Jeff Leen and Gene Weingarten, 'Linda's Trip', *Washington Post*,
   14 March 1998, https://www.washingtonpost.com/archive/lifestyle/
   1998/03/15/lindas-trip/18a54c9f-3e1f-40e1-8bf2-372db7feb52e/.

8 All the FBI documents relating to the Vince Foster case can be found
   here: https://vault.fbi.gov/vincent-foster/vincent-foster-part-01-of-04/
   view.

9 Ambrose Evans-Pritchard, *The Secret Life of Bill Clinton*
   (Washington: Regnery Publishing, 1997), p. 128.

10 For an exhaustive and reliable account of the failings and
   contradictions in the various investigations into Vince Foster's death,
   see Dan E. Moldea's excellent *A Washington Tragedy: Bill and Hillary
   Clinton and the Suicide of Vince Foster* (self-published, 2015).

11 This episode is described in detail in chapter 12 of Evans-Pritchard's
   book, *The Secret Life of Bill Clinton*.

12 *The Secret Life of Bill Clinton*, p. 174.

CHAPTER 3: THE SCANDAL FACTORY

1 Ambrose Evans-Pritchard used the same metaphor to describe Vince
   Foster's death.

2 https://apnews.com/general-news-1b111df51f1c475b956ef5895626f93f.

3 David Brock, *Blinded by the Right* (New York: Crown, 2002), p. 198.

4 Leon Neyfakh, *Slow Burn,* season 2, episode 8, https://slate.com/

news-and-politics/2018/10/slow-burn-season-2-episode-8-transcript. html.

5 Ibid.
6 Philip Weiss, 'NBC's Vetting of Juanita Broaddrick: Clinton's Accuser Discusses Agonizing Weeks as NBC Dragged It Out', *New York Observer*, 4 December 1999, https://observer.com/1999/04/nbcs-vetting-of-juanita-broaddrick-clintons-accuser-discusses-agonizing-weeks-as-nbc-dragged-it-out/.

CHAPTER 4: PERSISTENT MAKE-BELIEVE

1 Figure quoted by Anne Nelson in *The Shadow Network* (New York: Bloomsbury, 2019), p. 52.
2 Mike Fleming Jr, 'IFC Acquires "Knife Fight"', Deadline, 9 August 2012, https://deadline.com/2012/08/ifc-acquires-knife-fight-316325/.
3 *The Secret Life of Bill Clinton*, p. 205.
4 Ibid., p. 202.
5 *The Secret Life of Bill Clinton*, pp. 201–202.
6 William Rees-Mogg and James Dale Davidson, *The Sovereign Individual* (New York: Simon & Schuster, 1997), p. 369.
7 Ibid. p. 371.
8 Ibid., p. 57.
9 Ibid., p. 360.
10 Ibid., p. 259.
11 Ibid., p. 17.
12 Ibid., p. 19.
13 Ibid., p. 18.
14 Ibid., p. 394.
15 Interview with Jason Hartman, Nov 2016, https://www.jasonhartman.com/1692-fbf-the-breaking-point-profit-from-the-coming-money-cataclysm-with-james-dale-davidson/.
16 Karl Taro Greenfeld, 'The Next Ailes: Newsmax's Chris Ruddy Preps TV Rival to Fox News', Bloomberg, 6 March 2014, https://www.bloomberg.com/news/articles/2014-03-06/newsmaxs-chris-ruddy-preps-tv-network-to-rival-fox-news.

CHAPTER 5: REHEARSAL

1   Dana Canedy and Dexter Filkins, 'COUNTING THE VOTE: MIAMI-
    DADE COUNTY; A Wild Day in Miami, With an End to Recounting,
    and Democrats' Going to Court', *New York Times*, 23 November 2000,
    https://www.nytimes.com/2000/11/23/us/counting-vote-miami-dade-
    county-wild-day-miami-with-end-recounting-democrats.html.
2   Nick Kulish and Jim VandeHei, 'GOP Protest in Miami-Dade Is a
    Well-Organized Effort', *Wall Street Journal*, 27 November 2000,
    https://www.wsj.com/articles/SB975279431548753691.
3   Jeffrey Toobin, 'The Dirty Trickster', *New Yorker*, 23 May 2008,
    https://www.newyorker.com/magazine/2008/06/02/the-dirty-trickster.

CHAPTER 6: ANYONE CAN BE ANYTHING

1   For a brilliant account of the rise of 4chan, see Dale Beran, *It Came
    from Something Awful* (New York: All Points Books, 2019).
2   For a brilliant account of the rise of 4chan, see Simon Parkin, 'Zoe
    Quinn's Depression Quest', *New Yorker*, 9 September 2014, https://
    www.newyorker.com/tech/annals-of-technology/
    zoe-quinns-depression-quest.

CHAPTER 7: CONFLICT IS ATTENTION, ATTENTION IS
INFLUENCE

1   Daniel J. Boorstin, *The Image: A Guide to Pseudo-events in America*
    (New York: Vintage, 2012).
2   'Clinton Foundation investigated by Justice Department', BBC News,
    5 January 2018, https://www.bbc.co.uk/news/world-us-canada-42579732.
3   Andrew Marantz, 'Trolls for Trump', *New Yorker*, 24 October 2016,
    https://www.newyorker.com/magazine/2016/10/31/trolls-for-trump.

CHAPTER 8: MIMETIC WARFARE

1   Exchange with Zoe Chace of NPR's *This American Life*: https://www.
    thisamericanlife.org/608/transcript.
2   Jeff Giesea, 'It's Time to Embrace Mimetic Warfare', 2016, *Defence*

Strategic Communications 1, pp. 67–75, https://stratcomcoe.org/cuploads/pfiles/jeff_gisea.pdf.

3 Jack Posobiec, *Citizens for Trump: The Inside Story of the People's Movement to Take Back America* (self-published, 2017), p. 169.

4 Ibid., p. 168.

5 For a comprehensive account of Peter Thiel's rise, see Max Chafkin, *The Contrarian: Peter Thiel and Silicon Valley's Pursuit of Power*, (London: Bloomsbury, 2022).

6 Joseph Bernstein, 'Here's How Breitbart and Milo Smuggled White Nationalism into the Mainstream', Buzzfeed, 5 October 2017: https://www.buzzfeednews.com/article/josephbernstein/heres-how-breitbart-and-milo-smuggled-white-nationalism.

7 Lauren Etter, Vernon Silver and Sarah Frier, 'How Facebook's Political Unit Enables the Dark Art of Digital Propaganda', Bloomberg Technology, 21 December 2017, https://archive.is/iA6VU#selection-1881.12-1881.19.

8 Lauren Etter, 'How Rodrigo Duterte Turned Facebook into a Weapon with a Little Help from Facebook', Bloomberg, 7 December 2017, https://www.bloomberg.com/news/features/2017-12-07/how-rodrigo-duterte-turned-facebook-into-a-weapon-with-a-little-help-from-facebook/.

9 Michael Nunez, 'Former Facebook Workers: We Routinely Suppressed Conservative News', Gizmodo, 9 May 2016: https://gizmodo.com/former-facebook-workers-we-routinely-suppressed-conser-1775461006.

10 Jake Tapper, *Down and Dirty: The Plot to Steal the Presidency* (referenced by Benjamin Wofford, 'The Infinite Reach of Joel Kaplan, Facebook's Man in Washington', *Wired*, 10 March 2022 https://www.wired.com/story/facebook-joel-kaplan-washington-political-influence/).

11 Craig Timberg, 'How Conservatives Learned to Wield Power inside Facebook', 20 February 2020, https://www.washingtonpost.com/technology/2020/02/20/facebook-republican-shift/.

12 Benjamin Wofford, *The Infinite Reach of Joel Kaplan*, *Wired*, March 10, 2022 https://www.wired.com/story/facebook-joel-kaplan-washington-political-influence/.

13 Ibid.

14 Ibid.

CHAPTER 9: THE PATRIOT

1 Pamela Brown, Evan Perez and Shimon Prokupecz, 'First Charges Filed in Mueller Investigation', CNN, 27 October 2017 (updated 30 October), https://edition.cnn.com/2017/10/27/politics/first-charges-mueller-investigation/index.html.

2 Paris Martineau, 'The Storm Is the New Pizzagate – Only Worse', *New York Magazine*, 19 December 2017, https://nymag.com/intelligencer/2017/12/qanon-4chan-the-storm-conspiracy-explained.html.

3 David Kirkpatrick, 'Who Is Behind QAnon? Linguistic Detectives Find Fingerprints', *New York Times*, 19 February 2022 (updated 24 February), https://www.nytimes.com/2022/02/19/technology/qanon-messages-authors.html.

CHAPTER 10: THE CALM BEFORE THE STORM

1 'Meet the man keeping 8chan, the world's most vile website, alive', Splinter, 19 April 2016, https://www.splinter.com/meet-the-man-keeping-8chan-the-worlds-most-vile-websit-1793856249.

2 Michael Edison Hayden, 'Jack Posobiec Interviewed A Pro-Hitler Disinformation Poster On One America News Network', SPLC, 23 July 2020, https://www.splcenter.org/hatewatch/2020/07/23/jack-posobiec-interviewed-pro-hitler-disinformation-poster-one-america-news-network; for specific post see https://www.documentcloud.org/documents/6937738-MicrochipHitler.html.

3 *QAnonAnonymous*, episode 32 https://soundcloud.com/qanonanonymous/episode-32-4chan-8chan.

CHAPTER 11: YOU ARE THE PLAN

1 Poll published in November 2021 by PRRI https://www.prri.org/research/competing-visions-of-america-an-evolving-identity-or-a-culture-under-attack/.

2   See https://twitter.com/MC_Hyperbole/status/139912929724008448
    9?s=20.

CHAPTER 12: EVERYTHING IS CONNECTED

1   Wikisource contributors, 'McCormack–Dickstein Committee',
    Wikisource, 16 March 2024, https://en.wikisource.org/wiki/
    McCormack–Dickstein_Committee#Testimony_of_Gerald_C._
    Macguire.
2   Dave Troy, 'The Big History behind January 6th', Medium, https://
    davetroy.medium.com/the-big-history-behind-january-6th-the-entire-
    series-fcf432f391dd.
3   The Blue Book of the John Birch Society, https://archive.org/stream/
    WelchRobertBlueBook/Welch%2C%20Robert%20-%20Blue%20
    Book_djvu.txt.
4   Robert Welch, 'The Truth in Time' (1966 speech at 1:07'14") https://
    www.youtube.com/watch?v=4VbQGvsKXHc; text of speech here:
    http://www.ourrepubliconline.com/Article/21.
5   Ibid. (14'40").
6   Ibid. (22'15").
7   David Maraniss, 'Young Political Widow Eyes Joining the Battle',
    Washington Post, 4 September 1983, https://www.washingtonpost.
    com/archive/politics/1983/09/04/young-political-widow-eyes-joining-
    the-battle/e6d51e69-8e8f-4c71-88d6-107de36b89f0/.
8   Zach Dorfman, 'The Congressman Who Created His Own Deep
    State. Really.' *Politico*, 2 December 2018, https://www.politico.com/
    magazine/story/2018/12/02/larry-mcdonald-communists-deep-state-
    222726/.
9   John K. Singlaub and Malcolm McConnell, *Hazardous Duty* (New
    York: Summit Books, 1991), p. 439.
10 Sterling and Peggy Seagrave, *Gold Warriors: America's Secret Recovery
    of Yamashita's Gold*, (Verso Books), p. 18.
11 See Anne Nelson, *The Shadow Network*, for an in-depth investigation
    into the reach and power of the CNP.
12 General Michael T. Flynn's acceptance speech can be found here:
    https://www.youtube.com/watch?v=heLpUvhGMRg.

13 No longer available but quoted by David Armiak, 'Operatives Tied to Council for National Policy Organizing Protests Alleging Voter Fraud', Exposed by CMD, 6 November 2020, https://www.exposed bycmd.org/2020/11/06/operatives-tied-to-council-for-national-policy-organizing-protests-alleging-voter-fraud/.

14 Anne Nelson, 'How the CNP, a Republican Powerhouse, Helped Spawn Trumpism, Disrupted the Transfer of Power, and Stoked the Assault on the Capitol', *Washington Spectator*, 22 February 2021, https://washingtonspectator.org/nelson-cnp/.

CHAPTER 13: THE BLACK PILL

1 John Paul Mac Isaac told his story to Will Cain on a Fox News podcast: https://www.youtube.com/watch?v=kGoCW1prXs4.

2 Letter published in *Politico*, 19 October 2020: https://www.politico.com/f/?id=00000175-4393-d7aa-af77-579f9b330000.

3 John Dentinger, 'Hollywood Heretic', *Reason*, December 1985, https://www.unz.com/print/Reason-1985dec-00064.

4 YouGov poll, December 2023. https://today.yougov.com/politics/articles/48113-which-conspiracy-theories-do-americans-believe.

5 *Economist*/YouGov poll, March 2022. https://today.yougov.com/politics/articles/41874-which-groups-believe-conspiracies-ukraine-russia.

CHAPTER 14: WHATEVER IT TAKES

1 David Ferarra, 'Judge cuts defendant's testimony short in Bunkerville retrial', *Las Vegas Review Journal*, 10 August 2017, https://www.reviewjournal.com/crime/courts/judge-cuts-defendants-testimony-short-in-bunkerville-retrial/.

2 Maxine Bernstein, 'Cliven Bundy standoff case thrown out in another stunning blow to government', *The Oregonian*, 8 January 2018, https://www.oregonlive.com/oregon-standoff/2018/01/cliven_bundy_standoff_case_thr.html.

CHAPTER 15: AMONG THE GODS

1 Balaji first outlined his ideas in a presentation entitled *Silicon Valley's Ultimate Exit* at Y Combinator, a 'start-up accelerator', in 2013: https://www.youtube.com/watch?v=n1kfVAX7WGU.

2 Anna Tong, Jeffrey Dastin and Krystal Hu, 'OpenAI researchers warned board of AI breakthrough ahead of CEO ouster, sources say', Reuters, 23 November 2023, https://www.reuters.com/technology/sam-altmans-ouster-openai-was-precipitated-by-letter-board-about-ai-breakthrough-2023-11-22/.

3 'Planning for AGI and beyond', OpenAI, 24 February 2023, https://openai.com/index/planning-for-agi-and-beyond/.

4 'Introducing OpenAI', OpenAI, 11 December 2015, https://openai.com/index/introducing-openai/.

5 Helen Toner spoke to the TED AI show, a podcast devoted to topics related to artificial intelligence, hosted by TED: https://www.ted.com/talks/the_ted_ai_show_what_really_went_down_at_openai_and_the_future_of_regulation_w_helen_toner?subtitle=en.

6 David Freeman Engstrom, Daniel E. Ho, Catherine M. Sharkey and Mariano-Florentino Cuéllar, 'Government by Algorithm: Artificial Intelligence in Federal Administrative Agencies', February 2020, https://law.stanford.edu/wp-content/uploads/2020/02/ACUS-AI-Report.pdf.

7 Thiel talking to Bambi Francisco Roizen in 2021, https://www.youtube.com/watch?v=y1qf2MCzneU.

8 Lecture at Stanford University, 2014, https://www.youtube.com/watch?v=3Fx5Q8xGU8k.

9 'Peter Thiel Answers Student Questions at the ISFLC 2012', https://www.youtube.com/watch?v=5fsUMoHZ1cY (at 38'30").

ACKNOWLEDGEMENTS

This book would not exist without the people who agreed to speak to me: some are named, others are not; some became whole chapters; others were woven into the background fabric of the tale. I thank them all for trusting me with their stories and insights.

I would like to thank Albert DePetrillo, my editor at Ebury, whose enthusiasm for this project propelled me onward, and whose sensitive but incisive edits helped turn a monster of a tale into a more coherent whole. My thanks also to Jess Anderson, Shammah Banerjee, David Bamford, Vanessa Milton, Kirsty Howarth and the whole team at Penguin Random House.

I owe a huge debt of gratitude to my agent, Toby Mundy, who had faith in my writing, who helped structure the book at the proposal stage and gave essential feedback on the nearly finished manuscript.

To everyone at the BBC involved in making the podcast: Lucy Proctor, of course, who was my partner in crime; Dan Clarke, without whose intellectual curiosity and appetite for adventure this would never have happened; Mohit Bakaya, who invited us to plant a tree in his enchanted forest; Richard

Vadon, who kept us honest while contributing flashes of brilliance rooted in a deep knowledge of America; and many more supportive and inspiring people who bounced ideas, read drafts and added insights.

I must also say a special thanks to everyone at *Newsnight* – working with you lot turned me from a news reporter into someone with ambitions to tell bigger stories. I could mention two dozen names or more, but I'll just name a few: Ian Katz, who hired me; Esme Wren, who let me off the leash; and Warwick Harrington, who badgered me about signposting until I started to entertain the idea that I might make an actual writer.

I would like to thank my parents, Adam and Nicoline, who nurtured and encouraged me. Thanks to them, and to my mother-in-law, Venus, who also nurtured my kids so that I might escape to write in cafes and garden sheds; and to Alexander and Chloe, who likewise entertained, distracted and generally helped wrangle two small children, who are the joy of my life (and who I hope will one day read this book) but whose presence is not always conducive to getting words onto the page.

My greatest debt is to my partner, Afsaneh Gray, whose own writing inspires me and who is my sounding board, my structure-nut, my gentle critic: I couldn't do any of this without you.